STECK-VAUGHN

PreGED
Social Studies

REVIEWERS

Robert Christensen
Principal
Handlon Correctional Facility
Michigan Department
of Corrections
Ionia, MI

Linda Correnti
GED Staff Developer
Alternative Schools & Programs
New York City Department
of Education
New York, NY

Dr. Gary A. Eyre
Consultant
GED Testing Service
Advance Associates
and Consultants
Phoenix, AZ

Arnoldo Hinojosa
Senior Director
Community Initiatives
Harris County Department
of Education
Houston, TX

Nancy Lawrence
E-teacher
KC Distance Learning, Inc.
Butler, PA

Charan Lee
Director
Adult Education
Anderson School Districts 1 & 2
Williamston, SC

STECK-VAUGHN
 Harcourt Supplemental Publishers

www.steck-vaughn.com

Executive Editor: Ellen Northcutt

Senior Editor: Donna Townsend

Associate Design Director: Joyce Spicer

Senior Designer: Jim Cauthron

Senior Photo Researcher: Alyx Kellington

Editorial Development: Learning Unlimited, Oak Park, IL

Photograph and Political Cartoon Credits: P.12 ©Ed Gamble/Florida Times Union/Reprinted with Special Permission of King Features Syndicate; p.14 ©Pete Saloutos/CORBIS; p.31 ©The Granger Collection; p.36, 43a ©Brown Brothers; p.65 ©George Grantham Bain Collection/Library of Congress; p.66 ©José Fuste Raga/CORBIS; p.89 ©Bob Dornfried/Greenwich News; p.93 ©Scott Peterson/Liaison/Getty Images; p.101 ©Ben Sargent/Austin American Statesman; p.106 ©Bob Daemmrich/PictureQuest; p.110 ©Don Landgren; The Landmark; Holden, Mass. Reprinted with permission.; p.122 ©Paul Conrad/Tribune Media Services; p.128 ©Bob Grieser/AP/Wide World; p.138 ©Joseph Sohm; ChromoSohm Inc./CORBIS; p.143 ©Steve Greenberg; p.144 Courtesy of U.S. National Archives and Records Administration; p.145 ©Scott Stantis/The Birmingham News/Copley News Service; p.146 ©José Carrillo/PhotoEdit Inc.; p.162 Courtesy of Sports Cards Magazine; p.178 ©Strauss/Curtis/CORBIS; p.186 ©Steve Raymer/CORBIS; p.190 ©SuperStock; p.207 ©Dorothea Lange/CORBIS; p.212 ©Stewart Cohen/Index Stock Imagery, Inc.; p.222a,b ©AP/Wide World; p.226b ©Marshall Ramsey/Copley News Service. Additional photography by Getty Royalty Free and Park Street.

Acknowledgments: p. 123, West End Community Center, Hartford, CT. Leaflet reprinted by permission.

ISBN 0-7398-6699-0

2 3 4 5 6 7 8 9 10 CKV 09 08 07 06 05 04

CONTENTS

How to Use This Book

The purpose of this book is to help you develop the foundation you need to pass the *GED Social Studies* Test.

Throughout the five units of the book, you will learn a variety of thinking and reading skills. You will also learn several graphic skills, such as reading timelines, maps, political cartoons, and graphs. These skills will not only help you as you work through this book, but they are crucial to success on the GED.

Pretest and Posttest

The Pretest is a self-check of what you already know and what you need to study. After you complete all of the items on the Pretest, check your work in the Answers and Explanations section at the back of the book. Then fill out the Pretest Evaluation Chart. This chart tells you where each skill is taught in this book. When you have completed the book, you will take a Posttest. Compare your Posttest score to your Pretest score to see your progress.

Units

Unit 1: U.S. History. This unit covers such history skills as reading historical and political maps, understanding photos, and using timelines. The articles you read will increase your knowledge of major events in the history of the United States.

Unit 2: World History. In this unit you will learn about important events in the world's history. You will learn about cultural and economic realities for various people.

Unit 3: Civics and Government. In this unit you will learn about selected contents in political science. You will read diagrams, political ads, and political cartoons. You will also read about how laws are made and the roles of local, state, and federal governments.

Unit 4: Economics. This unit focuses on skills in economics. You will use graphic illustrations such as tables, line graphs, circle graphs, and bar graphs. You will gain an understanding of our economy by reading articles about supply and demand, world trade, and money management.

Unit 5: Geography. This unit covers geography skills, including how to read maps. You will use map keys and scales as you read maps and articles about the geography of the United States and other parts of the world.

Lessons

Each unit is divided into lessons. Each lesson is based on the Active Reading Process. This means doing something before reading, during reading, and after reading. By reading actively, you will improve your reading comprehension skills.

The first page of each lesson has three sections to help prepare you for what you are about to read. First, you will read some background information about the passage presented in the lesson. This is followed by the Relate to the Topic section, which includes a brief exercise designed to help you relate the topic of the reading to your life. Finally, Reading Strategies will provide you with a pre-reading strategy that will help you to understand what you read and a brief exercise that will allow you to practice using that strategy. These are the activities you do before reading. Vocabulary words important to the lesson are listed down the left-hand side of the page.

The articles you will read are about interesting topics in social studies. As you read each article, you will see two Skills Mini-Lessons. Here you learn a reading or graphic skill, and do a short activity. After completing the activity, continue reading the article. These are the activities you do during reading.

After reading the article, you answer fill-in-the-blank, short-answer, or multiple choice questions in the section called Thinking About the Article. Answering these questions will help you decide how well you understood what you read. The final question in this section relates information from the article to your own real-life experiences.

Social Studies at Work

Social Studies at Work is a two-page feature in each unit. Each Social Studies at Work feature introduces a specific job and describes the skills the job requires. It also gives information about other jobs in the same career area.

Mini-Tests and Unit Reviews

Unit Reviews tell you how well you have learned the skills covered in each unit. Each Unit Review includes a Social Studies Extension activity that provides an opportunity for further practice. Mini-Tests follow each Unit Review. These timed practice tests allow you to practice your skills with the kinds of questions that you will see on the actual GED Tests.

Setting Goals

A goal is something you aim for, something you want to achieve. What is your long-term goal for using this book? You may want to get your GED or you may just want to learn more about social studies. These are large goals that may take you some time to accomplish.

Write your long-term goal for social studies.

_____

_____

This section of the book will help you to think about how you already use social studies and then to set some goals for what you would like to learn in this book. These short-term goals will be stepping stones to the long-term goal you wrote.

Check each activity that you do. Add more activities.

I use social studies skills in my everyday life to

_____ use a map to find a location
_____ stay informed about current events
_____ plan a budget for my family
_____ interpret graphs and charts
_____ other _____

_____

_____

List your experiences with learning and using social studies.

What I've Liked	What I Haven't Liked
_____	_____
_____	_____
_____	_____
_____	_____
_____	_____

Think about your social studies goals.

1. I decided to improve my social studies skills when I _____

   _____

   _____

2. My social studies goals include (check as many as you like)

   ☐ understanding how government works

   ☐ understanding where my taxes go

   ☐ staying informed on political issues and different candidates
   for office

   ☐ knowing important events in U.S. and world history

   ☐ appreciating different cultures and regions in the world

   ☐ appreciating my rights and responsibilities as a citizen

   ☐ reading different types of maps

   ☐ understanding and interpreting political cartoons

   ☐ understanding diagrams and graphs

   ☐ other _____

   _____

3. I will have met my long-term goal for social studies when I am able to

   _____

   _____

Keep track of your goals.

As you work through this book, turn back often to this page. Add more goals at any time you wish. Check each goal that you complete.

Learn about the skills you have.

Complete the Pretest that begins on the next page. It will help you learn more about your strengths and weaknesses in social studies. You may wish to change some items in your list of goals after you have taken the Pretest and completed the Pretest Evaluation Chart on page 13.

Use this Pretest before you begin Unit 1. The Pretest will help you determine which content areas in social studies you understand well and which you must practice further. Read each article and study the graphics—map, timeline, graph, diagram, and cartoon. Then answer the questions on each page.

Check your answers on page 232. Mark the number of correct answers you have in each content area on the chart on page 13. Use the chart to figure out which content area(s) to work on and where to find practice pages in this book.

The Elevation of the United States

United States Elevation Map

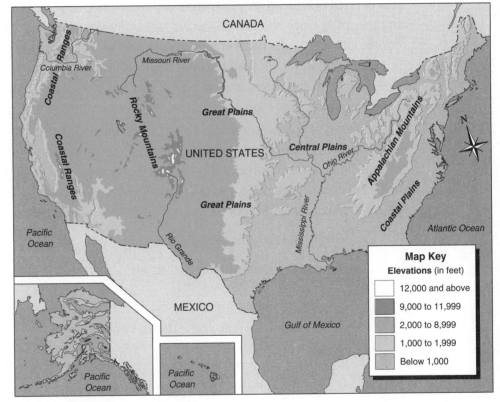

Write the answer to each question.

1. What is the elevation of the Coastal Plains?

_____

2. Are the Central Plains or the Great Plains higher in elevation?

_____

Desert Regions

Nearly every continent has at least one desert region. When people think of deserts, they often picture hot, dry, sandy, empty lands. Hot deserts are usually found at low latitudes and low elevations. The Sahara, a desert region in North Africa, is hot.

Indeed every desert is very dry with few or no plants at all. But not all deserts are hot. Some are cold. Cold deserts include the Gobi, a desert in northeastern Asia. Cold deserts are found at higher latitudes and higher elevations. The Gobi's elevations range from 3,000 to 5,000 feet above sea level.

Although many deserts have sand, most of them do not. Only five percent of the Gobi, for example, has sand.

Deserts are home to many different plants and animals. Desert plants and animals have adapted to the harsh environment. Desert plants have tough skins and few or thick leaves so they can keep any water they absorb. Some desert animals, like the mourning dove and the desert rat, are active at night when temperatures are cooler. Other animals need little water to survive. For example, kangaroo rats never actually drink water. Instead they get their water from the seeds they eat. Another desert animal, the camel, can live off fat stored in its hump and can go for long periods without water.

People have also found ways to live in the desert, just as they have in every other environment. Some people move from place to place with herds of camels, goats, or sheep. Other people farm in the desert. To do so, they must bring water to their fields from a distant underground spring or river. People have found oil and other natural resources in the desert. They often build cities in the desert, near the valuable resources.

Write the answer to each question.

3. Name one way all deserts are alike.

   _____

4. Name one way some deserts are different.

   _____

Circle the number of the best answer.

5. Which of the following is a conclusion that can be drawn from the article?
   (1) Animals can live only in hot deserts.
   (2) Living things have developed ways to survive in difficult environments.
   (3) Deserts can be cold as well as hot.
   (4) Not all deserts are sandy.
   (5) People survive better in a hot desert than a cold desert.

4

Ancient Greek Culture

Jutting out into the Mediterranean Sea is a country called Greece. From about 750 to 336 B.C., the people there developed an advanced **culture.** This culture is famous for its religion, art, architecture, and customs, which influenced people throughout the Mediterranean region.

The Greek family of gods was an important influence on Greek culture. Unlike ancient Egyptians, who pictured their gods as animals, the Greeks believed their gods looked like humans. The Greeks also believed the gods lived on Mount Olympus in northeastern Greece.

The Greeks thought that each god controlled a part of nature. The chief Greek god was Zeus. The Greeks considered him Lord of the Sky, the Rain God, and the Cloud Gatherer. He was often described as throwing thunderbolts to Earth when he became angry. He was considered the most powerful god of all.

Poseidon was Zeus's brother and second in power. He was the Ruler of the Sea and Earth Shaker. The Greeks admired Poseidon because he gave them the first horse. He was often described as holding a three-pronged spear, which he would shake to disturb the sea or land.

Athena was Zeus's favorite child. She did not have a mother. The Greeks believed that she sprang full-grown from her father's head. She was the Goddess of the City. Athens, one of Greece's first cities, was named after her. She was noted for her wisdom and artistic talents.

The people wanted to keep the gods happy so that the gods would bring good fortune to them. For this reason, the Greeks built temples, sacrificed animals, and prayed to the gods. They also honored the gods through festivals. For the glory of Zeus, the Greeks organized the first Olympic Games in 776 B.C. From that date on, they had a series of athletic contests every four years.

Write the answers to each question.

6. What was the purpose of the first Olympic Games?

_____

Circle the number of the best answer for each question.

7. Which definition for *culture* is intended in this passage?
   (1) expert training
   (2) medium for growing bacteria
   (3) to improve by study
   (4) way of life
   (5) taste in fine arts

The Korean War

The United Nations sends troops to help South Korea.

China sends troops to help North Korea.

United Nations troops retake South Korea's capital and push back the North Koreans to the border between the two countries. The two sides are at a stand-off.

A cease-fire is signed. Both sides return to pre-war borders.

| June 1950 | July 1950 | Sept. 1950 | Oct. 1950 | Jan. 1951 | Mar. 1951 | June 1952 | July 1953 |

North Korean troops invade South Korea. The United States sends troops to help South Korea.

United Nations troops under United States leadership push back the North Korean troops.

North Korea moves into the south again and takes over South Korea's capital.

Talks for a cease-fire begin.

Write the answer to each question.

8. What event started the Korean War?

9. Who fought on each side of the Korean War?

Circle the number of the best answer for each question.

10. Which event was probably a result of China's entry into the war?
    (1) North Korea gained control of South Korea's capital.
    (2) North and South Korea talked about a cease-fire.
    (3) United Nations' troops pushed back the North Koreans.
    (4) The United States sent troops to help South Korea.
    (5) The United Nations entered the war to help South Korea.

11. Based on the timeline, which of the following statements best summarizes the Korean War?
    (1) South Korea was winning the war at its start.
    (2) North Korea, with the help of Chinese troops, won the war.
    (3) The two sides were deadlocked for a year until truce talks began.
    (4) The two sides talked about a truce for more than one year.
    (5) Neither side gained territory from the war.

The American Revolution

The start of the American Revolution forced people in North America to take sides. Those who wanted to be free from Britain were called Patriots. Those who were loyal to Britain were called Loyalists. Most African Americans faced a hard choice. Many were enslaved. They chose the side that offered them their freedom.

Even before the colonies declared their independence, African Americans were taking sides. African-American soldiers fought in all the early battles of the war. Then in November 1775, Patriot leaders said African Americans could no longer serve in the Patriot army. Those who had already joined were sent home. Slave owners did not want any African Americans to have guns. They were afraid African Americans would use the guns to fight against slavery.

Then the British promised to free any slave who joined their army. Many slaves accepted the offer. As a result Patriot leaders changed their minds. However, they decided to allow only free African Americans, not slaves, to join their army. In December 1777 George Washington took his army of about 9,000 men to Valley Forge, Pennsylvania. By the spring of 1778, Washington had fewer than 6,000 soldiers. Many deserted, while others died of cold or hunger.

Washington desperately needed more soldiers. So the Patriot leaders finally decided to allow enslaved African Americans to enlist. By the end of the war, 5,000 African Americans had taken part in the American Revolution. They came from every state and fought in every major battle. The efforts of African-American soldiers during the war helped convince people who lived in the northern states that slavery should not be allowed.

Write the answer to each question.

12. What is the difference between a Patriot and a Loyalist?

_____

13. Why were African Americans turned away from the Patriot army in 1775?

_____

14. What were the effects of the British decision to free any slave who joined their army?

_____

Circle the number of the best answer.

15. What event permitted enslaved African Americans to join the Patriots' army?
    (1) the start of the American Revolution
    (2) Britain's decision to free slaves who joined its army
    (3) the loss of so many soldiers at Valley Forge
    (4) African-American participation in earlier battles
    (5) the end of the American Revolution

Women's Right to Vote

Women's Suffrage in the United States

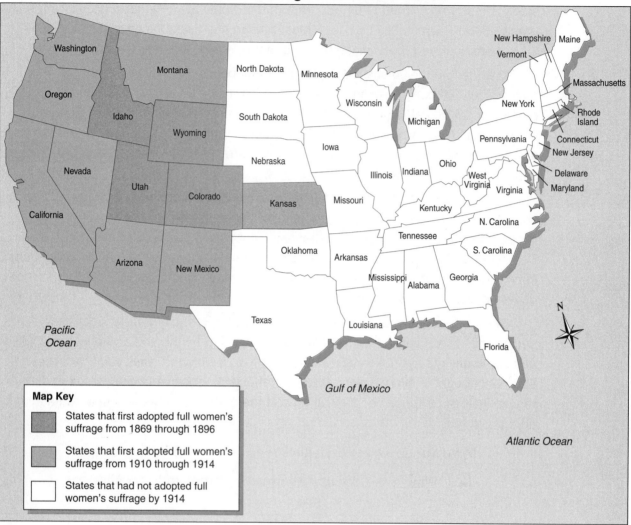

Map Key

States that first adopted full women's suffrage from 1869 through 1896

States that first adopted full women's suffrage from 1910 through 1914

States that had not adopted full women's suffrage by 1914

Write the answer to the question.

16. *Suffrage* means the right to vote. Which states first supported women voting in elections?

_____

Circle the number of the best answer.

17. Which statement is supported by the information in the map?
    (1) In 1900 men influenced American government more than women did.
    (2) Few women in eastern states wanted to vote.
    (3) Before 1914 fewer women lived in Colorado than in Pennsylvania.
    (4) By 1914 most states had given women the right to vote.
    (5) In 1920, the Nineteenth Amendment gave women the right to vote.

Civil Rights

For many years after the Civil War, African Americans worked for equal rights. In the North and the South, they faced **discrimination.** White Americans did not treat them as if they had the same rights that whites did. In many states, schools were segregated. As a result, African American and white children could not attend the same school. African Americans were not allowed to live in many neighborhoods or to hold certain jobs. Some state laws even kept African Americans out of such places as restaurants, public swimming pools, movie theaters, and hotels.

In August 1963, nearly one hundred years after the Civil War ended, more than 250,000 Americans marched down the streets of Washington, D.C. They included white Americans and African Americans from every state and several foreign countries. They demanded that Congress finally pass a civil rights bill that would end discrimination in the United States.

Dr. Martin Luther King, Jr., was among the marchers. He was an African-American minister who was well known for his inspiring sermons. King captured the mood of the day. He said to the crowd, "I have a dream that one day this nation will rise up and live out the true meaning of its creed: 'We hold these truths to be self-evident; that all men are created equal.'"

President John F. Kennedy supported King's cause. He called on Congress to pass a strong civil rights bill. Kennedy did not live to see the bill become law. After Kennedy's death, Congress passed the Civil Rights Act of 1964. It protected the right of all citizens to vote. It outlawed discrimination in hiring and education. It also ended segregation in public places.

Write the answer to each question.

18. What do you think the word *segregated* means from the way it is used in the fourth sentence?

_____

_____

19. Why did Americans march in Washington, D.C., in 1963?

_____

Circle the number of the best answer.

20. Dr. King was calling on all Americans to
    (1) change the nation's values and beliefs
    (2) live up to the nation's values and beliefs
    (3) march down the streets of Washington, D.C.
    (4) pass a civil rights bill
    (5) follow the leadership of President Kennedy

Electing a President and Vice President

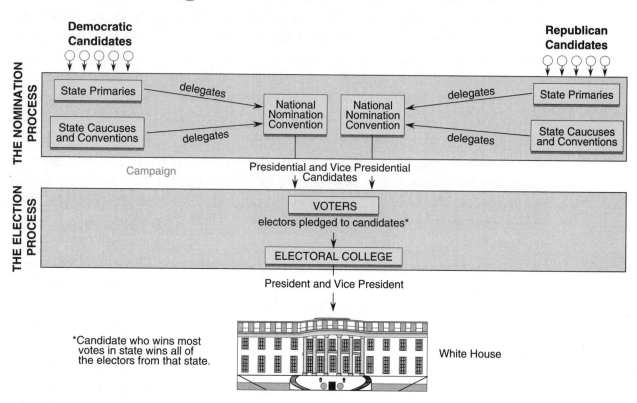

Democratic Candidates

Republican Candidates

THE NOMINATION PROCESS

State Primaries → delegates → National Nomination Convention

State Caucuses and Conventions → delegates → National Nomination Convention

delegates ← State Primaries

delegates ← State Caucuses and Conventions

Campaign

Presidential and Vice Presidential Candidates

THE ELECTION PROCESS

VOTERS
electors pledged to candidates*

ELECTORAL COLLEGE

President and Vice President

*Candidate who wins most votes in state wins all of the electors from that state.

White House

Write the answer to the question.

21. From what two sources are delegates chosen to represent both the Democratic and Republican parties at their nominating conventions?

_____

_____

Circle the number of the best answer.

22. Based on the information provided in the diagram, which group directly elects the president and vice president?
    (1) the voters for the national candidates
    (2) party delegates from the national conventions
    (3) electors of the Electoral College
    (4) party caucus of each political party
    (5) state primaries of each political party

Taxes

Government in the United States provides citizens with many goods and services. To pay for these, it collects taxes from individuals and businesses. Taxes are generally collected on income, sales, and property. Taxes collected in the United States usually follow one of two basic tax principles.

One is the benefit principle. This says that those who benefit the most should be the ones taxed. It also says that they should pay in proportion to the amount of benefit they receive. Gasoline taxes are an example of benefit taxes. Those people who use the most gasoline pay the most gasoline taxes. People who do not own a car do not pay any gasoline tax.

The second tax principle is the ability-to-pay principle. This says that those who have the most income should pay a higher rate of taxes than those who make less money. Most income taxes are based on this principle. The federal government, state governments, and some city governments charge income taxes using this principle. This idea comes from the belief that people with higher incomes can afford to pay higher taxes. So Americans pay different percentages based on their income. A single person in 2002 with $25,000 in taxable income paid 10 percent on the first $6,000 and 15 percent on the rest, or $3,450 in federal income taxes. A person with $50,000 of taxable income paid $9,846, or 10 percent on the first $6,000, 15 percent on $27,950, and 27 percent on the rest. A single person with $308,000 of taxable income in 2002 paid $95,085—close to one-third of this income, in federal income tax.

Many Americans object to the ability-to-pay principle. They argue that everyone should pay the same percentage of his or her income in federal tax. Such a tax is called a flat tax.

Write the answer to each question.

23. What is the difference between a benefit tax and an ability-to-pay tax?

_____

_____

24. If the government switched to a flat tax of 20 percent, whose taxes would go up—those who make $25,000 a year or those who make $308,000 a year?

_____

Circle the number of the best answer.

25. What American ideal is reflected by the principle the federal government currently uses to determine income tax.
    (1) loyalty
    (2) equality
    (3) punishment
    (4) fairness
    (5) freedom

The Global Economy

Write the answer to each question.

26. What does the man hanging from the limb represent?

_____

27. How does the cartoonist show that the United States economy is strong, although in danger?

_____

_____

Circle the number of the best answer.

28. What message is the cartoonist trying to communicate?
    (1) Asia is saving the United States economy.
    (2) A ball and chain can pull a man off a cliff.
    (3) Global economies succeed or fail together.
    (4) Business confidence is at an all-time high.
    (5) The American and Asian economies are not related.

Pretest Evaluation Chart

The chart below will help you determine your strengths and weaknesses in the five content areas of social studies.

Content Area	Question	Total Correct	Practice Pages
U.S. History (Pages 14–65)	12, 13, 14, 15, 16, 17	_____ out of 6	Pages 22–27 Pages 34–39
World History (Pages 66–105)	6, 7, 8, 9, 10, 11	_____ out of 6	Pages 68–73 Pages 92–97
Civics and Government (Pages 106–145)	18, 19, 20, 21, 22	_____ out of 5	Pages 120–125 Pages 126–131
Economics (Pages 146–185)	23, 24, 25 26, 27, 28	_____ out of 6	Pages 154–159 Pages 172–177
Geography (Pages 186–219)	1, 2, 3, 4, 5	_____ out of 5	Pages 194–199 Pages 188–193

Total Correct for Pretest _____ out of 28

Directions

Check your answers on page 232. In the Questions column, circle the number of each question that you answered correctly on the Pretest. Count the number of questions you answered correctly in each content area. Write the amount in the Total Correct blank in each row. (For example, in the Geography row, write the number correct in the blank before *out of 5*). Complete this process for the remaining rows. Then add the five totals to get your Total Correct for the whole Pretest.

If you answered fewer than 25 questions correctly, look more closely at the five content areas of social studies listed above. In which areas do you need more practice? Each content area makes up a part of this book. Look for the page numbers of that section in the chart's right-hand column. Then complete that part of the book for further practice.

UNIT 1

U.S. History

U.S. history tells an exciting story of native peoples and of immigrants from around the world; of everyday citizens and their leaders; of soldiers, teachers, farmers, and inventors. It is the story of how Americans have shaped—and continue to shape—this nation.

Name a historic event that has happened in your lifetime and one that

happened long ago. _____

_____

14

Thinking About U.S. History

You may be surprised to discover how much you already know about U.S. history. Think about what you learned in school, have read in newspapers, or heard on the television news.

Check the box for each fact that you already know.

☐ Christopher Columbus was an early explorer of the Americas.

☐ The Declaration of Independence declared the American colonists free of Great Britain's control.

☐ The Civil War led to the end of slavery in the United States.

☐ The first motion pictures were made by Thomas Alva Edison.

☐ There have been two world wars.

☐ The *Apollo 11* mission put the first Americans on the moon.

Write two other facts that you know about U.S. history.

_____

_____

Previewing the Unit

In this unit, you will learn:

● how European nations gained and then lost colonies in North America

● why Americans fought each other in the 1860s

● how reformers changed American society

● why the United States became involved in World War II and some conflicts that followed it

● how changes in the way we share information have shaped the modern world

Lesson 1	Establishing Colonies
Lesson 2	The American Revolution
Lesson 3	The U.S. Civil War
Lesson 4	The Reform Movement
Lesson 5	World War II
Lesson 6	The Cold War and the Vietnam War
Lesson 7	Communicating in the New Millennium

Establishing Colonies

Establishing Colonies
Establishing Colonies
Establishing Co

Vocabulary

immigrant

migrate

pueblo

conquistador

mission

colony

indentured servant

The first people to come to North America traveled east from Asia long ago. Over time they spread across the land and eventually inhabited all parts of North and South America. They were the original Americans— the Native Americans.

Many years later, Europeans sailed across the Atlantic Ocean. Spanish explorers, looking for riches, conquered Native Americans in the southern part of North America. Other Europeans settled along the Atlantic coast. The mixing of these cultures helped shape what would become the United States of America.

Relate to the Topic

This lesson is about the Americans who lived here first and the ones who came later. Think about your own background.

Where did each of your parents' families originally come from?

_____

How has your family background affected your life?

_____

_____

_____

Reading Strategy

SKIMMING   **Skimming** means to quickly look over something to get the main idea. A good way to do this is to start with the **title,** or name, of an article. The title will gives you a general idea about what the writer will discuss. Read the title on page 17. Then answer the questions.

1. Which groups of people will the writer discuss?

_____

Hint: What words describe the people?

2. What do you think is the basic difference between the two groups?

_____

Hint: In what order does the writer present the groups?

Check your answers on page 232.   **UNIT 1 U.S. HISTORY**

Native and New Americans

The United States is a land of **immigrants.** Immigrants come to a region or country where they were not born in order to live there. Scientists believe that the original Americans came at least 27,000 years ago. They may have walked from Asia to North America across land that today is underwater. Nearly 500 years ago, Europeans sailed to the eastern shores of what would become the United States of America. Even today immigrants from many parts of the world travel to America.

The Original Americans

Small bands of Asian hunters followed animals across a land bridge where water now separates Siberia and Alaska. These people and their descendants **migrated,** or gradually moved, across the continent from the Pacific Ocean to the Atlantic Ocean and south to South America. Over thousands of years, the hunters changed to fit their environment. They learned to farm and settled in villages. Groups in different areas developed their own crafts, language, and religion.

One group in North America was the Anasazi. From 100 B.C. to about A.D. 1300, these people lived in what is now the southwestern United States. They managed to raise corn, squash, and beans in a very dry climate. They built large **pueblos,** or settlements with apartment-like buildings made of sandy clay called "adobe." Anasazi buildings are believed to be the oldest in what today is the United States.

By the 1400s, some groups of Native Americans in what are now Mexico and Central America had empires with elaborate cities. The cities had canals, pyramids, temples, and markets. The Aztec people built the great city of Tenochtitlán, which was located where Mexico City stands today. In 1500, this Aztec city had about 300,000 people, which was twice the number of people that lived in London, England, at the time.

In the eastern woodlands of North America, many nations of American Indians shared the region's thick forests and rich soil. Groups often disagreed over farmland and hunting grounds. In what is now New York, Indians from five nations often trespassed on one another's land. Trespassing led to fighting. Tired of war, the nations finally decided to work together. About 1570 they formed the Iroquois League. Each nation governed itself but also chose members to serve on a Great Council. The council made decisions on important matters, such as trade and war.

European Explorers and Traders

The first Europeans to visit North America were sailors from Scandinavia. They reached Newfoundland about A.D. 1000 but did not stay. European exploration and settlement of the Americas did not really begin until Spain sent Christopher Columbus on a voyage in 1492. He was looking for a sea route from Europe to Asia. He wanted to trade for Asian spices. Instead he found the Americas, or what Europeans called the New World.

Europeans soon realized that the New World was full of riches. Spanish **conquistadors** (conquerors), fired by dreams of gold and silver, looted the rich empires of Mexico and South America. At first the Native Americans did not resist because they thought the Spaniards were gods. Later the Native Americans were unable to resist because so many had died from European diseases.

In North America the explorers found little gold. Nevertheless, Roman Catholic priests who came with the Spanish explorers built missions in what is now Mexico, Texas, California, and Florida. A **mission** is a settlement centered around a church. The priests who ran the missions were called missionaries. The Spanish missionaries invited Native Americans into their missions and taught them about Christianity. Many missionaries thought the Native Americans were savages and tried to make them give up their ways.

The English, French, and Dutch also searched for a water route through the Americas to the markets of Asia. In this search, they explored the northern regions of North America. By 1610 France had a profitable fur trade with Native Americans in what is now Canada.

Reading a Historical Map A map can show how different groups moved from one place to another. A map key can indicate when each move took place. Look closely at the map below. How many years before the English did the Spanish establish a settlement in what is now the eastern United States?

    a. 42 years   b. 55 years

Some European Voyages to North America

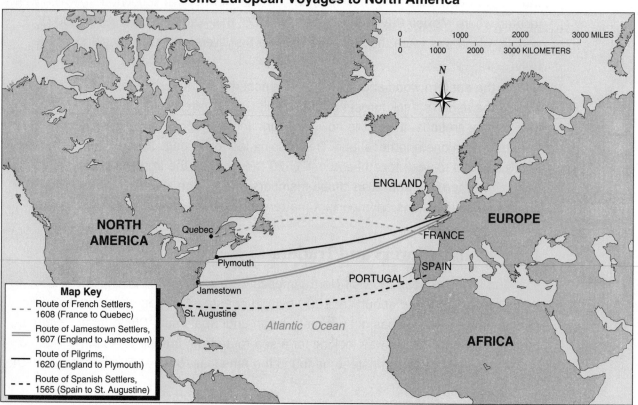

Map Key
- - - Route of French Settlers, 1608 (France to Quebec)
—— Route of Jamestown Settlers, 1607 (England to Jamestown)
━━ Route of Pilgrims, 1620 (England to Plymouth)
- ‑ - Route of Spanish Settlers, 1565 (Spain to St. Augustine)

New Americans

The English began their settlement of North America in the early 1600s. Their **colonies** lasted longer and grew larger than many other European settlements. Most English who settled in North America came for religious, political, or economic reasons.

The first long-lasting English settlement in North America was Jamestown, Virginia. Three ships carrying 144 settlers landed there in 1607. That first winter, the settlers faced disease, starvation, and attacks by Native Americans. In time, however, they learned to grow food crops and tobacco.

In 1620 the *Mayflower* set sail from Plymouth, England, with 73 men and boys and 29 women and girls. They were seeking religious freedom from the official Church of England. Their ship landed along the coast of Massachusetts. These settlers, who called themselves Pilgrims, also had a difficult first year. Almost half of them died. But a Native American named Squanto taught the survivors how to plant corn, catch fish, and find their way in the wilderness.

Later a religious group known as Puritans started the Massachusetts Bay Colony. They permitted only followers of their religion to live in their settlements. So some colonists who wanted religious freedom left Massachusetts and set up the colonies of Rhode Island in 1644 and New Hampshire in 1662. Quakers, another religious group, founded Pennsylvania in 1681. They welcomed Spanish Jews, Irish Catholics, and German Lutherans.

As news of these colonies returned to England, more people came to North America looking for land and freedom. Those who had no money to pay their way became **indentured servants.** They promised to work for two to seven years in exchange for their passage to the colonies. Convicted criminals served their sentences in the colonies as indentured servants. Africans were kidnapped and also forced to work in America as indentured servants. By the 1660s, however, colonies were passing laws that made slaves of African-American servants.

Gradually the 13 British colonies developed their own way of life. This strained their ties with England. By the 1770s some colonists were ready for independence.

Sequencing Events The **sequence** of events is the order in which things happen. This is also called chronological order. Specific dates and words like *first, second, next,* and *finally* provide clues to the order of events. Reread the paragraphs under "New Americans." Then number the names of the colonies below in the order that they were established.

_____ Pennsylvania

_____ Massachusetts

_____ Virginia

_____ Rhode Island

Check your answers on page 233.

Thinking About the Article

Practice Vocabulary

The words below are in the passage in bold type. Study the way each word is used. Then complete each sentence by writing the correct word.

immigrants	migrated	pueblos
conquistadors	missions	indentured servants

1. The Spanish _____ came to America seeking wealth and adventure.

2. Europeans with little money became _____ to pay their way to America.

3. Scientists believe that over many generations the first Americans slowly _____ across North and South America.

4. Spanish priests invited Native Americans to live and learn at the

   _____ .

5. The Anasazi lived in settlements known as _____.

6. _____ from many parts of the world have moved to North America for a better life.

Understand the Article

Write the answer to each question.

7. Why did Asians first come to North America?

   _____

8. Later settlers came from Spain, France, and Britain. Why did each of these groups come to North America?

   _____

   _____

9. What difficulties did settlers have in establishing a colony in Jamestown?

   _____

   _____

10. Why did some Massachusetts colonists found Rhode Island?

    _____

    _____

Apply Your Skills

Circle the number of the best answer for each question.

11. Look at the map on page 18. Based on the map, which of the following statements describes the beginnings of European settlement?
    (1) European settlers moved west across North America over a long period.
    (2) Early English settlements lay north of Spanish settlements.
    (3) French settlers arrived about 40 years before the English.
    (4) The Spanish first landed in Asia on their way to North America.
    (5) The English settled before the Spanish.

12. Review the article, and then select the most recent event below.
    (1) The Anasazi raised corn, beans, and squash in what today is the southwestern United States.
    (2) The Aztecs in Mexico built an empire with a great city.
    (3) The first Americans migrated across a land bridge from Asia.
    (4) The English settled at Jamestown, Virginia.
    (5) Sailors from Scandinavia first arrived in Newfoundland.

13. Which of the following colonies was the last to be established?
    (1) Massachusetts
    (2) Virginia
    (3) Pennsylvania
    (4) Rhode Island
    (5) New Hampshire

Connect with the Article

Write your answer to each question.

14. The Pilgrims and Squanto were better neighbors than later colonists and Native Americans. Give two reasons why you think this was the case.

    _____

    _____

    _____

15. At one time or another, members of your family moved to North America. Why do you think they came?

    _____

    _____

    _____

The American Revolution

The years from 1688 to 1763 were a time of war. France, Spain, and Great Britain fought one another for control of Europe and the Americas. In 1763 Great Britain won a seven-year war with the French in North America.

Great Britain had created one of the largest empires in the world, but the nation was deeply in debt. British King George III decided that his American colonies must help pay the bill. The colonists disagreed and started down the road to war with Great Britain.

Vocabulary

prime minister

legislature

boycott

exports

repealed

imports

minutemen

Relate to the Topic

This lesson is about the conflict between Great Britain and its American colonies. Describe how this kind of conflict could be similar to conflicts between parents and their teenage children.

_____

_____

_____

_____

Reading Strategy

SKIMMING   A title usually gives the main topic of an article. **Headings** are the names of sections within the article. Headings are set in smaller type, and tell you what supporting details are discussed in each section. Read the headings on pages 23 through 25. Then answer the questions.

1. Name three places that the writer will discuss. _____

   _____

   Hint: Look for words that name places rather than things.

2. What do the words "disagreements" and "battles" suggest about the

   article? _____

   _____

   Hint: Think about how you would use these words.

Check your answers on page 233. UNIT 1 U.S. HISTORY

The Fight for Independence

After Great Britain's long war with France, the British Parliament became more involved in its American colonies. The colonists, who had done as they pleased for many years, did not welcome this new interest. Parliament pushed and the colonists pushed back. In time, the disagreements grew more serious. They led to a war known as the American Revolution.

Growing Disagreements

Great Britain faced a huge bill after the war with France. Nearly half the debt was from the fighting in North America. Therefore Parliament decided that Americans should help pay the bill because they shared the benefits from the victory over France. Britain's **prime minister,** or head of the Parliament, realized that enforcing some old trade laws in the colonies might help the Treasury.

The money raised from these laws was still not enough to pay the bill. More taxes would raise money, but people in Great Britain already were paying high taxes. So in 1765 Parliament passed the Stamp Act. Colonists who bought certain items or documents had to buy stamps that proved they had paid the necessary tax. Without the stamp, the item was considered stolen or the document illegal. Marriage licenses, newspapers, diplomas, and playing cards were among the items that needed stamps.

The colonists were angry when they heard about the Stamp Act. In many colonies, mobs forced tax collectors out of town. The colonists knew the principles that British government followed. In Great Britain, people could not be taxed unless they had a representative in Parliament. The colonists did not have any representatives in Parliament. Therefore they believed that Parliament had no right to tax them. They felt that only a colony's **legislature,** or lawmakers, had that right.

Parliament said its members acted in everyone's interest, including that of the colonists. But the colonists did not accept this. They protested, "No taxation without representation." They **boycotted,** or refused to buy, British products. British merchants suffered when colonists refused to buy their **exports.** These were the products made in Great Britain and sold in the colonies. One year later, Parliament **repealed,** or did away with, the Stamp Act. Colonists celebrated with bonfires and parades.

Identifying Cause and Effect Every event has at least one cause and one effect. The **cause** is <u>why</u> something happened. Words like *because, since,* and *reason* signal a cause. The **effect** tells <u>what happened</u> as a result of the cause. Words such as *so, therefore,* and *as a result* signal an effect. Reread the first paragraph under "Growing Disagreements." Then circle the letter of the effect of Great Britain's debt.

    a. Parliament passed new taxes for the colonies.
    b. Britain fought a seven-year war with France.

The next British prime minister still believed the colonists should be taxed. This time the money raised would help pay the salaries of royal governors and judges in the American colonies. Parliament passed a new law in 1767 that taxed imports to the colonies such as glass, lead, paper, silk, and tea. **Imports** are goods brought into a country from another country. The colonies protested the new taxes, and Great Britain sent troops to the colonies to enforce the law.

British soldiers and American colonists did not get along. On March 5, 1770, in Boston, Massachusetts, about sixty colonists taunted ten British soldiers. Colonists knocked down two soldiers. The squad opened fire on the colonists. The British killed three colonists and wounded eight others. Two of the wounded colonists later died. This clash is called the Boston Massacre.

A Tea Party in Boston

A month after the clash in Boston, Parliament repealed all the taxes except the tea tax. British lawmakers wanted to remind the colonists that Parliament had the right and power to tax them. Unexpectedly, the colonists boycotted tea. Parliament lowered the price of tea but kept the tax. The British were sure the colonists would buy tea again. Nevertheless, on the night of December 16, 1773, a group of colonists in Boston dressed up like Native Americans. They boarded British ships and dumped more than three hundred chests of tea into Boston's harbor. This protest against the tea tax became known as the Boston Tea Party.

The British were outraged. In 1774 Parliament passed new laws to punish the colonists. One law closed Boston's harbor until the colonists paid for the tea. Another law strengthened the power of the king's governor in Massachusetts. Still another law required the colonists to provide housing for British soldiers. Colonists called the laws the Intolerable Acts because Americans thought the laws made life unbearable.

Events Leading to the American Revolution

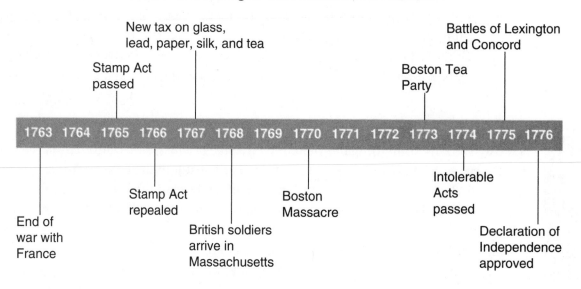

Because of the Intolerable Acts, representatives from 12 of the 13 colonies met in Philadelphia, Pennsylvania, in 1774. They called the meeting the First Continental Congress. The delegates were still willing to remain part of Britain. But they wanted the harsh laws repealed. The colonists also wanted Parliament to know it could not tax them. The delegates voted to meet again in May 1775. The American Revolution began before that meeting was held.

The Battles of Lexington and Concord

Few colonists wanted a war. Nevertheless, some farmers, blacksmiths, and other workers trained for battle. They called themselves **minutemen** because they were ready to fight at a minute's notice.

The British also prepared for war. British troops in Massachusetts planned to capture two colonial leaders, John Hancock and Samuel Adams, and to raid the colonists' military supplies. The supplies were stored in the small town of Concord, about twenty miles from Boston.

Paul Revere and other colonists learned of the British plan. On the night of April 18, 1775, they rode ahead of the British troops to alert the minutemen. The next morning when the British soldiers arrived at Lexington, a town near Concord, the minutemen were waiting.

The minutemen and the British soldiers were under orders to hold their fire. Nevertheless, someone opened fire and the shooting began. Eight minutemen were killed. The battle gave Hancock and Adams time to get away.

Next the British marched to Concord. There they found only a few weapons. Just outside Concord, three British soldiers and two minutemen died during a brief battle. At about noon, the outnumbered British soldiers headed back to Boston. Minutemen hid behind fences, barns, and farmhouses along the road. They fired at the soldiers. By the time the British reached their camp near Boston, 73 more soldiers had died. Another 200 were wounded or missing.

The American Revolution had begun. In the weeks that followed, the fighting spread. On July 4, 1776, the Second Continental Congress officially approved the Declaration of Independence. It told the world why the 13 colonies were fighting to be free of British rule. Americans' fight for independence continued until 1781.

Reading a Timeline A **timeline** shows when a series of events took place. It also shows the order of events. It helps you figure out the time between events as well as cause-and-effect relationships. Look at the timeline on page 24. Then answer the questions.

1. In what year were the colonies first taxed by Britain? _____

2. In what year were protesting colonists killed in Boston? _____

3. Was the Declaration of Independence approved before or after the Battles of Lexington and Concord? _____

Check your answers on page 233.

Thinking About the Article

Practice Vocabulary

The words below are in the passage in bold type. Study the way each word is used. Then complete each sentence by writing the correct word.

exports	legislature	boycotted
repealed	imports	minutemen

1. Colonists protested the Stamp Act by refusing to buy British

   _____ .

2. Parliament _____ the Stamp Act in 1766.

3. Each colony had its own _____ , which made laws for its people.

4. _____ were waiting for the British soldiers when they came to Lexington.

5. Tea, glass, and silk were some of the _____ on which colonists had to pay taxes.

6. British trade was hurt after the colonists _____ goods from Great Britain.

Understand the Article

Write the answer to each question.

7. How did the colonists react to the Stamp Act?

   _____

   _____

8. Why did the colonists throw the Boston Tea Party?

   _____

9. What is the Declaration of Independence about?

   _____

   _____

10. How did the minutemen manage to shoot so many British while the soldiers retreated to Boston?

    _____

    _____

Apply Your Skills

Circle the number of the best answer for each question.

11. Which event caused the British to pass the Intolerable Acts?
    (1) the colonial boycott of British products
    (2) the Boston Massacre
    (3) the enforcement of the tea tax
    (4) the Boston Tea Party
    (5) the signing of the Declaration of Independence

12. Which of the following was an effect of the battles of Lexington and Concord?
    (1) The colonists planned the Boston Tea Party.
    (2) The First Continental Congress met.
    (3) Parliament passed the Intolerable Acts.
    (4) Parliament passed the Tea Act.
    (5) The American Revolution began.

13. Look again at the timeline on page 24. How many years passed between the end of Great Britain's war with France and the beginning of its war with the American colonies?
    (1) 7
    (2) 10
    (3) 11
    (4) 12
    (5) 15

Connect with the Article

Write your answer to each question.

14. How do you think news of the American Revolution affected American colonists ruled by Spain?

    _____

    _____

    _____

15. Using the American Revolution as an example, how do you think people today might react if laws are enforced unfairly over a long period of time?

    _____

    _____

    _____

LESSON 3

The U.S. Civil War

Vocabulary

cash crop

Union

Confederacy

abolitionist

Emancipation Proclamation

discrimination

regiment

In the early 1800s, the United States doubled its territory. Each region—the North, the South, and the new West—developed its own character. In the North, many farm workers moved to cities, where they could find work at textile mills. In the South, enslaved African Americans worked long hours on plantations. The cotton that they picked went to mills in the North and in Europe. Other Americans migrated to western lands. There they built towns, farms, and plantations of their own.

These different ways of life led to disagreements. The disagreements became so serious that they threatened to tear the United States apart.

Relate to the Topic

This lesson is about why Americans during the 1860s fought one another in a war that split the country. Think of a time when you and a friend disagreed about an issue that was very important to you. Describe how you tried to resolve your difference. If the issue is unresolved, describe how you feel about it now.

_____

_____

_____

_____

Reading Strategy

SKIMMING PICTURES   In most informational reading, pictures can add to your understanding of the text. They can also help you preview a passage. Skim the picture on page 31. Then answer the questions.

1. What kind of scene does the picture show? _____

   _Hint: Complete this sentence: The picture is about _____._

2. Based on the picture, name a topic that you think the writer might discuss in the article.

   _____

   Hint: Decide which details seem especially important

Differences Lead to War

In the North many people were leaving farms to become factory workers. Textile mills, where workers wove cotton and wool into cloth, were among the first factories in the North. Thousands of job-seeking immigrants arrived through northern seaports. By 1860 the North's population was nearing twenty million.

The South's eleven million people included four million enslaved African Americans. Many white Southerners depended on slave labor to grow cash crops, such as tobacco and cotton. A **cash crop** is grown to be sold rather than for personal use. Most Southerners did not hold slaves, but those who did were the South's leaders.

The Many-Sided Slavery Issue

In Congress and in newspapers throughout the country, Americans debated the issue of slavery. Many Northerners saw slavery as immoral. Southerners saw it as necessary for their economy. In coastal regions of South Carolina and Georgia, enslaved African Americans made up 50 to 75 percent of the population. Many plantation owners feared financial ruin if slavery was outlawed.

The most heated debates centered on whether new states in the West should allow slavery. Congress created plans in 1820 and 1850 to answer this question. Each plan tried to satisfy both the North and the South. But in the end, neither was satisfied. Abraham Lincoln, who was against the expansion of slavery, was elected the United States President in 1860. Several states soon left the United States to form a new nation. In 1861 the Civil War began.

The Civil War was fought between 23 northern states, called the **Union,** and 11 southern states, called the **Confederacy.** Southerners in the Confederacy no longer wanted to be part of the United States. Most Northerners did not think the South had a right to declare itself a separate country. They were willing to fight to keep the nation together. African Americans hoped the Civil War would end slavery.

Before the war started, people held slaves in 15 states. Four of these slave states stayed in the Union. They are called the border states. When Lincoln asked for volunteers to fight for the Union, thousands of free African Americans rushed to sign up. But Lincoln thought the Union might lose the four border states to the Confederacy if he allowed African Americans to fight. He did not want people in these states to think the Union was fighting to end slavery. So the armed forces turned away African-American volunteers. Lincoln explained his war goals in a letter to the owner of a New York newspaper:

> My paramount object in this struggle is to save the Union, and is not either to save or destroy slavery. If I could save the Union without freeing any slave I would do it; and if I could save it by freeing all the slaves, I would [do] it; and if I could do it by freeing some and leaving others alone, I would also do that.

Understanding the Main Idea The main idea of a paragraph is often stated in a sentence called the topic sentence. It is usually the first sentence in a paragraph but is sometimes the last. It tells what the paragraph is about. Underline the topic sentence from Lincoln's letter. Then circle the letter of the statement below that best describes his main idea.

    a.   The Civil War must save the Union.

    b.   The Civil War must destroy slavery.

The Emancipation Proclamation

Lincoln wanted a quick end to the war, and **abolitionists**—people opposed to slavery—were pressuring him to act. They wanted him to free enslaved African Americans.

Lincoln thought he should wait for a Union victory before announcing any decision. The North won a battle at Antietam in Maryland, in September 1862. Five days later, Lincoln issued a written statement. It said that on January 1, 1863, all slaves in states fighting against the United States would be "forever free." This action was called the **Emancipation Proclamation.** Lincoln was still concerned that the border states might leave the Union. He was very clear that he had not freed the enslaved people in those states. But the war took on a new meaning. African Americans and white Northerners who were against slavery celebrated.

The proclamation did not end slavery in the Confederacy. Lincoln knew that the South would have to be defeated before all the people there would be free. The proclamation also did not end discrimination. **Discrimination** is the unequal and unfair treatment of a person or group. Even free African Americans in the North did not enjoy the same rights that Whites enjoyed. In most states African Americans could not vote or attend public schools. Many states did not allow them to own property. However the Emancipation Proclamation opened the door for African Americans to join the military. By the end of the war, about 200,000 African Americans served in the Union army and navy. Many of them had escaped from slavery in the South.

African-American soldiers faced discrimination. They were not allowed to fight beside white soldiers. At first they were paid only half as much as white soldiers. But by the war's end, both groups were paid the same amount.

African Americans' Proud Record

Massachusetts was one of the first states to form African-American regiments, including the famous 54th regiment. A **regiment** is a large military group. In July 1863 the 54th attacked Fort Wagner near Charleston, South Carolina. Nearly fifty percent of the regiment was killed.

The fighting record of African-American soldiers in the Civil War was outstanding. Only the bravest members of the armed forces receive the Congressional Medal of Honor. Twenty-three African Americans received this honor during the Civil War.

At the war's start, African Americans gave their support in other ways besides fighting. They acted as camp cooks, barbers, gravediggers, messengers, nurses, scouts, and spies. In 1862 a small group of enslaved African Americans in South Carolina took over a Confederate steamer named *The Planter*. Robert Smalls led the group. He had been forced as a slave to serve in the Confederate Navy. He sailed the ship out of Charleston harbor and turned it over to Union forces. Later he said:

> Although born a slave I always felt that I was a man and ought to be free, and I would be free or die. While at the wheel of *The Planter* . . . it occurred to me that I could not only secure my own freedom but that of numbers of my comrades.

Another one-time slave, Harriet Tubman, had been helping African Americans escape from the South since the 1850s. During the war, she helped the Union forces as a nurse, scout, and spy.

The South surrendered in April 1865, ending the Civil War. African Americans had won their freedom. However, the fight to end discrimination in the United States was just beginning.

The 54th Massachusetts Volunteers Regiment attacks Fort Wagner in Charleston, South Carolina, on July 18, 1863.

Identifying Point of View in a Historic Context Writers express their point of view using words. Artists use pictures to show how they feel. Look at the picture above. It shows the Union's Massachusetts 54th Regiment attacking Fort Wagner in South Carolina. Which detail in the picture suggests that the artist sided with the North?

    a.   The American flag is at the center of the picture.

    b.   The Confederate fort looks strongly fortified.

THE U.S. CIVIL WAR

Check your answer on page 234.

Thinking About the Article

Practice Vocabulary

The words below are in the passage in bold type. Study the way each word is used. Then complete each sentence by writing the correct word.

cash crop **Union** **Confederacy** **abolitionists**

Emancipation Proclamation **discrimination** **regiment**

1. Eleven southern states left the Union and formed the

   _____ .

2. In 1862 President Lincoln announced the _____ .

3. _____ tried to persuade President Lincoln to end slavery.

4. Even free African Americans in the North suffered from

   _____ .

5. Massachusetts formed a _____ of African-American soldiers.

6. Abraham Lincoln's major concern was preserving the

   _____ .

7. An example of a(n) _____ is tobacco.

Understand the Article

Write the answer to each question.

8. Why did plantation owners defend slavery?

   _____

9. Why did the Union hesitate to enlist African Americans as soldiers?

   _____

10. What were two ways African Americans supported the war before they were allowed to fight?

    _____

    _____

11. How did the Union discriminate against African-American soldiers during the Civil War?

    _____

Apply Your Skills

Circle the number of the best answer for each question.

12. Which description <u>best</u> expresses the main idea of the picture on page 31?
    (1) African-American soldiers fought bravely for the Union.
    (2) Confederate soldiers won the 1863 battle.
    (3) African-American soldiers pushed back Confederate soldiers as the Confederates attacked the fort.
    (4) Union ships supported the attack on Fort Wagner.
    (5) The American flag is at the center of the picture.

13. Who was least likely to view Robert Smalls as a hero?
    (1) Abraham Lincoln
    (2) Harriet Tubman
    (3) an abolitionist
    (4) a plantation owner
    (5) a European who opposed slavery

14. Which of the following statements expresses the main idea of the Emancipation Proclamation?
    (1) All enslaved African Americans were freed.
    (2) The Union was winning the war.
    (3) Enslaved persons in the border states were freed.
    (4) African Americans would have the same rights as whites.
    (5) Freeing slaves in the Confederacy was a Union goal.

Connect with the Article

Write your answer to each question.

15. In what two ways did the North and South differ before the Civil War began?

    _____

    _____

    _____

16. What is a problem of discrimination in your community? Write a three-step plan to help fight this problem.

    _____

    _____

    _____

    _____

    _____

LESSON 4

The Reform Movement

Vocabulary

child labor

apprentice

master

reformer

literate

In colonial times, a family worked as a team. All family members—even children—shared the work. They tended to animals, planted crops, cooked meals, and cleaned the house and barns together. Children worked six days a week from sunup to sundown. Few went to school.

In the 1800s, Americans began leaving their farms. They found jobs in growing cities and new factory towns. Business owners encouraged their workers' children to work, too. Soon children were doing work that was as hard or as dangerous as adults' work. In addition, child workers earned only a fraction of an adult's pay. The situation cried out for change.

Relate to the Topic

This lesson is about how some Americans in the early 1900s wanted laws to protect children in the workplace. Write a sentence or two about your early work experiences. How old were you when you first earned money? When did you start your first job? How many hours did you work each week? On what did you spend your wages?

_____

_____

_____

_____

Reading Strategy

RELATING TO WHAT YOU KNOW   There are several ways to help yourself make sense of informational reading. One way is to compare the facts with what you already have read or learned about the topic. Read the paragraph that begins the article on page 35. Then answer the questions.

1. What do you already know about this topic? _____

_____

Hint: When or where might you have heard the term child labor?

2. Write one fact that is new to you. _____

_____

Hint: What dates and other numbers does the writer mention?

Check your answers on page 234.   UNIT 1 U.S. HISTORY

Child Labor

As factories spread throughout the United States, so did the practice of **child labor,** or in other words, using children as workers. By 1890 one million children had jobs. In the South most child laborers worked in textile mills, where cotton was made into cloth. In Chicago many children worked in the meat-packing industry. In New York they worked in the garment industry. By 1900 more than 1.7 million Americans under 16 years of age had jobs.

Learning a Trade

Child labor was not a new idea. Learning from skilled masters was a common practice in ancient Egypt, Greece, and Rome. It was still the way young people learned a trade in Europe when the American colonies were founded.

During colonial times, many children were working as apprentices by the time they were 12 years old. An **apprentice** is someone who learns a trade, or skill, from an expert called a **master.** Apprentices learned how to make clothing from master tailors. They learned how to make shoes from master cobblers. Hatmakers, blacksmiths, silversmiths, and other skilled business people all trained apprentices. Apprentices worked long, hard days. Being an apprentice was an opportunity for a boy to get ahead. Girls, on the other hand, rarely had the chance to become apprentices.

At the age of 12, Benjamin Franklin became an apprentice to his older brother, James. The older brother was a printer. James agreed to teach Benjamin how to become a good printer. He also provided Benjamin with food, clothing, and a place to live. He promised to take care of Benjamin if he became ill. In return Benjamin had to work hard for five years. He also had to promise not to give away any of his master's printing secrets.

When Franklin finished his apprenticeship at age 17, he had valuable skills. His skills made him capable of contributing to a business. Because he had a trade, he would earn more wages than someone with no special skills. When he could not find work in Boston or New York, he moved to Philadelphia. Within weeks, he was working for a printer. By the time he was 22, he had enough experience to start his own printing shop. Franklin became one of Philadelphia's most respected business leaders.

Comparing and Contrasting. To **compare** people, events, or things is to show how they are alike. The words *also, as well as,* and *like* signal a comparison. To **contrast** is to show how people, events, or things are different. Words that signal a contrast include *however, on the other hand, unlike, although,* and *yet.* Reread the second paragraph under "Learning a Trade." In one sentence, the phrase *on the other hand* signals a contrast. Which two persons are being contrasted?

   a.   an apprentice and a master

   b.   a boy and a girl

Check your answer on page 234.

A Child's Life

Factory owners in the 1800s had jobs that needed little or no training. A ten-year-old child could often handle the work. In fact, some factory owners hired only children. They claimed that children could do certain jobs better than adults. Children ran errands, helped machine operators, and cleaned. Factory owners also paid children less than adults. Unskilled adult workers made about one dime per hour, which came to one dollar for a ten-hour day. Children worked for as little as 50 cents a day.

By the mid-1800s, many states had free public schools. In 1850 nearly 3.3 million children went to elementary schools. Most parents wanted their children to go to school. But because factory jobs paid adults so little, some parents needed their children to work, too. Before 1900 most workers made only about $400 to $500 per year. Yet the basic cost of living was about $600. Many parents could not pay their family's living expenses without the money their children earned. They could not afford to let their children go to school.

Children did not work only in factories. Some worked in coal mines. Others worked in country stables. Some worked on city sidewalks, selling newspapers or shining shoes. Many children still worked on farms. They harvested berries, tobacco, sugar beets, and other vegetables. However, children in factories and mines worked under the most dangerous and unhealthy conditions. In paint factories child workers breathed in toxic fumes. In the garment industry, young laborers hunched over sewing machines and developed curved spines. In coal mines boys as young as nine years old inhaled coal dust all day.

Children worked in canneries in the early 1900s.

The Push for Reform

People who work to change things for the better are called **reformers.** In the 1890s and early 1900s, many Americans worked hard to improve the lives of children. These reformers wanted laws that set a minimum working age. They also wanted to limit the number of hours children could work. They felt children should be kept out of dangerous jobs. Most reformers believed that every child should have the chance to go to school.

Reformers worked to make people aware of the conditions that children faced in the workplace. Some reformers created the National Child Labor Committee. This group hired people to investigate factories and mines. One of these investigators was Lewis Hine. He wrote about the children he met and took photos of them at work. In 1910 he took the photo shown on page 36.

Factory owners hired guards to keep Hine away. The owners did not want anyone to take pictures of their workers. They were afraid to let people see what conditions were like. But Hine found ways to get inside the factories. He often disguised himself as a Bible salesman or a fire inspector. Sometimes he pretended to be a photographer eager to take pictures of the latest machines. He always kept his notebook hidden in a pocket. He used his notes to write many articles. His photographs, however, were more powerful than any words he wrote.

Several states passed laws to protect children as the result of the work of Hine and others. For example, the Illinois Factory Act of 1893 stopped employers from hiring children under 14 to work more than eight hours a day. By 1914 every state but one had child-labor laws with a minimum age limit. The age was 12 in several states in the South, 15 in South Dakota, and 16 in Montana. Most laws also banned children from working until they were **literate,** or could read and write.

Often states failed to enforce their laws. As a result, many Americans demanded a national law that the United States government and its federal agents would enforce. But business people across the nation disapproved of any such law.

Several times Congress passed child-labor laws, but the Supreme Court ruled them unconstitutional. In 1925 reformers even proposed a Constitutional amendment that would limit child labor. However, the amendment failed to win enough support. Finally, in 1938 Congress passed a national child-labor law. The law made it illegal for most businesses to hire children under the age of 16. Children under the age of 18 could not work at dangerous jobs. But the law failed to protect all children. For example, it did not include farm workers. It also failed to stop child labor during World War II. When adults left their jobs to join the armed forces, states ignored the law and allowed young teenagers to work long hours.

Understanding a Photo As proof of the need for laws to protect children, Hine used photos like the one on page 36. Which charge would the details in the photo support?

a. Child workers lack adult supervision.

b. Children work in unhealthy conditions.

Thinking About the Article

Practice Vocabulary

The words below are in the passage in bold type. Study the way each word is used. Then complete each sentence by writing the correct word.

child labor   **apprentice**   **master**

reformers   **literate**

1. _____ was common from the nation's beginning.

2. Other _____ at the turn of the century worked to gain women the right to vote and to help the poor in cities.

3. From ancient times, the best way for a young person to learn a skill was to study under a(n) _____ .

4. In the early 1900s, many immigrants moved to the United States and needed to become _____ in English.

5. A(n) _____ spent years learning a trade from an expert.

Understand the Article

Write the answer to each question.

6. How was a master like a parent?

   _____

   _____

7. Why did some parents send their children to work?

   _____

   _____

8. Why did many factory owners hire children?

   _____

   _____

9. Why did factory owners try to keep Lewis Hine from visiting their factories?

   _____

   _____

Apply Your Skills

Circle the number of the best answer for each question.

10. Which statement is an example of a comparison?
    (1) Work in garment factories as well as in coal mines posed health hazards for children.
    (2) Hine often disguised himself as a Bible salesman or as a fire inspector.
    (3) Several states passed laws to protect children as the result of the work of Hine and others.
    (4) As a result, many Americans demanded a national law that the United States government and its federal agents would enforce.
    (5) In 1938 Congress passed a law making it illegal for most businesses to hire anyone younger than age 16.

11. Look again at the photograph on page 36. Which phrase <u>best</u> describes the working conditions?
    (1) no fresh air
    (2) dirty workplace
    (3) dangerous tasks
    (4) unsafe machinery
    (5) loud noises

12. Which sentence states a true contrast between apprentices in colonial times and child workers in the early 1900s?
    (1) Both apprentices and boys in coal mines worked long hours.
    (2) Masters and factory owners supplied their workers with clothing.
    (3) An apprentice earned better wages than a child worker in a factory.
    (4) An apprentice learned more valuable skills than a factory worker.
    (5) Factory owners taught young workers to read while masters did not.

Connect with the Article

Write your answer to each question.

13. There is an old saying that "one picture is worth a thousand words." How does this saying apply to Hine's photograph on page 36?

    _____

    _____

14. Many teenagers have part-time jobs in which they work 20 to 30 hours a week during the school year. To help protect young workers, suggest two guidelines for an employer of teenagers.

    _____

    _____

World War II

Vocabulary

Allies

defense industry

labor union

defense contract

stock market

labor force

Only 21 years after the end of World War I, countries across the globe clashed again. By the late 1930s, Germany, Italy, and Japan had built up their armed forces. They began threatening their neighbors.

As in World War I, the United States was not involved at the start of World War II. The nation still was recovering from the serious economic problems of the Great Depression. President Franklin D. Roosevelt had created programs that helped people keep their farms, get jobs, and stay in business. Putting people to work boosted the economy. World War II, however, helped American industry really regain its strength.

Relate to the Topic

This lesson is about how Americans fighting overseas and working in factories at home helped win World War II. Write a sentence or two about being part of a team. Have you been a member of a sports team or any other type of group effort? What united the team? Why do you think your team accomplished what it did?

_____

_____

_____

_____

Reading Strategy

SCANNING A GRAPH   Social studies materials often use graphs to illustrate information. You can scan, or quickly look over, a graph to find out what kinds of information it includes. **Scanning** is another way to preview something. Skim the title, labels of the graph, and key of the graph on page 43. Then answer the questions.

1.   What information does the graph illustrate? _____
     Hint: Look at the title and the words along the side.

2.   What years does the graph cover? _____

     _____

     Hint: Look at the numbers along the bottom.

Check your answers on page 235.   **UNIT 1 U.S. HISTORY**

The Search for New Workers

On December 7, 1941, Japanese planes bombed the American fleet in Pearl Harbor, Hawaii. The next day the United States declared war on Japan. Thousands of young workers left their jobs to join the armed forces. This meant fewer workers in factories. Yet war production required millions of skilled workers.

American factories had to make military supplies for American troops and the rest of the **Allies**—the British, the French, and the Soviets. The Allies fought together against the Germans, the Italians, and the Japanese. Enemy bombs had destroyed many weapons factories in other Allied countries. As a result, the American defense industry had more work than ever. The **defense industry** produced weapons, planes, and other military supplies.

The Doors Open

For years American employers had discriminated against African-American workers. Many companies in the defense industry had policies against hiring any African Americans. Others had labor unions that did not welcome African-American members. **Labor unions** are organizations that workers create to protect their interests. Unions help workers get higher wages and better work rules from employers.

African-American leaders wanted to end discrimination in the workplace. They planned a march on Washington, D.C., in 1941 to get the attention of President Roosevelt and the nation. Leaders of the march wanted to convince Roosevelt that African Americans had a right to be treated as most white Americans were treated.

One week before the scheduled march, Roosevelt issued a presidential order. It was the first time since the Reconstruction era (right after the Civil War) that the federal government took action against discrimination. The order required that factories with defense contracts end discrimination in hiring and promoting employees. **Defense contracts** are agreements that a government makes with companies so that they will produce goods needed by the military. To keep their defense contracts, these companies could no longer refuse to hire or promote workers because of race or religion. An African-American woman who found a job in a shipyard described the change:

> As the manpower in the country was getting pulled into the service, all of the industries were wide open. So they decided, "Well, we better let some of those blacks come in." Then, after the source of men dried up, they began to let women come in.

Summarizing Information When you **summarize,** you shorten a large amount of information into its major points. Reread the text under the heading "The Doors Open." Which statement best summarizes that information?
   a.   A need for workers during World War II opened doors for minorities and women.
   b.   Women faced discrimination in labor unions before World War II.

Soldiers Without Guns

The United States government helped the defense industry by recruiting workers for the industry. The government hired advertising experts in New York City and Hollywood to work on an advertising campaign. The ads encouraged Americans to join the war effort. They showed how people could help win the war by taking factory jobs. Government posters and movies called defense-industry workers "soldiers without guns."

Only lucky Americans had jobs during the Great Depression. This was the period that started after the United States stock market crashed in 1929. The **stock market** measures how companies in the United States are doing. After the crash, businesses failed, and millions of people lost their jobs. For many years, the economy was in major trouble because the country was producing very few goods. World War II renewed the American economy. The war gave American workers jobs and hope.

Early in the war, the advertising campaign created a poster for an airplane company. The ad showed a woman named Rosie working as a riveter. Riveters joined large metal sections with fasteners called rivets. The idea of a woman putting together an airplane was new to Americans. The poster was an overnight success. Songs were written about Rosie. She appeared in movies and on the cover of a magazine. Rosie became a symbol of all the women who worked in the defense industry. The number of women in the industry increased 460 percent from 1940 to 1945.

When the war began, women made up about 25 percent of the labor force. The **labor force** consists of all the people who are working or looking for work. Before the war most women had low-paying jobs in offices, shops, and factories.

The war opened the door to higher paying jobs. Some women helped build airplanes and ships. Others worked in steel mills. Women began driving buses, trucks, and trains. They flew airplanes from factories to battlefields. By the end of the war, women made up 36 percent of the labor force.

A Changing Labor Force

World War II brought great changes to the United States labor force. Americans produced twice as many military supplies as Germany, Italy, and Japan combined. During 1939 American workers made about 6,000 planes. In 1944 they made almost 100,000 planes. American workers made military supplies in less time than ever before. The time for making an aircraft carrier was cut from 35 months to 15 months. Factories were open day and night.

World War II affected the wages of American factory workers. Women and African Americans earned more than they had before the war. Yet women still earned about 60 percent less than men who were doing the same job. Women were often placed in unskilled jobs even though they had the skills for higher paying jobs.

American workers were a critical part of the war effort. Working for the Allies' victory was an experience many workers would never forget. A welder in New York explained the change. She said: "Rosie the Riveter was the woman who got up early in the morning when it was still dark and went to work and came in smiling, drinking coffee, working hard, finding herself as a new person."

Yet many of these new workers were unemployed within a year after the war ended. Soldiers returned from the war, and employers were eager to place the war heroes back in their old jobs. About four million women either lost or left their jobs between 1944 and 1946. Three-fourths of the women workers during the war were married, and many husbands did not want their wives working outside the home.

Neither women nor African Americans were willing to return to the way things were before the war. They now knew what it was like to have good jobs. They had enjoyed the benefits of a good wage. An African-American woman years later recalled the feeling:

> A lot of blacks . . . decided they did not want to go back to what they were doing before. They did not want to walk behind a plow. They wouldn't get on the back of the bus anymore.

Women contributed to the war effort.

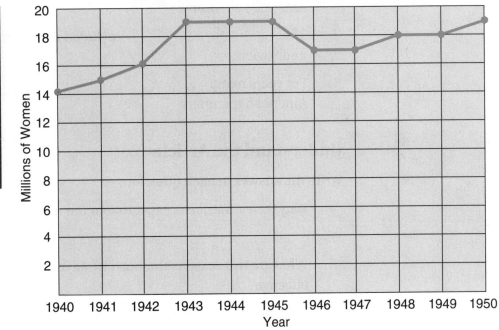

Women in the Labor Force, 1940–1950

Millions of Women (y-axis)

Year (x-axis: 1940, 1941, 1942, 1943, 1944, 1945, 1946, 1947, 1948, 1949, 1950)

Reading a Line Graph A **line graph** usually shows how something has changed over time. According to the graph above, which statement best sums up what happened between the beginning of World War II and the height of the war in 1943?

a. The number of women in the labor force increased.
b. The number of women in the labor force decreased.

Check your answer on page 235.

43

Thinking About the Article

Practice Vocabulary

The words below are in the passage in bold type. Study the way each word is used. Then complete each sentence by writing the correct word.

Allies	**defense industry**	**defense contracts**
labor unions	**stock market**	**labor force**

1. The government got the weapons and military supplies that it needed through _____ with private companies.

2. Advertisements sponsored by the United States government helped the _____ attract more workers.

3. The wartime _____ included many women and African Americans.

4. The _____ crash began a downturn in the American economy.

5. The _____ included the Americans, British, French, and Soviets.

6. For years many _____ did not welcome African-American members.

Understand the Article

Write the answer to each question.

7. Why were Americans eager to join the wartime labor force?

_____

8. What are two reasons the wartime advertising campaign was so effective?

_____

_____

9. How did the workplace change when former soldiers returned to their jobs in the United States?

_____

10. Why were African Americans unwilling to return to the way life was before the war?

_____

Apply Your Skills

Circle the number of the best answer for each question.

11. President Roosevelt issued a presidential order in 1941. Which statement <u>best</u> summarizes why it was important?
    (1) It ended all discrimination against African Americans in the workplace.
    (2) It ended racial and religious discrimination in all American factories.
    (3) It protected the rights of women in the workplace.
    (4) It raised the pay for women and African Americans.
    (5) It ended discrimination in companies with national defense contracts.

12. Look at the line graph on page 43. Which statement <u>best</u> summarizes what the changes on the graph show?
    (1) Many women were unwilling to return to the way life was before the war.
    (2) World War II affected the wages of American factory workers.
    (3) Former soldiers returned to their old jobs after the war.
    (4) No job seemed too tough for women.
    (5) The number of women in the work force continued to decrease five years after the war ended.

13. Which of the following phrases <u>best</u> summarizes what Rosie the Riveter symbolized during the war?
    (1) women driving trucks, buses, and trains
    (2) women acting in the movie industry
    (3) women putting together airplanes
    (4) women working in the defense industry
    (5) women modeling for magazines

Connect with the Article

Write your answer to each question.

14. World War II marked the end of serious problems for the American economy. Do you think war is "big business?" Explain your answer.

    _____

    _____

15. If you had lived during World War II, how would you have helped the war effort? Describe the job you would have wanted.

    _____

    _____

    _____

The Cold War and the Vietnam War

Vocabulary

communism

containment

Cold War

guerrilla

civilian

draft

deferment

The Soviet Union, the United States, Great Britain, and France were Allies during World War II. Afterward, however, they had very different ideas about how to treat the defeated Germany. The Soviet Union took over East Germany. The United States, Great Britain, and France controlled West Germany. The Allies even divided Berlin, Germany's capital.

The Soviet Union wanted control over even more of Europe. The other Allies wanted all European countries to become independent. These differences led the Soviet Union and the United States into a tense struggle for world power called the Cold War.

Relate to the Topic

This lesson is about how world politics changed after World War II, leading to the Cold War and the Vietnam War. Think about what you have heard or seen about the Vietnam War. Then write two facts that you know about the war.

_____

_____

Reading Strategy

SKIMMING A MAP   Maps can be an excellent way to present information. You can skim a map to find out what kind of information it includes, such as the title, labels, and key. Skim the map on page 48. Based on what you see there, write two questions that you expect the article to answer.

_____

_____

_____

_____

Check your answers on page 235.

The Race for World Power

World War II had left much of the Soviet Union's western lands in shambles. The Soviet people were starting over. Many had lost not only family members but also their homes during the war. With so much destruction, the Soviet leaders and people were bitter. They wanted to punish Germany. The Soviets believed that a weak Germany was their best protection against another war. So they stripped East Germany of its factories and other resources. The Soviets also wanted to control their eastern European neighbors, some of whom had once belonged to Russia.

The Cold War

After World War II, the United States, Great Britain, and France were still allies. They believed that a rich Germany was the best protection against another war. These Allies worked to return West Germany to normal. Americans gave West Germans financial help to rebuild their shops, factories, and homes.

The Soviet Union had a different point of view. It wanted to force its communist system on all of eastern Europe. **Communism** is both a political system and an economic system. A small group of people, those who lead the Communist Party, run the government. The party also controls the economy and most property.

Eventually the Soviets gained control of Poland, Czechoslovakia, Hungary, Romania, Bulgaria, and Albania. They made sure each country, including East Germany, had a communist government. In 1949 the West made West Germany an independent nation. The Soviets soon made East Germany an independent nation, too, but they continued to control its leaders and those of other eastern European countries. The Soviets also helped Communists in China, the Soviets' neighbor to the east. The Chinese Communists gained control of China in 1949.

Some Americans feared that the Communists might take over the world. In 1947 the United States announced a policy called **containment.** This policy was designed to stop communism from spreading without going to war. Instead, the United States sent military and economic aid to help threatened countries fight the Communists themselves.

From 1945 to 1989, the United States and the Soviet Union struggled for world power in what has been called the **Cold War.** The two countries' military forces never fought each other directly, even though tensions were often high.

The Vietnam War

The Soviet and Chinese Communists had their eyes on Southeast Asia. Vietnam was a French colony before World War II. The Japanese conquered Vietnam during the war. When the war ended, the French tried to return after the Japanese left. But the Vietnamese wanted independence. In 1946 the French went to war against the Vietnamese, who were backed by Soviet and Chinese Communists.

The American containment policy was put to its greatest test in Southeast Asia. American generals thought that if Communists came to power in Vietnam, all of Southeast Asia eventually would become communist. At first, the United States sent supplies to the French. In 1954 the Vietnamese defeated the French forces. Vietnam was then divided. North Vietnam had a communist government. South Vietnam was to become a democratic nation after it had elections.

The United States sent military advisors in 1955 to help Ngo Dinh Diem, the new South Vietnamese leader. He was against communism but did not allow free elections. More and more people in South Vietnam thought communism might be a better way. These people formed the Viet Cong and rebelled against Diem. North Vietnam supported the Viet Cong. By 1960 the Viet Cong had 10,000 soldiers. They began attacking Diem's bases. U.S. military support to Vietnam increased year after year. By 1963 more than 16,000 United States military advisors were in South Vietnam.

Southeast Asia During the Vietnam War

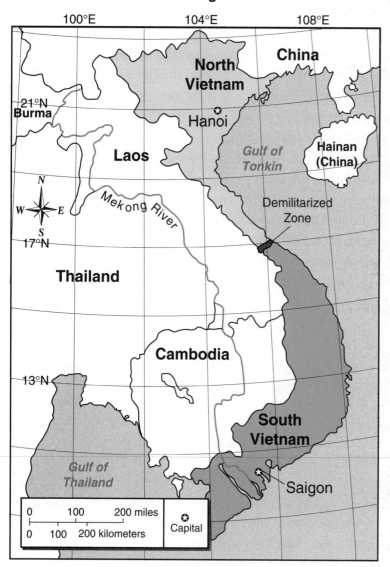

By 1964 the Viet Cong had taken control of about 75 percent of South Vietnam's population. In 1965 the first U.S. combat troops went to South Vietnam. Many American soldiers believed they were fighting against communism and defending freedom. As the war dragged on, the United States sent more and more soldiers, weapons, and supplies to South Vietnam.

American forces struggled to fight effectively in the South Vietnam countryside. The land is mostly mountainous with many forests, except along the coast. Temperatures were hot, and the rain was heavy. Because the Viet Cong were part of the South Vietnamese people, American troops could not tell who the enemy was. The Viet Cong used **guerrilla** tactics. Small units of Viet Cong fighters hid in forests and attacked villages as well as military targets. As a result, many innocent **civilians,** or nonmilitary people, suffered.

48

Reading a Political Map Maps that focus on showing boundaries between countries are called **political maps.** The map on page 48 is a political map. Its key shows the symbol that stands for a capital. North Vietnamese Communists set up camp in another Southeast Asian country. Which country gave them better access to South Vietnam's capital?

    a. Laos   b. Cambodia

The Controversy Over the War

As more United States troops headed to Vietnam, many Americans began to question the war. Every night on TV, people watched pictures of soldiers dying, villages burning, and children crying. A peace movement sprang up and used demonstrations and educational programs to spread its message. At the same time, other Americans believed that all citizens should support their government. These people reacted to the peace movement with anger and resentment.

Some Americans who opposed the war did not want U.S. soldiers fighting halfway around the world. Others felt the United States should not interfere in another nation's politics. Some thought the war's cost in money and lives was too high. Money spent on the war meant that less money was available for Americans who needed help at home.

Many who opposed the war were also against the **draft**—a system of required military service. If men were in college, they could get a **deferment,** which meant they could avoid military service until after they completed school. Those who did not go to college were drafted. As a result a high percentage of the American troops were young men from low-income families, who could not afford college. African Americans made up a large part of the American soldiers in Vietnam.

Many demonstrations against the draft and the war took place on college campuses. Most protests were peaceful. But in May 1970 National Guard troops shot into a crowd of antiwar protesters at Kent State University in Ohio, killing four students. The antiwar movement grew dramatically after the deaths.

As a result of growing opposition to the war, American troops withdrew from Vietnam in 1973. American military aid was cut, too. Within two years South Vietnam fell to communist forces. About 58,000 Americans, more than one million South Vietnamese, and nearly one million North Vietnamese died in the war.

Drawing Conclusions To draw a conclusion, you must identify what facts about a subject are important. Then you judge or decide what the facts tell you about the subject. A judgment made from examining facts is a conclusion. Which of the following facts supports the conclusion that the Vietnam War was splitting the American people?

    a. Some parents and children didn't speak to each other for years because of differing positions on the war.

    b. The people who opposed the Vietnam War had different reasons for their opposition.

Thinking About the Article

Practice Vocabulary

The words below are in the passage in bold type. Study the way each word is used. Then complete each sentence by writing the correct word.

communism	containment	Cold War
guerrilla	draft	deferment

1. In the _____ , Soviets and Americans opposed each other without any direct military conflict between them.

2. Americans thought that the _____ policy was the answer to stopping the spread of communism.

3. During the Vietnam War, young males faced the

   _____ .

4. A student could get a _____ until after he finished college.

5. Under _____ one political party controls the government.

6. The Viet Cong used _____ tactics such as shooting from the cover of forests.

Understand the Article

Write the answer to each question.

7. Why did the Soviets try to control other European countries?

   _____

8. Why did the United States begin to send help to Vietnam?

   _____

   _____

9. What were two reasons why Americans opposed the war in Vietnam?

   _____

   _____

10. How did the peace movement try to spread its message?

   _____

   _____

Apply Your Skills

Circle the number of the best answer for each question.

11. Which conclusion about the Vietnam War can be drawn from facts presented in the article?
    (1) The United States should have sent combat troops to help the French fight the Vietnamese.
    (2) Holding elections in South Vietnam would have stopped any North Vietnamese influence.
    (3) Most South Vietnamese favored democracy.
    (4) Guerrilla tactics made the job of American soldiers difficult.
    (5) The Viet Cong were members of the North Vietnamese Communist Party.

12. Look closely at the map on page 48. What feature formed the approximate boundary between North Vietnam and South Vietnam?
    (1) the Mekong River
    (2) the 104° E meridian
    (3) the 17° N parallel
    (4) the Gulf of Tonkin
    (5) the 21° N Parallel

13. Look again at the map on page 48. What fact about South Vietnam might you conclude gave the nation its best advantage in defending against North Vietnamese attack?
    (1) South Vietnam has a long western border.
    (2) South Vietnam is narrow and close to the South China Sea.
    (3) Mountains and forests cover most of North and South Vietnam.
    (4) South Vietnam is farther away from China than North Vietnam.
    (5) South Vietnam's capital is a far distance from North Vietnam.

Connect with the Article

Write your answer to each question.

14. Why do you think the United States and the Soviet Union had different attitudes toward Germany after World War II?

    _____

    _____

15. If you were advising the President, what would you recommend about sending troops to another country? What are some good reasons? What are reasons to be avoided?

    _____

    _____

LESSON 7

Communicating in the New Millennium

Communicating in the New Millennium
Communicating in the New Millen

Vocabulary

technology

communicate

telecommunication

broadcast

laser

computer

transistor

microchip

Internet

switchboard

email

In the late 1700s, people invented machines that manufactured products faster and at lower costs. This began the Industrial Revolution. As a result, many people turned from farming to factory work. Also in the 1700s, an inventor discovered a way to use steam power. In time this discovery helped replace sailing ships with steamships and stagecoaches with railroads. This began the Transportation Revolution. As a result, people and products moved from one place to another more quickly and easily.

Today we are in the middle of another major change—the Information Revolution. A variety of inventions have made it possible to send and receive information even faster than ever before.

Relate to the Topic

This lesson is about the ways that we get and share information, and the ways in which the information affects our lives. What kinds of machines have you used in the past 24 hours for getting and sending information?

_____

_____

_____

Reading Strategy

SCANNING A GRAPH Several different kinds of graphs are used to present social studies information. You can apply the same previewing strategies to any kind of graph. Scan the graph on page 54. Then answer the questions.

1. About what communications device is information given?

    _____

    Hint: What invention is named in the heading?

2. What time period does the graph cover? _____
    Hint: Look at the dates along the bottom of the graph.

Check your answers on page 236.

UNIT 1 U.S. HISTORY

Technology Changes the Way We Live

Technology has a way of changing the world. **Technology** includes the tools and methods used to increase production. Over the past 150 years, the world has witnessed great changes in communications and information technology. We can communicate faster, at lower cost, to a greater number of people than ever before. This revolution has made a huge difference in the ways people learn and work.

The Information Revolution

The Information Revolution is actually a series of inventions that changed the way we **communicate,** or send and receive information. The revolution started with American Samuel Morse's telegraph, which sent electrical impulses through a cable. By 1844 the telegraph used a dot-and-dash code for the messages. In 1876 another American, Alexander Graham Bell, invented the telephone. It sent voice messages over wire. In 1901 the first communication was sent without wires, and radio was born. Each invention led to improved **telecommunications,** or ways to send messages over long distances using either wires or radio waves.

In the early 1900s, adding telephone technology to radio technology led to voice radio **broadcasts.** These sent messages long distances over invisible radio waves. Radio stations soon sprang up across the United States. Not long after came television, which sent pictures as well as sounds over radio waves. By 1948 about one million American families had televisions in their homes.

Radio and television are two examples of wireless technology. Their signals travel through the air as radio waves, not through wires as electrical impulses. Both devices have been around for as long as you can probably remember. Some other wireless devices are newer, but they developed from the same basic technology. Cellular phones and "smart" phones (which can send and receive information as well as voices) are two examples. So are personal digital assistants (PDAs) and other handheld electronic data devices. You may remember when these items were new. In just a few years, they have become more powerful and less expensive. As a result, more and more people now use them each day, and wireless technology has changed the way we live.

Better communications have helped scientists develop and apply other discoveries quickly. For example, two scientists first proposed the idea of a laser in 1958. A **laser** is a narrow beam of intense light. Just over ten years later, American astronauts placed a laser reflector on the moon to measure the precise distance to Earth. Today lasers help surgeons remove tissue, artists clean centuries-old artwork, and supermarket workers scan prices at the checkout counter.

The Development of Computers

Another important technology owes much to two American engineers. In 1930 Vannevar Bush invented a "mechanical brain," which performed calculations quickly.

In 1944 Howard Aiken designed a machine that could store large amounts of information. Combining the engineers' work led to **computers**—electronic machines that process, store, and recall information.

Computers of the 1940s and 1950s were huge. Then, in 1947, came the invention of the **transistor,** a tiny device that controls the flow of electricity in electronic equipment. Transistors' small size and light weight made it possible to launch communications satellites into space. These satellites enable sound and pictures to be sent easily from one part of the world to another. A more recent invention is the **microchip,** a tiny electrical circuit that carries messages. Microchips form the computer's "brain." Today microchips help make computers more powerful and less expensive. They also help power a variety of other electronic devices, from robots on automobile assembly lines to artificial legs and arms.

Computers have affected the way we work, too. In factories computerized robots complete tasks that workers once had to do over and over. Fast-food restaurant workers take orders on a touch-screen ordering system. Mechanics at the repair shop hook a car to a computer to find out what is wrong with the engine.

Furthermore, computers have influenced education. Students sometimes read lessons on computers instead of in books. Most libraries now store information about their books on computers instead of in card catalogs. Teachers can instruct students in many locations at the same time instead of only those in a single classroom.

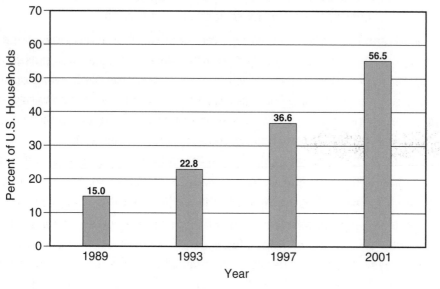

U.S. Households with Personal Computers

Percent of U.S. Households

- 1989: 15.0
- 1993: 22.8
- 1997: 36.6
- 2001: 56.5

Year

Reading a Bar Graph A **bar graph** is often used to make comparisons. The title tells what information the graph displays. The labels along the side and bottom of the graph tell the categories of this information. Look at the bar graph on this page. Compare the information about U.S. homes with personal computers by looking at the bars. Circle the letter before the year when close to one-fourth of American households had personal computers.

a. 1993   b. 1997

Exploring the Internet

Another modern communications technology is the Internet. The **Internet** is a network that connects many thousands of computers all over the globe through telephone lines. The idea of the Internet came out of the Cold War. In the 1960s the United States government was afraid that the Soviet Union would launch missiles to destroy its military bases. American leaders wanted to be sure that, even if some bases were hit, the others could communicate with one another. Scientists developed a way for computers to communicate without going through a central switchboard. A **switchboard** connects, controls, and disconnects the many phone lines in one building or location.

In 1985 the National Science Foundation (NSF) set up five supercomputer centers at large universities. It wanted to give science researchers an easier way to share research data. Using the government's technology, NSF linked these centers. It also helped connect other computer centers to the supercomputer centers. Computer users on the network found they could quickly send messages and share documents through electronic mail, or **email.**

In 1992 the network's capabilities grew. Swiss scientists created a single computer language that all computers could use for text on the Internet. Later, graphics were added. Now from any computer on the Internet, a person can find information stored in this language on computers all over the world. The World Wide Web is a system of Internet resources that provides documents in this special language. Anyone with an Internet connection can search the Web to find these documents, which may include words, pictures, and sounds.

In its short life, the Internet has shown many benefits. It encourages people from different cultures to exchange ideas. It removes distance and the high cost of travel as roadblocks to communication. It offers a visual way of learning. Internet users swap messages, share jokes, check the weather, debate politics, play games, look for job openings, and read newspapers on-line. People can also buy and sell things on the Internet, do scientific research, and study any subject they want.

In time many more people will have access to computers at home and at work. Many Americans already have several home phone lines, a cellular phone, a fax machine, PDA, and an Internet connection. With an Internet connection and a computer, many people work at home and send their work electronically to their company's office. Some home builders have even included telecommunications centers with large-screen televisions and computer components in new homes.

Applying an Idea to a New Context Ideas are often presented in one particular situation or **context.** You have just read about how scientists applied the Internet to a new situation or context. However, the Internet itself has created a need for new ideas. For example, some Internet users want to limit the messages they receive on their computers. Which telephone technology might be applied so that the user can decide who communicates with him or her over the computer?

a. call waiting   b. caller identification

Thinking About the Article

Practice Vocabulary

The words below are in the passage in bold type. Study the way each word is used. Then complete each sentence by writing the correct word.

technology	communicate	telecommunications
laser	Internet	transistors

1. Advances in _____ often change the way people live and work.

2. _____ made communication satellites possible.

3. The _____ connects computers around the world.

4. The telegraph was among the first uses of _____ technology.

5. Astronauts placed a(n) _____ reflector on the moon to measure the precise distance to Earth.

6. To _____ is to send and receive information.

Understand the Article

Write the answer to each question.

7. How do telecommunications help people communicate?

_____

_____

8. When people speak of *wireless technology,* what do they mean?

_____

_____

9. What is one way that computers have changed learning?

_____

10. What is one way that computers have changed working?

_____

11. What are two ways the Internet has changed communication?

_____

_____

Apply Your Skills

Circle the number of the best answer for each question.

12. Look at the bar graph on page 54. What do the numbers along the vertical axis represent?
    (1) the years that personal computers have been available
    (2) the percentage of U.S. homes with personal computers
    (3) the number of personal computers in use
    (4) the prices of personal computers over the years
    (5) the areas of the U.S. with the most personal computers

13. Look again at the bar graph. Which of the following general statements does the graphed information support?
    (1) The U.S. leads the world in the use of personal computers.
    (2) Most U.S. households that own personal computers replace them with newer models every four years.
    (3) The percentage of U.S. households having one or more personal computers more than tripled between 1989 and 2001.
    (4) Between 1993 and 1997 the percentage of U.S. households having one or more personal computers remained essentially the same.
    (5) After Americans rushed to buy their first personal computers for home use, purchases of home computers dropped dramatically.

14. The National Science Foundation applied technology used by the United States government in a new context and created the Internet. Which technology is a comparable blend of telephone and radio technologies?
    (1) television
    (2) voice broadcasts
    (3) laser reflectors
    (4) transistors in satellites
    (5) facsimile machines

Connect with the Article

Write your answer to each question.

15. Why do you think scientific ideas led to practical new technologies more quickly during the late 1900s than during the late 1800s?

    _____

    _____

16. Are you using a computer to help you prepare for the GED exam? If so, how is it helping you?

    _____

    _____

History at Work

Service: Sales Associates

Some Careers in Service

Over the past decade, museum stores and gift shops have become one important way for many museums to help fund their operations. You find them at historic places you visit. The sales associates at these stores are important to the financial success of the stores and the satisfaction of the customers.

Sales associates must be familiar with all the goods for sale in the store. They see that the displays are attractive and well stocked and that objects are placed in appropriate arrangements. They also handle sales, returns, and exchanges.

Because a sales associate assists customers, he or she should know how the goods in the store relate to the focus of the museum or historic place. A sales associate must also have good communication skills and a pleasant personality and appearance. They may need to write notes to fellow workers or provide written follow up to a customer's request. Strong math and computer skills are also expected for sales and inventory management.

Look at the chart of Some Careers in Service.

- Do any of the careers interest you? If so, which ones?

- What information would you like to find out about those careers? On a separate piece of paper, write some questions that you would like answered. You can find out more information about those careers in the *Occupational Outlook Handbook* at your local library or online.

Education Aide prepares activities and assists museum visitors and groups with the activities

Security Guard monitors exhibits and visitor traffic; provides information as needed

Tour Guide leads visitors through museums and historic sites; makes presentations and conducts demonstrations

Museum Library Aide assists patrons in finding requested information, using library facilities, and obtaining desired material

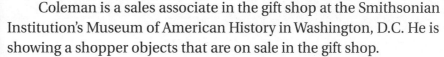

Use the material below to answer the questions that follow.

Coleman is a sales associate in the gift shop at the Smithsonian Institution's Museum of American History in Washington, D.C. He is showing a shopper objects that are on sale in the gift shop.

Coleman: Here we have a copy of an iron from the colonial days. Notice the size of this iron compared to the irons of today. Today's irons are much larger. They are made of plastic and metal; their handles are plastic and the base is metal. This colonial iron is made completely of metal and is about one-third the size of a modern iron. Hot coals were used to heat the colonial iron. The little door at the back of the iron was opened and hot coals were put inside. The door was closed and the coals heated up the metal. Before the iron could be used, a damp cloth was wrapped around the handle so the person ironing wouldn't get burned.

1. Which of the following materials was used to heat the colonial iron?
   (1) electricity
   (2) plastic
   (3) hot coals
   (4) a damp cloth
   (5) hot metal

2. Which of the following statements makes an accurate comparison?
   (1) Colonial irons and modern irons both have plastic handles.
   (2) Modern irons are much heavier than colonial irons.
   (3) Modern irons are smaller than colonial irons.
   (4) Colonial irons were smaller than modern irons.
   (5) Colonial irons were easier to use than modern irons.

3. Why would it be important to close the door of the colonial iron before using it?
   (1) to prevent the coals from cooling off too quickly
   (2) to prevent the coals from spilling onto the material
   (3) to help the iron heat up more quickly
   (4) all of the above
   (5) none of the above

4. Many of the objects we use today were invented years ago, like the colonial iron demonstrated by Coleman. Compare and contrast an object or invention we use today with its predecessor. Use a separate piece of paper to discuss how they are the same and how they are different.

Unit 1 Review
U.S. History

The St. Augustine Colony

Juan Ponce de León, a young Spanish noble, was one of the first Europeans to explore the Americas. He was part of Christopher Columbus's 1493 return voyage. The Spanish king had heard of gold in Puerto Rico, and in 1508 he sent Ponce de León to explore. Within a year the island was inhabited by settlers, who made the Native Americans dig for gold. The king appointed Ponce de León governor of Puerto Rico.

Legend says that Ponce de León went in search of the "Fountain of Youth." In 1513 he sailed north to a land that he named La Florida. He was the first European to set foot on the North American mainland. During the next several years, Ponce de León tried to colonize La Florida. But at each site Native Americans drove him out.

In 1564 the king of Spain learned that a group of French Protestants had started a colony in northeastern Florida. The king was angry because he believed all of La Florida belonged to Spain. The king sent his most experienced admiral, Pedro Menéndez de Avilés, to destroy the French colony. Menéndez de Avilés and his soldiers surprised the French colonists and killed them all. Then the Spanish built a colony called St. Augustine near the place where their fleet had landed.

By the time the first permanent English colony in America was founded, St. Augustine was already 40 years old. It became an important military base for the Spaniards. The soldiers guarded the Spanish ships carrying gold and silver from Mexico to Spain. They also kept out French and English colonists. St. Augustine now has its place in history as the oldest permanent European settlement in what is now the United States.

Circle the number of the best answer for each question.

1. Why did the king of Spain want to build a colony in La Florida?
   (1) to protect Spain's claim to La Florida
   (2) to help the French build a colony
   (3) to prove to Ponce de León that La Florida had gold
   (4) to beat the English and French to the Americas
   (5) to prove that Menéndez de Avilés was his best admiral

2. According to the passage, which of the following events happened first?
   (1) The king of Spain sent Menéndez de Avilés to secure Florida.
   (2) Juan Ponce de León came to the Americas from Spain.
   (3) English settlers established a colony in North America.
   (4) French Protestants established a colony in Florida.
   (5) The Spanish established a colony called St. Augustine in Florida.

The United States in 1863

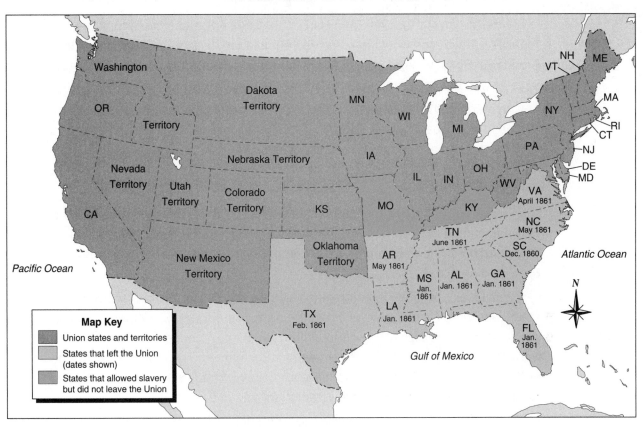

Correctly complete each statement.

3. The first state to leave the Union was _____ .

4. The last state to leave the Union was _____ .

5. The number of states that left the Union was _____ .

Circle the number of the best answer for the question.

6. Why were states that allowed slavery but did not leave the Union called border states?
   (1) They all lay along the southern border of the Confederacy.
   (2) They formed the northern border of the United States.
   (3) They all separated the rest of the states from the western territories.
   (4) They separated the Union and the Confederacy.
   (5) They all lay along the Gulf of Mexico.

The Internment of Japanese Americans

After Japan's attack on Pearl Harbor, the United States government feared that Japanese Americans would become spies for Japan. In January 1942 President Franklin D. Roosevelt ordered all **aliens,** or people who were not American citizens, to register with the government.

In March, officials began arrangements to move Japanese Americans from their homes in west coast states. More than 120,000 Japanese Americans were forced to sell their homes and most of their belongings. About 77,000 of these Japanese Americans were American citizens. Many had been born in the United States. But that did not seem to matter.

Then the Japanese-American families were interned. **Interned** means to be forced to live in camps away from home. Families were rounded up and taken to out-of-the-way places, often in the middle of a desert. Internment camps were in California, Colorado, Utah, and Arkansas.

Yet Japanese Americans remained loyal to the United States. In 1943 Japanese Americans were permitted to enlist in the Army. More than 1,200 men from the internment camps signed up. Although the Japanese-American soldiers' war records were outstanding, their families remained in the camps. The last Japanese Americans at the camps were not allowed to leave until six months after the war ended. No Japanese American was ever convicted of spying.

In 1988 the United States government under President Ronald Reagan formally apologized to 60,000 surviving Japanese Americans who had lived in the internment camps. The government gave each survivor $20,000 as **reparations,** or payment for damages.

Circle the number of the best answer for each question.

7. Why were Japanese Americans interned?
   (1) The government wanted Japanese workers in defense industries.
   (2) The government feared that Japanese Americans were responsible for World War II.
   (3) The government feared that Japanese Americans might be spies for Japan.
   (4) The government feared that Japanese Americans would refuse to join the armed forces.
   (5) The government feared that Japanese Americans would move to Japan.

8. Which conclusion does the article support best?
   (1) Japanese Americans were spies for Japan.
   (2) The internment of Japanese Americans was an injustice.
   (3) Japanese Americans didn't mind the internment camps.
   (4) The United States won the war with Japan.
   (5) Japanese Americans should have joined the Japanese army.

American Workers and Labor Unions

Union Membership in the United States, 1930–1995

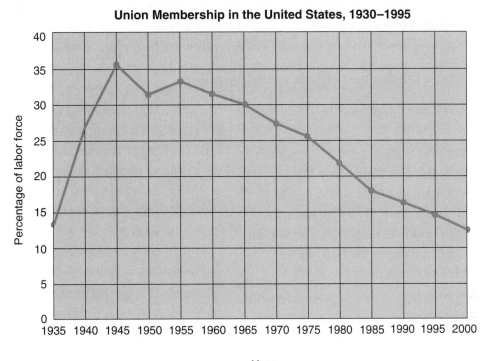

Year

Write the answers to each question.

9. Union membership kept increasing until what year?

_____

10. What happened after union membership increased in 1955?

_____

11. What might explain the steep rise in membership from 1940 to 1945?

_____

Circle the number of the best answer for each question.

12. Which two years had similar percentages for union membership?
    (1) 1935 and 1965
    (2) 1935 and 1980
    (3) 1935 and 2000
    (4) 1950 and 1975
    (5) 1965 and 2000

Social Studies Extension

For the next two weeks, collect the front sections of daily newspapers and read the headlines. Which news items indicate progress for your town or our nation? Which indicate conflict? Which will have lasting impact and make history?

Mini-Test • Unit 1

This is a 15-minute practice test. After 15 minutes, mark the last number you finished. Then complete the test and check your answers. If most of your answers were correct but you did not finish, try to work faster next time.

Directions: Choose the <u>one best answer</u> to each question.

<u>Questions 1 and 2</u> are based on the following information.

Crispus Attucks's life is a mystery, but his death was one of the most famous in the American Revolution. In 1750 he had been sought as a runaway slave. By 1770, he had become a sailor on whaling ships that sailed out of Boston Harbor. In this job, he had many conflicts with British soldiers.

On the night of March 7, 1770, Attucks and others harassed a British custom guard. British soldiers fired on the crowd. Attucks and several others were killed in what later became known as the Boston Massacre. Thus, Crispus Attucks, a former slave, became the first casualty of the American Revolution. Attucks has been remembered as, "the first to defy; the first to die." A Crispus Attucks monument was erected in Boston Common in 1888.

1. What was the cause of Crispus Attuck's death?

   He was killed because he
   (1) was a runaway slave
   (2) had become a sailor on a whaling ship
   (3) had become a guard at a custom office
   (4) was in a confrontation with British soldiers
   (5) became a symbol of the revolution

2. Which is most likely the reason that Boston erected a Crispus Attucks monument?
   (1) to remember early Boston
   (2) to remember runaway slaves
   (3) as a memorial to the British soldiers
   (4) as a memorial to African-American whalers
   (5) as a memorial to the Revolution

<u>Question 3</u> is based on the line graph below.

U.S. Immigration and Emigration, 1901–1950

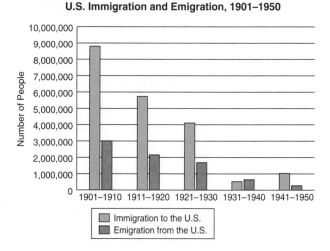

3. In which years was the number of people immigrating to the United States most similar to the number leaving?
   (1) 1901–1910
   (2) 1911–1920
   (3) 1921–1930
   (4) 1931–1940
   (5) 1941–1950

Questions 4 and 5 refer to the following photograph of unemployed workers during the early 1900s.

4. What is the main point of the photograph?

   Unemployed workers

   (1) started receiving benefits in the early 1900s
   (2) marched for jobs and against discrimination
   (3) wanted to stay in municipal shelters
   (4) demanded that the military be used against demonstrators.
   (5) could get jobs only if they protested

5. Which point of view does this picture support best?

   (1) We must unite to fight for our rights.
   (2) The army should give us all jobs.
   (3) We need to stay in shelters until we are able to find work.
   (4) All able-bodied people should receive unemployment compensation.
   (6) Anyone who wants work can find work.

Questions 6 and 7 are based on the following information.

The third chief justice of the U.S. Supreme Court, John Marshall, wrote one of the most important Supreme Court decisions in history. In the case *Marbury v. Madison* (1803), his decision made the Supreme Court the final authority on which laws are constitutional and which are not. This decision clarified the power of the judicial branch in relation to the executive and legislative branches of government.

6. What influence has *Marbury v. Madison* had on the Supreme Court?

   (1) The Supreme Court consists of a Chief Justice and associate justices.
   (2) The decisions of the Supreme Court are made in writing.
   (3) Supreme Court justices are nominated for life terms.
   (4) Supreme Court decisions are based on specific sections of the Constitution.
   (5) The Chief Justice is the head of the Supreme Court.

7. Which of the following conclusions is supported by the information?

   (1) John Marshall was a minor figure in U.S. history.
   (2) *Marbury v. Madison* ensured that the judicial branch became an equal partner with the other two branches.
   (3) The Supreme Court building in Washington, D.C., should be named after John Marshall.
   (4) After John Marshall presented his decision in *Marbury v. Madison,* the Supreme Court became the nation's highest court.
   (5) *Marbury v. Madison* was the first important decision the Supreme Court made.

 Check your answers on page 237.

UNIT 2

World History

World History

World History

World history is the story of people and events around our planet. It is the story of ancient times and of current events.

Events throughout the world have had a strong impact on Americans. They continue to influence us today. As Americans, we are neighbors with all nations and peoples. We can benefit from learning about people in other times and places.

Name two events that you think were important to the world's history.

_____

_____

Thinking About World History

You may not realize how much world history you already know. Think of what you may have heard or read about events in other parts of the world.

Check the box for each fact that you already know.

☐ Many ancient civilizations developed along major rivers.

☐ Persia, Rome, and China all had large, long-lasting empires.

☐ Europeans began to colonize the Americas about 500 years ago.

☐ The Industrial Revolution began in Europe and changed people's lives around the world.

☐ Mexico was a Spanish colony and became an independent nation in the early 1800s.

☐ The United Nations was established in the mid-1900s after the second world war.

☐ During the 1990s South Africa dropped the discriminatory policy of apartheid and held open elections.

Write two other facts that you know about world history.

_____

_____

Previewing the Unit

In this unit, you will learn:

● how Chinese emperors protected their land from invaders

● how various European inventions changed life around the world

● how Mexico became a modern country

● how the government of South Africa changed over time to become a full democracy

● how the United Nations tries to keep peace in the world

Lesson 8	The Age of Empires
Lesson 9	A Time of Enlightenment
Lesson 10	The Rise of Nations
Lesson 11	Democracy and Independence
Lesson 12	Global Interdependence

LESSON 8

The Age of Empires

The Age of Em

Vocabulary

empire

civilization

barbarian

peasant

dynasty

Long ago, China was made up of many kingdoms. Qin (pronounced "Chin") was one of the largest kingdoms. The ruler of Qin set out to conquer his neighbors. By 221 B.C. he had united all of China's kingdoms. He took the name of Qin Shi Huangdi—"First Emperor of China."

Some people who lived north of China invaded Shi Huangdi's newly conquered lands because they thought that these kingdoms were without leaders. In response, Shi Huangdi sent his leading general and 300,000 troops to drive out the invaders. He also ordered his army to build a wall to keep out enemies. This was the beginning of the Great Wall of China.

Relate to the Topic

This lesson is about the development of the Great Wall of China during the rule of several Chinese emperors. Imagine an emperor as being like the head of a large company. Why do you think many emperors and business leaders want to make their kingdoms and companies larger?

_____

_____

_____

_____

Reading Strategy

SCANNING A MAP   Maps can give you a lot of information more quickly than words alone. The **scale** on a map helps you measure distances represented the map. Scan the map on page 69 and find the scale in the lower right-hand corner. Then answer the questions.

1. What is the map about? _____
   Hint: Read the title of the map.

2. What is the distance between Beijing and Jiayuguan?

   _____

   Hint: Use the scale to find the approximate distance.

The Great Wall of China

The Great Wall of China runs from the western city of Jiayuguan to the Yellow Sea. Between these points, the wall zigzags across 2,150 miles. It is so long that astronauts can see the wall as they orbit Earth. Building this marvel took 1,800 years and millions of laborers.

Beginning the Great Wall

As early as 500 B.C., local Chinese rulers had walls erected to mark their borders and to keep out invaders. This piecemeal wall building went on for about 300 years. Then Shi Huangdi established his empire. An **empire** is a group of countries or territories governed by one ruler. These early Chinese kingdoms were independent states. But their people shared similar ways and values, such as love for learning. In other words, they had a common **civilization.**

Huns and other groups who wandered Mongolia—the land north of China— followed a different way of life. They valued strength in battle and skill with horses. The Chinese considered them barbarians. A **barbarian** is someone whom others regard as inferior and ignorant.

Shi Huangdi decided to keep barbarians out of China and to mark his empire's northern border with a great wall. He had his army and half a million **peasants**—poor, uneducated farmers—create this wall from the many earlier walls. Most of the early walls were crude structures, so the workers rebuilt them as well as building the connecting sections. The wall followed the land. It snaked along rivers rather than across them and up hills rather than around them. By the end of Shi Huangdi's 15-year rule, about 1,200 miles of wall had been completed.

The Great Wall of China

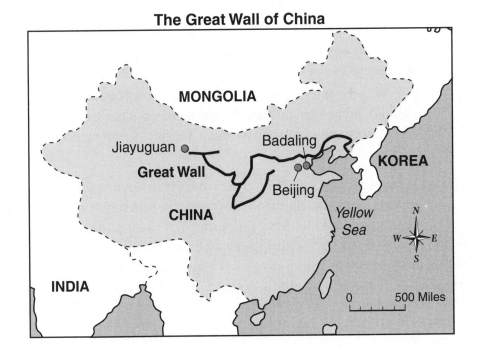

Shi Huangdi's workers put up a closed, wooden framework along the planned route of the wall. Then they packed the space inside the frame with three to four inches of dirt at a time. They pounded each layer of dirt before adding the next layer. Eventually the wall rose more than 20 feet.

Shi Huangdi's wall was only the beginning. In A.D. 446 another emperor drafted 300,000 people to work on the wall. About 100 years later, another emperor forced 1.8 million peasants to continue building the wall. The last work on the Great Wall for several centuries was finished by A.D. 618 under the Sui dynasty. A **dynasty** is a ruling family whose members govern over a long time.

Mongol Rule in China

After the Sui dynasty, the Tang and following dynasties built up the army rather than the Great Wall. Meanwhile, the tribes of Mongolia united under Genghis Khan and conquered lands from Korea to Russia and into India. In 1279 Mongols led by Kublai Khan, the grandson of Genghis, crossed the crumbling wall. They defeated the Chinese army and added China to their empire.

Kublai Khan established the Yuan dynasty, which ruled China for about one hundred years. The Mongols put themselves and foreigners, such as Italian Marco Polo, into high positions. The Chinese resented the way their Mongol rulers tolerated people who did not follow age-old Chinese beliefs.

In the mid 1300s, famine and flooding in China sparked uprisings. A peasant leader and his followers drove the Mongols out and founded the Ming dynasty. To keep the Mongols out, Ming rulers chose to rebuild the wall rather than the army.

The Ming Dynasty

Much of the Great Wall that remains today dates back to the Ming dynasty. To build new sections of wall, workers laid foundations of stone. Other workers set up ovens called kilns to make bricks and tiles and to burn lime for mortar.

With the bricks, workers built facing walls. They filled the space between the walls with dirt, stones, and rubble. Finally bricklayers topped the sections of wall with brick walks. Where the wall rose at steep angles, the workers laid steps.

Comparing and Contrasting To compare ideas is to figure out how they are alike. To contrast ideas is to figure out how they are different. Compare and contrast the method that builders used during Shi Huangdi's rule with the one that builders used during the Ming dynasty. Write *s* in the space before the Ming building method that is similar to one used during the Sui dynasty. Write *d* in the space before the Ming building method that differed from those used during the Qin dynasty.

_____ a. They filled the space between the walls with dirt.

_____ b. Workers topped the sections of wall with brick walks.

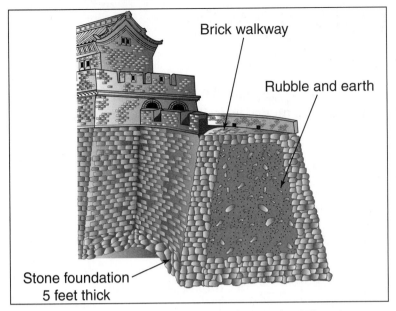

Brick walkway

Rubble and earth

Stone foundation
5 feet thick

Cross-section of the Great Wall built during the Ming dynasty

The wall served as a pathway as well as a barrier. Every 200 yards the builders erected a stairway on the Chinese side of the wall. Soldiers climbed the stairway to the top of the wall, where they could march ten abreast. In this way, they could rush to any part of the wall under attack.

The builders also included about 25,000 watchtowers in the wall. Each tower housed 30 to 50 soldiers. In peacetime, the soldiers kept the wall repaired and oversaw the traders who entered through the wall's gates. During wartime, the soldiers drove off invaders with cannons atop the towers.

The Great Wall proved a good defense for almost 300 years. But in 1644, a Chinese traitor opened a gate in the wall to let in Manchu warriors. They were wanderers like the Mongols and came from the land northeast of China. The Manchus defeated the Ming army and set up the Qing (pronounced "ching") dynasty, which ruled China until 1911.

The best-preserved part of the Great Wall is probably the Badaling section built during the Ming dynasty. From its top, you can still see the mounds where soldiers built fires for sending smoke signals. These signals warned troops miles away of approaching invaders.

Other sections of the wall have not fared as well as Badaling. The government of China has allowed many parts out of tourists' reach to decay. Even so, historians today consider the Great Wall a wonder of the world. It affirms, for all to see, a people's ingenuity.

Applying an Idea to a New Context Ideas, such as the Great Wall of China, are often presented in one particular situation, or context. Many peoples in other parts of the world also built walls on their borders or around their cities. Hundreds of years ago the Hausa people of West Africa built a large wall around Kano, a major business and cultural center. This wall was about 15 miles long and more than 65 feet high. Did the Hausa and the Chinese build walls for the same reason? Circle the letter of a reason that they most likely shared.

    a.   to serve as a market site

    b.   to protect people from invaders

    c.   to set up a marching route for guards

Thinking About the Article

Practice Vocabulary

The words below are in the passage in bold type. Study the way each word is used. Then complete each sentence by writing the correct word.

empire   **civilization**   **barbarian**

peasants   **dynasty**

1. Sui emperors considered a Mongol a(n) _____ .

2. The emperor of China depended on the _____ for food and labor.

3. The last _____ in China was the Qing.

4. Warriors and riders held honored places in Mongol

   _____ .

5. In 1279 Kublai Khan made China part of the Mongol

   _____ .

Understand the Article

Write the answer to each question.

6. Why did Shi Huangdi have the Great Wall built?

   _____

   _____

7. How did emperors immediately following the Sui dynasty try to stop invaders?

   _____

   _____

   _____

8. Why did the Chinese resent their Mongol rulers?

   _____

   _____

9. Why do you think sections of the Great Wall that builders constructed during the Ming dynasty are still standing?

   _____

   _____

Apply Your Skills

Circle the number of the best answer for each question.

10. Contrast the Mongols with the Chinese they conquered. How did they differ?
    (1) The Mongols were Christians.
    (2) The Mongols relied on the strength of their army.
    (3) The Chinese had built a vast empire.
    (4) The Mongols resented Europeans.
    (5) The Chinese valued learning over physical strength.

11. Compare the following dynasties. Which were the most alike?
    (1) Yuan and Ming
    (2) Sui and Ming
    (3) Tang and Sui
    (4) Ming and Tang
    (5) Mongol and Yuan

12. The United States government spends much of its defense budget on the military and weapons. Which dynasty applied this same idea for defense in early China?
    (1) Qin
    (2) Sui
    (3) Tang
    (4) Mongol
    (5) Ming

Connect with the Article

Write your answer to each question.

13. The Great Wall can no longer keep invaders out of China. How do you think aircraft helped make the wall an ineffective defense in wartime?

    _____

    _____

    _____

14. Do you consider any structures in the United States as awe-inspiring as the Great Wall of China? Explain your answer.

    _____

    _____

    _____

    _____

LESSON 9

A Time of Enlightenment

Vocabulary

century

composer

orchestra

navigator

latitude

longitude

chronometer

pendulum

smallpox

vaccination

immune

The 1700s were an exciting time in Western Europe and North America. Historians call this period the Enlightenment. During the Enlightenment, some thoughtful people began questioning the right of their rulers to govern. They also took a fresh look at nature and the arts.

The biggest influence on the thinkers of the Enlightenment was modern science. The new scientific method held that knowledge came not from following tradition without question but instead from observing and experimenting. One result of all the new observations and experimentation was a flood of inventions.

Relate to the Topic

This lesson is about inventions from the 1700s. It describes advances made in music, timekeeping, and medicine. List two ways your life might be different without music, watches, and modern medical care.

_____

_____

_____

Reading Strategy

USING A TITLE TO PREVIEW   The title, or name, of an article can help you focus your reading. Read the title at the top of page 75. Then answer the questions.

1. What is the main topic of the article? . _____

    _____

    Hint: Decide which is the most important word in the title.

2. How does knowing the topic help you plan your reading of the article?

    _____

    Hint: What information will you look for as you read?

Check your answers on page 238.   UNIT 2 WORLD HISTORY

The Age of Inventions

The eighteenth **century,** or 1700s, was a fruitful time for inventors. They produced advances in many fields—music, timekeeping, and medicine, to name just a few. Their contributions to history and culture amounted to more than inventions. They made possible richer music, a keener sense of time, and longer lives.

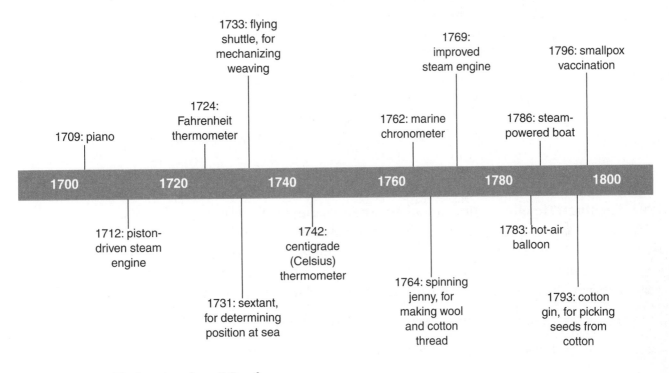

1733: flying shuttle, for mechanizing weaving

1769: improved steam engine

1796: smallpox vaccination

1724: Fahrenheit thermometer

1762: marine chronometer

1786: steam-powered boat

1709: piano

| 1700 | 1720 | 1740 | 1760 | 1780 | 1800 |

1712: piston-driven steam engine

1742: centigrade (Celsius) thermometer

1783: hot-air balloon

1731: sextant, for determining position at sea

1764: spinning jenny, for making wool and cotton thread

1793: cotton gin, for picking seeds from cotton

Reinventing Music

Since the early 1400s, musicians had been making do with a keyboard instrument called a harpsichord. When a player pressed one of the keys, a pick inside the harpsichord popped up and plucked a tight metal string. The string vibrated and made a sound. How lightly or firmly the player touched the key made little difference in tone. All sounds that the harpsichord made were equally loud. Any musician who wanted to play softly or build to a loud finish was unable to do so.

In 1709 Italian Bartolomeo Cristofori replaced the picks in a harpsichord with hammers. Instead of plucking the strings, the hammers hit them with the same force that the fingers struck the keys. Now players could control how softly or loudly a note sounded. Cristofori named the new instrument "harpsichord with softness and loudness." In Italian the words for the last part are *piano e forte*. Over the years, English-speaking people shortened the instrument's name to *pianoforte* or *piano*.

The piano was only one of several new or improved instruments that came out in the eighteenth century. Many instruments achieved a greater range of sound. For example, between 1775 and 1780, French violin maker François Tourte developed the modern shape of the violin bow. Rubbing the bow on an instrument's strings makes sound. Tourte's bow allowed the same violin to make powerful or delicate music.

Great eighteenth-century **composers**—Franz Joseph Haydn, Wolfgang Amadeus Mozart, and Ludwig van Beethoven—embraced the variety of sounds. A piece of music they wrote might require pianos, violins, drums, and flutes. To play this kind of music, the orchestra emerged.

Once, the word *orchestra* meant only "the space in front of a stage." During the early 1700s, **orchestra** also came to mean "a group of musicians performing music together." By the mid 1700s, the modern orchestra's four sections—woodwinds, brass, percussion, and strings—were already in place. Music had blossomed into a rich and complex art.

Reading a Timeline A timeline shows when a series of events took place. It also shows the order in which these events happened. It can be used to find the amount of time between events. Look at the timeline on page 75. Then match each pair of inventions below with the correct number of years that passed between the appearance of the first invention and the second one.

_____ Fahrenheit thermometer/Celsius thermometer	a.	18 years
_____ piston-driven steam engine/improved steam engine	b.	31 years
_____ piano/steam-powered boat	c.	29 years
_____ spinning jenny/cotton gin	d.	57 years
_____ sextant/marine chronometer	e.	82 years

Taking Clocks to Sea

In early times, ships sometimes lost their way going long distances at sea. During the 1700s, however, the oceans became the main channels of trade. A **navigator**—the person who charts the position and course of a ship—already knew how to figure out **latitude,** the distance north or south of the equator. He also knew that in one hour, Earth turns 15 degrees of **longitude,** the distance east or west on Earth relative to Greenwich, England. But in 1700 the only way know ship's longitude was by observing the moon, and a navigator often lacked clear weather at sea.

But if a navigator had a **chronometer,** or very accurate clock, he could easily find the ship's longitude. How? The clock would be set at London time. When the sun shone directly overhead, the time aboard ship was noon. If the clock said that the time in London was 2:00 P.M., then the navigator would know that the ship was 30 degrees west of London.

In 1700 most clocks were run with pendulums. A **pendulum** is a weight that swings back and forth at regular intervals, ticking away the minutes. On a rolling ship, a pendulum clock could not stay accurate because movement would disturb its regularity. A mistake of one minute could mean going 450 miles off course.

The British government offered a prize for the invention of a seagoing chronometer. English carpenter John Harrison wanted the prize. He observed clocks in which springs did the work of pendulums. In the clocks that Harrison made, he added a second spring that kept the first spring moving. In 1762, after 34 years of experimenting, Harrison had a small clock that kept accurate time despite heat, cold, humidity, or the motion of a ship on a 156-day voyage. Harrison's chronometer won the prize. It also gave the world a model for portable and accurate clocks that people called *watches*. Watches allowed people to always know the time, anywhere they went.

Preventing Disease

At one time, people feared **smallpox** more than any other disease. Smallpox spreads, by way of sneezes, coughs, or items handled by someone with the disease. Smallpox symptoms included a rash that fill with pus. Four out of ten people who came down with the disease died. Those who survived had deep pits in their skin where the rash had been. Some survivors were left blind.

English doctor Edward Jenner observed many milkmaids—women who milked cows for a living—with cowpox. This was a mild form of smallpox passed from cows to humans. Jenner noted that milkmaids who had had cowpox never caught smallpox.

In 1796 Jenner tried an experiment. He injected the pus from a cowpox sore into a healthy boy, who then developed cowpox. Afterward Jenner injected the same boy with pus from a smallpox sore. The disease failed to develop.

Jenner had invented the first practical smallpox **vaccination,** which got its name from the *vaccinia* virus that produces cowpox. He encouraged other doctors to vaccinate against smallpox. Through their success, *vaccination* came to mean "injecting a substance that makes a person **immune,** or safe, from a disease that spreads."

In 1980 the World Health Organization declared smallpox a disease of the past. Today, however, there are fears that terrorists could use smallpox as a weapon. Many countries are making plans to deal with possible new outbreaks of smallpox.

Summarizing When you summarize something, you reduce a large amount of information to a few sentences. These sentences restate only the major points of the information. For example, the sentence that defines vaccination in the last paragraph summarizes Jenner's process. Reread the information under "Preventing Disease." Then summarize it by completing the sentences below.

a.   Dr. Edward Jenner observed that _____

b.   He experimented by _____

c.   The results of the experiment were _____

Thinking About the Article

Practice Vocabulary

The words below are in the passage in bold type. Study the way each word is used. Then complete each sentence by writing the correct word.

century   orchestra   chronometer

smallpox   vaccination   immune

1. One of the worst diseases of the 1700s was _____ .

2. Violins and French horns are instruments in a(n)

   _____ .

3. A(n) _____ helps prevent disease, not cure it.

4. A navigator uses a(n) _____ to figure out the exact position of a ship at sea.

5. A vaccine for polio was developed in the twentieth

   _____ .

6. Jenner injected a boy with the cowpox virus to make him

   _____ from a worse disease.

Understand the Article

Write the answer to each question.

7. How do a harpsichord and piano differ?

   _____

8. Why was a pendulum clock useless at sea?

   _____

   _____

9. Why were watches not practical until John Harrison invented his chronometer?

   _____

   _____

10. How did Edward Jenner get the idea that smallpox can be prevented?

    _____

    _____

Apply Your Skills

Circle the number of the best answer for each question.

11. You have read that accurate watches were developed from the chronometer. Which other inventions on the timeline on page 75 were probably linked in a similar way?
    (1) steam engine and hot-air balloon
    (2) steam engine and steam-powered boat
    (3) piano and flying shuttle
    (4) sextant and thermometers
    (5) spinning jenny and cotton gin

12. What time span does the timeline on page 75 cover?
    (1) 10 years
    (2) 15 years
    (3) a century
    (4) the 17th century
    (5) from 1700 to the present

13. Which of the following sentences best summarizes the last paragraph under "Taking Clocks to Sea"?
    (1) John Harrison's chronometer kept accurate time during a 156-day voyage.
    (2) Harrison adapted and improved a spring-driven clock.
    (3) Harrison's clock was simply a pendulum clock without a pendulum.
    (4) To win a prize, John Harrison spent thirty-four years inventing a seagoing chronometer.
    (5) All clocks were pendulum-driven until Harrison's chronometer.

Connect with the Article

Write your answer to each question.

14. Think of a musical instrument you play or like to hear. How is sound produced?

    _____

    _____

15. Name two diseases for which you would like researchers to find a vaccine and governments to require widespread vaccinations. Explain why you chose these diseases.

    _____

    _____

    _____

The Rise of Nations

The Rise of Nations

Vocabulary

conservative

liberal

diplomat

democracy

duties

capital

gross national
   product

strike

union

In 1521 the land that is now Mexico became a part of Spain's large empire in the Americas. Mexico stayed under Spain's rule for 300 years, until a revolution brought independence in 1821. Then one leader after another used force to gain control of the young nation's government.

Mexico's unstable politics kept its economy from developing. Meanwhile, other countries were using new inventions to industrialize. Fifty-five years after independence, Porfirio Díaz took control of Mexico. He modernized the country's economy on the eve of the twentieth century.

Relate to the Topic

This lesson is about how Porfirio Díaz modernized Mexico's economy between 1876 and 1911. His improvements, however, came at a high price for most Mexicans. Think about the expression *Do it for your own good.* Explain why you think that some people would have mixed feelings about that advice.

_____

_____

_____

Reading Strategy

SCANNING A TABLE   Tables can be an excellent way to present information—especially statistics—in social studies material. A **table** is a type of list that organizes information in rows and columns. Look briefly at the table on page 82. Be sure to scan the various labels. Then answer the questions.

1. What is the general topic of the table? _____
   Hint: Read the title at the top of the columns.

2. Name two activities other than agriculture for which figures are given.

   _____

   Hint: Study the labels across the tops of the columns.

Modernizing Mexico

After Mexico became independent, different groups fought for control of the government. In its first 55 years, Mexico had 75 leaders. These leaders were either conservatives or liberals. **Conservatives** wanted little change. They were wealthy landowners whose ancestors had come from Spain. They wanted a government with a strong army to enforce laws. Most Mexicans, however, were of Indian or mixed ancestry. Many were poor farmers. They wanted a government that would act on their behalf. They were called **liberals.**

A Struggling Nation

Porfirio Díaz had both Indian and Spanish ancestry. He had fought on the side of the liberals in a civil war against the conservatives. Many Mexicans considered Díaz a hero and thought he should lead Mexico. After liberal President Benito Juárez died, Díaz and his soldiers drove out the president who followed Juárez.

Díaz took over the Mexican government in 1876. At the time, Mexico's economy was in shambles. One reason was that Mexico had spent more money on the goods it bought than it received for the goods it sold. Also, wealthy Mexicans and foreign investors would not risk their money in a nation without strong leadership. So Mexico had little of the advanced technology seen elsewhere in the world.

Díaz realized that Mexico had a low standing among nations. Few diplomats lived there. A **diplomat** is a person whom a nation's leader chooses to handle relations with another nation. Díaz invited diplomats from the United States, Europe, and Asia to Mexico. He wanted to show them that Mexico had a firm leader in charge. He thought that perhaps their countries then would invest in Mexico's economy.

Identifying Faulty Logic A statement with faulty logic may seem reasonable at first. However, when you think about it, the statement makes little sense. Often such statements contain a hasty generalization. A **hasty generalization** is based on little or no evidence. Words such as *all, none, never,* and *always* may signal hasty generalizations. Review the article above. Then select the statement with faulty logic from the following sentences.

a. After independence Mexicans spent all their time on politics and none on their economy.

b. Liberal Mexicans outnumbered conservatives, so the liberals sometimes took control of the government from the wealthy.

Díaz Modernizes

Díaz's motto was "Order, Then Progress." His advisors told him to improve the economy first and to put democracy on hold. **Democracy** is a system of government that gives all of its citizens the power to make choices.

Check your answer on page 239. **81**

Díaz sent soldiers to all parts of the country. He added more *rurales* (rural police) to rid the countryside of bandits. He had the police shoot criminals who tried to escape. Mexico also needed the money from **duties,** or taxes collected on goods entering the nation. But smugglers paid no duties. If caught, they suffered heavy penalties.

Next Díaz worked on progress. Land belonging to Indians was put up for sale. When some Indian peoples protested, Díaz's troops enslaved them and made them work for wealthy landowners.

Investors began spending on Mexico's economy. Foreign **capital**—money spent for production or investment—was put to immediate use. It bought modern equipment for textile, paper, and steel mills. It also paid for developing Mexico's natural resources. An American investor bought land and explored for oil. As a result, Mexico became one of the world's largest oil suppliers by the early 1900s.

Figures below show the growth in Mexico's gross national product. The **gross national product** is the total value of everything a nation produces. A country's gross national product indicates the growth and health of its economy.

MEXICO'S ECONOMIC GROWTH INDICATORS

Gross National Product*							
Year	Mining	Agriculture	Manufacturing	Oil	Transportation	Other Activities	Total
1895	431	2,107	806	none	204	5,315	8,863
1900	541	1,991	1,232	none	237	5,890	9,891
1905	848	2,543	1,475	1	299	7,294	12,460
1910	1,022	2,692	1,663	19	295	7,833	13,524

*in millions of pesos at 1950 prices

Foreign Capital in Mexican Mining and Industry 1896–1907

United States
$336,991,000

Great Britain
$253,544,824

Germany
$25,204,375

France
$16,751,500

Spain
$2,466,860

Austria-Hungary
$400,000

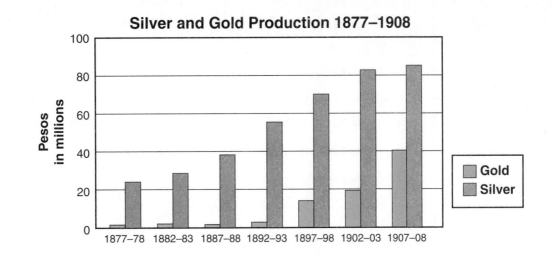

Silver and Gold Production 1877–1908

Pesos in millions

Gold
Silver

1877–78 1882–83 1887–88 1892–93 1897–98 1902–03 1907–08

Drawing Conclusions from Tables and Graphs To draw a conclusion, you must identify which facts are important. Then you decide what they tell you about the topic. One way of presenting facts is a graph, a special kind of drawing that is used to compare information. A table is a kind of list with information organized in columns and rows. Look at the table and graphs on pages 82 and 83. They show facts about Mexico's economic growth under Díaz's leadership. Based on the facts in the table and graphs, which of the following conclusions can you draw?

a. The value of agricultural products outstripped the value of mining products because of foreign investments.

b. Foreign capital and modern equipment helped Mexico uncover its gold and silver.

The Toll on Mexicans

Mexico's economic boom did not help most Mexicans. They worked at difficult and dangerous jobs. Factories stayed open 15 hours a day. Workers, including children, worked the entire time with only two short breaks for meals. Mines were very unsafe. One reported 500 deaths in five years.

Díaz made sure that workers had little power. He made **strikes** illegal. In some industrial towns, joining a **union** was a crime. Without labor unions, workers had no protection against their bosses' abuse.

Mexico's population went from 8.7 million in 1876 to more than 15 million in 1911. With such growth, proper housing was a major problem. Many people lived in rundown shacks. Several families often lived together in very small quarters. These conditions led to increased illnesses and deaths. Between 1895 and 1911, more people died in Mexico City alone than in the entire United States.

By 1910 Díaz had achieved his peaceful and united nation, but Mexicans were far from happy. Most had longed for democracy. Instead they experienced violence and growing poverty. The Mexican people would have to face another revolution before they achieved democracy.

Thinking About the Article

Practice Vocabulary

The words below are in the passage in bold type. Study the way each word is used. Then complete each sentence by writing the correct word.

conservatives	liberals	diplomat
democracy	duties	capital

1. The _____ invested in Mexico by business people from other countries helped Porfirio Díaz modernize Mexico.

2. The majority of Mexicans were _____ who wanted a democratic government.

3. _____ collected on goods at the American border helped Mexico build up its treasury.

4. Wealthy Mexicans who wanted the strong protection of the military behind the government were called _____ .

5. A _____ from Japan was one of the first from Asia to visit Mexico.

6. Mexicans would go through a second revolution before they achieved _____ .

Understand the Article

Write the answer to each question.

7. How did Porfirio Díaz create order in Mexico?

_____

_____

_____

8. Why did Díaz invite diplomats to Mexico?

_____

_____

_____

9. Why did so many people die in Mexico City between 1895 and 1910?

_____

_____

Apply Your Skills

Circle the number of the best answer for each question.

10. Which statement about Mexico under Díaz is a hasty generalization?
    (1) Soldiers tried to collect duties on imports at the borders.
    (2) Capital from industrial countries was used to boost industry.
    (3) Díaz kept order by increasing the number of police.
    (4) All foreign diplomats to Mexico approved of its government.
    (5) Díaz decided to delay democracy.

11. Look at the table on page 82. Which of the following conclusions is supported by the economic facts?
    (1) Mining production decreased during Díaz's presidency.
    (2) Manufacturing doubled while Díaz was in office.
    (3) The gross national product tripled under Díaz's leadership.
    (4) Mexico had a growing oil industry in the 1800s.
    (5) Agricultural production remained the same between 1895 and 1910.

12. Based on the graph from page 82, which conclusion can you draw about investors in Mexico?
    (1) Americans invested more money than the combined investment from Europeans.
    (2) Germany invested more in Mexico than any other European country.
    (3) Spain invested the least money of all the countries shown.
    (4) Great Britain's investment equaled the combined money from Germany, France, Spain, and Austria-Hungary.
    (5) Foreigners invested more than one billion pesos in Mexico between 1896 and 1907.

Connect with the Article

Write your answer to each question.

13. Another popular slogan during Díaz's time in office was *pan y palo,* or "bread and the stick." What do you think this slogan meant to Mexican workers?

    _____

    _____

14. Would you give up your rights and freedom for a well-paying job? Explain why or why not.

    _____

    _____

Democracy and Independence

ndence

Democracy and Independence

Vocabulary

republic

suffrage

civil rights

parliament

apartheid

racist

sanctions

Black South Africans will long remember 1994. That was the year in which they were first allowed to participate in government elections in their country.

For decades, laws had stripped them of all political rights and freedoms. Laws also had separated them from white South Africans. Finally the years of oppression and protest had ended. Black and white South Africans faced the challenge of working together to build harmony in their new government.

Relate to the Topic

This lesson is about change in South Africa's long-standing policy of separating blacks and whites. Hostility between the races can lead to crimes committed out of racial hatred. In the United States, some states' laws give stiffer punishments to persons who commit such hate crimes. Do you think that our court system should handle hate crimes differently from other crimes? Explain.

_____

_____

Reading Strategy

PREVIEWING A POLITICAL CARTOON Some social studies materials contain political cartoons. A **political cartoon** is a special type of cartoon that presents an opinion about a controversial topic. Previewing political cartoons helps you know what information to look for as you read. Look at the cartoon on page 89. Then answer the questions.

1. What two groups of people do the boaters represent? _____

_____

   Hint: Look at the way the boaters are drawn and the words on the buckets.

2. What problem do the boaters share?

_____

   Hint: Look at what is happening in the boat.

Check your answers on page 239.   **UNIT 2 WORLD HISTORY**

Against Apartheid

For nearly 600 years, native black Africans and descendants of white Europeans have lived in South Africa. During most of this time, the whites ruled and mistreated the blacks. However, in the 1990s, black South Africans gained political power in their homeland.

The Fight over Land

Thousands of years ago, hunters and food-gatherers called the San made what is now South Africa their home. Their descendants, the Khoikhoi (KOY koy), raised sheep, goats, and cattle. Other black African groups who spoke the Bantu language migrated to the area from the north. They farmed the fertile soil and developed tools that helped improve their harvests. They fashioned some tools from iron.

In the 1400s and 1500s, Europeans searched for trade routes to Asia. One route went around the Cape of Good Hope at the southern tip of Africa. Portuguese sailors stopped on their way to Asia. They traded goods with the Khoikhoi. Later Dutch traders built a colony at the cape where sailors could rest on their long voyages. These Dutch were the first Europeans to settle in southern Africa.

During the 1600s, the mountains and rich valleys on the Cape of Good Hope attracted settlers from other European countries. All the Europeans called themselves Boers, the Dutch word for "farmers." The Boers stole Khoikhoi land and livestock to start farms of their own.

At first, the black Africans viewed the Europeans as mere visitors. The black Africans welcomed the trade, especially when they received iron in return for animal hides. But when they saw the Europeans planned to stay, some Khoikhoi rebelled. In 1659 they attacked the Boers, hoping to gain back herds they had lost. The attempt failed.

The Khoikhoi could not win against the Boers' firearms. In 1713 smallpox, a disease brought from Europe, killed many Boers and nearly all the Khoikhoi. The population decline brought a decline in the Khoikhoi's way of life and culture. Many Khoikhoi became servants of the Boers.

Recognizing Values A people's culture influences the values that they hold. **Values** are what people feel are important, right, and good. People may indicate their values by what they say. Yet people's actions often reveal more about their values than words do. Reread the third and fourth paragraphs under "The Fight Over Land." Then match each beginning and ending below to form statements about the values of the European settlers and the native Africans.

1. The Boers stole from the Khoikhoi because _____

2. The black Africans welcomed European trade because _____
   a. they valued land.
   b. they valued iron for tools.

The White Minority and the Black Majority

European domination of South Africa only began with the Boers. During the 1800s, the British built an empire in Africa. They saw the riches of South Africa much as the Boers had. The Boers, however, refused to share the land that they considered theirs. By 1854 they had carved out two republics, the Transvaal and the Orange Free State. A **republic** is a self-governing territory. The British started colonies in a place called Natal and on the Cape of Good Hope.

British rule angered the Boers who lived on the cape. Some decided to leave. As Boer settlers moved north and east from the cape, they met Bantu-speaking groups, such as the Xhosa (KOH suh), Sotho, and Zulu. The Boers captured black Africans and enslaved them. The white Africans believed that owning slaves was their right even though blacks outnumbered the whites.

Discoveries of gold and diamonds in present-day South Africa led to war between the British and the Boers. The British eventually won the Boer War, which lasted from 1899 to 1902. As a result, the Boer republics became British colonies. In exchange, the British guaranteed positions of power to the white residents, who now called themselves *Afrikaners*. The British also refused to grant the black majority **suffrage,** or the right to vote.

In 1910 the four South African provinces united under one constitution. Black Africans still could not vote. So they organized a political group devoted to gaining their civil rights. **Civil rights** are peoples' freedoms, including the right to be treated equally with other people. This political group would later be known as the African National Congress (ANC).

Soon after the union, the South African **parliament,** or law-making body, passed laws that caused hardships for black Africans. For example, a law in 1911 reserved high-paying jobs for whites. The law forced even skilled blacks into the lowest-paying jobs. A 1913 land act set aside just ten percent of the country's land for blacks—although blacks made up nearly 80 percent of South Africa's population.

In 1948 the white government passed a formal policy that separated whites from blacks. Called **apartheid,** which means "apartness," the policy described who was "black," who was "white," and who was "colored"—a person of mixed race. Blacks and coloreds had to carry cards showing their race. In the 1950s, black Africans also had to carry small books with their fingerprints, racial background, and other details of their lives. Police demanded to see this book whenever a black African was in a city or in a whites-only area. If the person was not carrying the book, the police could put him or her in jail.

Apartheid caused much pain among black South African families. Most were very poor. Families broke apart when fathers went to jail. The government-run schools paid low salaries to the poorly trained teachers of black students. Officials decided what was taught, and they discouraged important subjects, such as mathematics. When the ANC decided to start its own schools, the government outlawed private schools.

The Long Road to Democracy

The ANC knew it needed to take stronger action against apartheid policies. It joined with other groups to encourage protest among black Africans. During the early 1950s, the police arrested nearly 9,000 blacks for purposefully disobeying apartheid laws. By the 1960s, the ANC promoted even stronger opposition. New young leaders, such as Nelson Mandela, spoke of a government with equality for all Africans. ANC members also began training for an armed uprising. In 1962, when word of the ANC plans reached the government, it arrested Mandela and 17 other leaders.

Other nations became keenly aware that South Africa's government was **racist,** or favored one race over another. News stories began to cover the protests and riots between the police and black South Africans. The Olympic organizers even banned South Africa from the 1968 and 1972 games. In 1976 thousands of black children in Soweto, near Johannesburg, marched to protest their poor schooling. As they sang freedom songs, police used tear gas. When the children threw rocks, the police opened fire and killed 176 people. To show disapproval of South African policies, many nations started sanctions. **Sanctions** are economic or military measures that nations use to pressure another nation to stop violating some international law or human right.

During the 1980s, global economic sanctions hurt South Africa's economy. Cries to release Nelson Mandela, who had been in prison for more than 20 years, grew louder. In 1990 the white government freed Mandela. It began to work toward equal rights for blacks and coloreds. In 1994 South Africa held elections that were open to all races. Seventeen million black voters went to the polls for the first time. As a result of the election, Nelson Mandela became South Africa's president.

South Africa adopted a new constitution, with a detailed bill of rights, in 1996. Three years later, Mandela stepped down. Another black South African, Thabo Mbeki, was elected in his place. Today South Africa struggles with unemployment, a high crime rate, and the growing incidence of AIDS. However, the country's success in ending apartheid provides hope that it will be able to deal with its other challenges.

Reading a Political Cartoon A political cartoon expresses an opinion on an issue. The artist uses symbols and exaggerated drawings to express his or her views. Labels often provide important clues to what the cartoonist is trying to say. Study the cartoon above. What does the boat represent?

a. the government of South Africa
b. peace between the people of South Africa

Thinking About the Article

Practice Vocabulary

The words below are in the passage in bold type. Study the way each word is used. Then complete each sentence by writing the correct word.

republic   **suffrage**   **civil rights**   **parliament**

apartheid   **racist**   **sanctions**

1. The South African _____ began making anti-black laws in the early 1900s.

2. In 1948 the government's abuse of black South Africans' rights became a policy called _____ .

3. Black South Africans wanted the same _____ that white South Africans had.

4. _____ practices in South Africa date back to the Boers who enslaved the black Africans they defeated in battle.

5. South Africa was a colony in the British empire, but in 1961 the colony became a(n) _____ .

6. One way a government shows its disapproval of another government's actions is through _____ .

7. Black South Africans practiced their newly won _____ in 1994 when they voted for Nelson Mandela to lead their government.

Understand the Article

Write the answer to each question.

8. Why did the Boers resist British control in South Africa?

_____

9. List three ways that apartheid violated the basic freedoms of black South Africans.

_____

_____

10. How did the African National Congress try to resist apartheid?

_____

Apply Your Skills

Circle the number of the best answer for each question.

11. Which of the following actions of ANC members is evidence that they valued learning?
    (1) They planned to fight the government, if necessary.
    (2) They devoted time to working for civil rights.
    (3) They joined other groups to encourage resistance among black Africans.
    (4) They sent their leaders to universities in Europe.
    (5) They tried to open nongovernment schools for black children.

12. Look again at the cartoon on page 89. What is the cartoonist trying to show about the men who refuse to bail out their boat?
    (1) They are lazy.
    (2) They are proud.
    (3) They are afraid.
    (4) They are sleepy.
    (5) They don't care.

13. In the cartoon, what is used to symbolize the problems that were destroying peace in South Africa?
    (1) the buckets
    (2) the boat
    (3) the water
    (4) white clothing
    (5) black clothing

Connect with the Article

Write your answer to each question.

14. Why did sanctions against South Africa discourage apartheid?

    _____

    _____

15. Nelson Mandela became the leader of South Africa after the 1994 election. If you had been elected president of South Africa instead of Mandela, what would your first actions as the head of its government have been?

    _____

    _____

    _____

    _____

LESSON 12

Global Interdependence

Vocabulary

charter

neutral

cease-fire

mediator

allies

deadlocked

province

civil war

The year was 1944, and World War II was still raging. Even so, Great Britain, the United States, and China were looking ahead to peacetime. Their delegates met in Washington, D.C., to draw up a plan for a world organization called the United Nations. Its purpose was to stand up to national leaders who bullied their neighbors or their own people, as Germany and Japan had done at the start of the war.

Relate to the Topic

This lesson is about United Nations peacekeeping forces. It describes who they are and what they do in the troubled spots they protect. Think about a recent newspaper or television report about fighting in a distant region of the world. Where was the fighting, and what was it about?

_____

_____

_____

Reading Strategy

USING HEADINGS TO ASK QUESTIONS   The headings of an article can help guide your reading. They also can help you review what you have read. Skim the headings in the article that begins on page 93. Then answer the questions.

1. What is one question that you could ask about a group of people?

    _____

    _____

    Hint: Start a question with the word Who.

2. Write a question that you could ask about a place.

    _____

    _____

    Hint: Start a question with the word Where.

UN Peacekeeping Forces

By the end of World War II, most leaders had realized that they needed the combined strength of several nations to stand up to powerful enemies. So 51 countries formed the United Nations (UN) in 1945. Their representatives approved its **charter,** or plan, at a meeting in San Francisco.

The UN Charter created a Security Council. The Security Council is responsible for maintaining peace in the world. The United States, Great Britain, Russia, China, and France are permanent members of the Security Council. The General Assembly—delegates from the 191 countries who now belong to the United Nations—elects ten temporary members.

Peacekeepers to the Rescue

The members of the Security Council decide how to handle trouble-making governments, warring countries, or warring groups within a country. The council's actions can range from scolding publicly to sending troops. Troops under UN command are known as peacekeeping forces. The secretary-general, the chief officer of the UN, appoints their commander.

Peacekeeper forces must be **neutral.** In other words, they cannot take sides. So the soldiers come from countries that are not directly involved with the conflict at hand. The soldiers fall into two groups—observers and peacekeepers.

The observers are unarmed officers who visit an area in small numbers simply to watch. Then they report back to the UN. They wear blue helmets or berets. The jeeps and other vehicles that accompany them are white and marked with *UN* in large, dark letters. Observers monitor situations such as an election or a **cease-fire**—a pause in fighting. For example, in the 1990s the UN sent observers to Nicaragua in Central America to witness the change from civil war to a democratic government.

Refugees leaving the capital of Rwanda

Lightly armed soldiers do the actual peacekeeping. They often do not have tanks or heavy weapons. They sometimes do their job by coming between warring parties. Either side must then attack UN soldiers first in order to get to its enemy. The UN soldiers also act as **mediators,** or go-betweens, to settle disagreements between enemies. Both kinds of peacekeeping are often necessary to maintain a cease-fire.

Understanding a Photo Pictures often contain as much information as words do. Look at the photo on page 93. It shows people fleeing the capital of Rwanda where warring groups were battling for control of the government in 1994. What does this photo suggest about the UN's goals in Rwanda?

a. UN troops were trying to keep order.

b. UN troops were trying to help people flee from Rwanda.

Early Missions in the Middle East and Africa

On several occasions, UN troops have stepped in to make peace in the Middle East. One of the earliest instances was the Suez Crisis in 1956. The United States and Great Britain had offered to help pay for the Aswan High Dam project in Egypt. But Egypt's President Gamal Nasser also asked the Soviet Union for money. The Americans and British distrusted the Soviet Union and withdrew their offer. On July 26, 1956, an angry President Nasser responded by claiming that the Egyptian government owned the Suez Canal.

The Suez Canal was an important shipping lane. Until Egypt seized the canal, a company half-owned by the British ran it. So with the help of its **allies,** France and Israel, Britain tried to retake the canal by force. Israel attacked Egypt from the air on October 29, and British and French troops landed on its Mediterranean shore on November 5.

President Nasser requested help from the UN. Members of the Security Council were **deadlocked**—unable to agree on what to do. So the General Assembly voted to send troops. A cease-fire took effect on November 6, and Great Britain, France, and Israel withdrew from Egypt. Six thousand UN troops guarded the borders after the withdrawal.

On this mission, none of the troops were from Great Britain, France, the United States, or the Soviet Union. For the first time, an international police force took action without a major power involved. Since then, United Nations peacekeepers have gone several more times to the Middle East. To this day, UN observers continue to monitor borders there.

In the 1960s, the Congo crisis brought UN peacekeepers to Africa. The Congo declared independence from Belgian rule in 1960 and renamed itself Zaire. But the new central government could not control the far-flung parts of the country. Katanga and other **provinces**—regions similar to states in the United States—tried to pull out and establish their own countries.

Zaire's Prime Minister Patrice Lumumba requested aid from the UN. In 1962 UN forces arrived to keep order. Despite their presence, Zaire collapsed into **civil war,** and the most that the 20,000 UN soldiers could do was to protect civilians, or nonmilitary persons.

In 1988 the United Nations peacekeeping forces received the Nobel peace prize. This award recognized the growing importance of international forces. In the 1990s, the UN definition of "keeping peace" became broader. Some missions, like the one in Somalia, focused on saving a country's people rather than its government.

Saving Somalis

Siad Barre was the ruler of Somalia. For years his harsh treatment of the people had caused revolts. Several groups of rebels came together in the United Somali Congress (USC) and overthrew Siad in 1991.

Groups in the USC then quarreled about who would take Siad's place. Heavy fighting broke out in a major grain-growing region of the country. The fighting drove out the farmers. Harvests had already fallen off because of a drought that began in 1989. As a result of the drought and the fighting, the country had almost no food.

By spring of 1992, civil war had killed about 30,000 Somalis. However, ten times more people had died from hunger. By June about 3,000 people were dying each day.

Agencies from all over the world flew in food. But the warring groups hijacked the food before the Red Cross and similar nongovernmental organizations (NGOs) could distribute it. So the UN Security Council approved a peacekeeping force to help deliver the food. Over six months, American planes flew 28,000 tons of food to Somalia, and 500 UN peacekeepers from Pakistan arrived to protect it. Still the food could not reach central Somalia, where people needed it most.

Relief to the hungry took many more soldiers. On December 12, 1992, thousands of troops from Canada and France began arriving to protect the trucks that would deliver the food. More soldiers spread out to the relief stations where the food would be distributed to the people. American soldiers and sailors began building and improving roads to the stations.

By February 1993, food and other aid was being distributed in all parts of the country. Famine was no longer a danger, and convoys full of supplies were rolling along on new or improved roads. Cooperation among governments, UN agencies, and NGOs had accomplished a truly humane mission.

Getting Meaning from Context Sometimes you can figure out the meaning of an unfamiliar word from its context, or the sentences around it. Find the word *famine* in the last paragraph and choose the definition that fits the word's context.

    a.   a scarcity of food
    b.   a lack of rainfall

Thinking About the Article

Practice Vocabulary

The words below are in the passage in bold type. Study the way each word is used. Then complete each sentence by writing the correct word.

charter	neutral	cease-fire
deadlocked	provinces	mediator

1. The peacekeeping officer acted as a _____ between leaders of Somali groups.

2. The United States was _____ in the Bosnia conflict, and so American troops were included in the UN force sent to Bosnia.

3. The new secretary-general scanned the _____ for a description of his duties.

4. When the Security Council was _____ , the General Assembly approved the use of UN troops in Egypt.

5. The rebels in Katanga and other _____ declared a

_____ so they could discuss their demands with Zaire's prime minister.

Understand the Article

Write the answer to each question.

6. How does a UN observer differ from a UN peacekeeper?

_____

_____

_____

7. Why was the Suez Canal important to Great Britain?

_____

_____

_____

8. Why did Somalis have so little food in 1992?

_____

_____

Apply Your Skills

Circle the number of the best answer for each question.

9. Look again at the photo on page 93. What might you conclude based on clues in the picture?
   (1) All Rwanda's men were engaged in the fighting.
   (2) More than half the refugees were women and children.
   (3) UN soldiers were indifferent to the refugees' hardships.
   (4) Most Rwandans could afford cars or trucks.
   (5) The UN soldiers in Rwanda were only observers.

10. Find the term *civil war* in the first paragraph on page 95. Then reread the paragraph as well as the paragraph before it. Which of the following meanings best fits *civil war* in the context of the two paragraphs?
    (1) a quarrel among staff members
    (2) war according to international rules
    (3) fighting between people of the same country
    (4) a disagreement about private rights
    (5) violence among people out of uniform

11. Find the word *allies* in the second paragraph under "Early Missions in the Middle East and Africa." Which meaning best fits *allies* in the context of the paragraph?
    (1) living things with similar traits
    (2) countries that help each other
    (3) assistants to government officials
    (4) mixtures of different things
    (5) narrow streets behind buildings

Connect with the Article

Write your answer to each question.

12. "The UN peacekeeping mission to Zaire was a failure." Do you agree or disagree with this statement? Explain your answer.

_____

_____

13. If you were going to be a mediator in a disagreement between two friends, why would it be important that you remain neutral in the dispute?

_____

_____

_____

History at Work

Service: National Historic Park Guide

Some people enjoy studying and talking about history, sharing information with others, and helping others appreciate our nation's cultural resources. If that describes you, a job in one of the U.S. national historic parks may be just what you are looking for.

Every year, millions of U.S. residents and foreign visitors tour America's 379 national parks and sites. Park guides help visitors learn about and enjoy these historic sites and areas. National historic parks such as Ellis Island, the battlefield at Gettysburg, and the Lyndon B. Johnson National Historical Park in the photo above have a rich history that guides enjoy sharing with visitors.

Park guides must have a good understanding of the historic events related to their specific park. They are expected to be well read and know interesting facts about the people, times, and places associated with the site. Guides must also have good personal skills. They need to be patient and resourceful in order to answer people's questions. They must also have good public speaking skills since they often need to make presentations to groups.

Look at the *Some Careers in Service* chart.

- Do any of the careers interest you? If so, which ones?
- What information would you need to find out more about those careers? On a separate piece of paper, write some questions that you would like answered. You can find more information about those careers in the *Occupational Outlook Handbook* at your local library or online.

Some Careers in Service

Park rangers enforce laws and safety rules and provide assistance to visitors

Site managers supervise staff, organize special activities, and oversee the budget for the maintenance of the site

Visitor assistants tally visitor fees, answer questions, and provide assistance to visitors

Preservation specialists maintain and repair historic buildings and relics, help prepare site exhibits

National park guides need to read information about the history of the park or site in which they work. **Read the excerpt below from an informational brochure about Liberty Island National Park. Then answer the questions.**

The Statue of Liberty

It now stands as the ultimate symbol of immigration and welcome to the U.S. But in the beginning, "Liberty Enlightening the World," better known as the Statue of Liberty, was a gift from the French to the people of the United States. This 151-foot-tall gift celebrated the partnership of these two countries in the American Revolution and America's independence from England.

The statue was presented on October 28, 1886, at Bedloe Island. Thousands of invited guests witnessed the incredible unveiling ceremony of the world's tallest freestanding statue and New York's tallest structure. The statue's artist, Frèdèric-Auguste Bartholdi, was given the honor of releasing the French flag draped across Liberty's 14-foot-long face.

Today the copper-covered Statue of Liberty is no longer the tallest structure in New York. However, it is among the top New York sites visited by Americans and tourists from around the world.

1. Which of the following best describes "Liberty Enlightening the World"?
   (1) building
   (2) statue
   (3) country
   (4) island
   (5) national park

2. The Statue of Liberty was a gift from which of the following?
   (1) England
   (2) the United States
   (3) France
   (4) New York
   (5) Bedloe Island

3. List four facts a guide at Liberty Island National Park should be expected to know about the Statue of Liberty.

   _____

   _____

   _____

   _____

Unit 2 Review
World History

Russia's Democratic Challenge

Russians have been taking lessons in democracy. Because they have had a long history of rule by one person, they have found the lessons difficult. Before the 1400s, princes ruled different parts of what is now Russia. In the 1400s, Ivan the Great conquered the parts and formed an empire. Only for a few months in 1917, immediately after the Russian Revolution, did rebels set up a government "by the people."

The Communist party, however, quickly took control of Russia and its empire. The Communists formed the Soviet Union, which survived for about 70 years. By 1991, however, peoples in the Soviet Union who were not Russians wanted to rule themselves. Russia also exchanged communist government for a more democratic system in 1991.

With little experience in democracy, Russians had to start at the beginning. First they created words in their language for *democracy, president,* and *constitution.* Then citizens voted for leaders. In the first seven years of the republic, Russians went to the polls five times to vote for a president and parliament, their law-making body. But political change came slowly. In 1999 most Russians felt that it was important to have free elections. They appreciated such rights as freedom of expression and freedom of religion. More than half the people, however, believed that their current government was not a democracy.

In the spring of 2000 Russians elected Vladimir Putin as their president. Since then, some observers say that Russia has become less democratic. They point to corruption in Russia's law enforcement system, the closing of some newspapers, and possible tampering with regional election results. They suggest that Putin is not committed to true democracy. Other observers note that there have been some legal reforms and that a high percentage of Russians now vote. Reforms take time, they say, and Russia continues to move toward democracy.

Circle the number of the best answer.

1. What is the main idea of this passage?
   (1) Communists ruled Russia more years than emperors did.
   (2) Russians do not appreciate democracy.
   (3) Russia provides a strong example of democratic government in action.
   (4) Russia's new government is struggling.
   (5) The Russian Revolution was unsuccessful.

Write the answer to each question.

2. What does the bear represent in the cartoon? What does the pan represent?

_____

_____

3. Why is the pan on fire?

_____

_____

4. What is the main idea the cartoonist communicates in this cartoon?

_____

_____

Circle the number of the best answer.

5. Based on the information in the passage, what values do the Russian people equate with democracy?
   (1) respect, honesty, courage in battle
   (2) citizenship, loyalty, uniformity of beliefs
   (3) wealth, military power, order at all costs
   (4) authority, law, strength of purpose
   (5) freedom, impartial justice, and honest elections

The Spanish Empire Tumbles

By 1588 Spain had built the world's largest empire. It included land in nearly every part of the world. But this was not enough for Spain's King Philip II. He had his eye on England and its Protestant queen, Elizabeth I. Under Elizabeth's rule, English sea pirates had been raiding Spanish ships and stealing the treasures they carried from Spain's colonies. So Philip planned to attack the island nation.

The Spanish king built a magnificent fleet of ships, which the Spanish called an **armada.** Many of its 150 ships were huge, with enough space for mules, horses, food, weapons, and hundreds of soldiers. Each ship bore the name of an apostle or saint. To command the armada, Philip chose a high-ranking nobleman who had no experience at sea. The more than 25,000 soldiers on the armada considered this attack a mission to bring England back into the Catholic Church.

England's navy could not defend the nation by itself. Elizabeth asked the Dutch for help. She also called upon English merchant ships to join the Royal Navy. Nearly 200 ships met the armada, but they were only half as big as the Spanish ships.

In July 1588, fierce storms and rough seas made sailing difficult in the English Channel. England's small ships were light and fast, and their sailors moved them expertly through the rough waters. After two days of heavy fighting, the English set fire to eight of their own ships and sent them, loaded with ammunition, toward the armada.

The Spanish Empire 1588

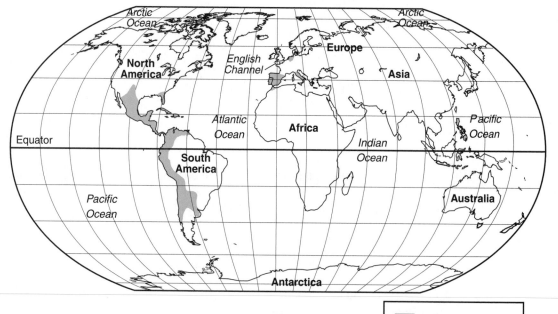

Spanish Empire

The Spanish ships headed north to dodge the attack, but even more English ships chased them. Wild storms wrecked 17 Spanish ships along Ireland's coast. Only a few hundred Spaniards returned home. England had defeated the grand Spanish armada.

Spain's empire was never the same. Its power seemed to sink with its ships. England would become the next great power in Europe.

Write or circle the answer to each question.

6. Reread the first two paragraphs of the article on page 102. From the context, what does *armada* mean?
   (1) naval commander
   (2) Spanish empire
   (3) raiding sea pirates
   (4) fleet of ships
   (5) treasure ships

7. Which part of Philip's plan to attack England is the best example of faulty logic?
   (1) He told his soldiers they were winning England back into the Catholic Church.
   (2) He named a high ranking but inexperienced nobleman as fleet commander.
   (3) He named the ships after apostles and saints.
   (4) He brought 25,000 soldiers.
   (5) He set fire to his smaller ships.

8. What was faulty about Philip's overall plan?

   _____

   _____

   _____

Look at the map on page 102. Then answer the question.

9. Why do you think so many areas under Spanish control were along coastlines?

   _____

   _____

Social Studies Extension

Think about a person with whom you often disagree. Choose an issue over which you have disagreed. List points you made in the disagreement, and then list the other person's points. Compare and contrast them. What values do you share? What values are yours alone? What opposite values does the other person hold? What seems to be the reason that you disagree?

Mini-Test • Unit 2

Directions: Choose the <u>one best answer</u> to each question.

<u>Questions 1</u> refers to the following timeline.

Latin American Independence

1. What can you conclude about Latin American independence?

   (1) The countries that won independence in the 1800s all broke free of Spain.

   (2) Most of the movement's leaders were born in Latin America, not in Europe.

   (3) Almost all of these countries became independent within a fifteen-year period.

   (4) The independence movement took place only in South America.

   (5) Leaders of the United States generally supported the independence movement.

<u>Questions 2 and 3</u> refer to the following information.

In the 1700s, many Enlightenment thinkers believed that human reason was the best way to understand people, the universe, and God, and that it was the key to improving the world.

The French writer Voltaire blasted "unreasonable" leaders and government policies. He also condemned the Church and traditional Christianity. Voltaire did not believe in democracy. Instead, he wanted well-educated nobles to turn to reason and take charge of making the world a better place for everyone.

Jean-Jacques Rousseau believed that emotion, as well as reason, was important. He opposed the aristocracy and believed that everyone should have a voice in government. Rousseau and Voltaire became enemies.

2. Which statement <u>best</u> summarizes the main idea of this passage?

   (1) Voltaire attacked traditional religion; to Rousseau the Church was important.

   (2) Rousseau and Voltaire were the two most powerful voices for the Enlightenment.

   (3) The Enlightenment began in France and spread through Europe.

   (4) Enlightenment thinkers believed that reason alone would improve society.

   (5) Voltaire and Rousseau were part of the same movement but disagreed.

3. According to the passage, what did both writers consider to be important?

   (1) using emotion as well as reason

   (2) reforming the government

   (3) trusting in the average person

   (4) using the Bible as a guide to morality

   (5) receiving a formal education

Questions 4 and 5 refer to the following table about ancient Egypt.

Some Rulers of Egypt's New Kingdom
1567–1085 B.C.

Name/Reign	Accomplishment
Amenhotep I (1546–1526 B.C.)	He began building an Egyptian empire by attacking neighboring countries
Hatshepsut (1503–1482 B.C.)	She seized power from her stepson and ruled as a Pharaoh
Akhenaten (1379–1362 B.C.)	He replaced traditional state religion with a monotheistic religion, based on belief in one god
Tutankhamen (1361–1352 B.C.)	He began returning Egypt to the traditional state religion but died young
Ramses II (1304–1237 B.C.)	He made peace with Egypt's enemies, the Hittites, and started a massive building program

4. In what way was Hatshepsut different from the other rulers listed in the table?

   Hapshepsut

   (1) ruled much earlier than the other rulers did
   (2) had no wish to build an empire
   (3) was a monotheist
   (4) was a woman
   (5) made peace with Egypt's enemies

5. Napoleon Bonaparte tried to conquer much of Europe in the early 1800s. Which Egyptian ruler could have been an inspiration to Napoleon?

   (1) Amenhotep I
   (2) Hatshepsut
   (3) Akhenaten
   (4) Tutankhamen
   (5) Ramses II

Questions 6 and 7 refer to the following information.

In the early 1950s, six European nations agreed to cooperate on a number of economic matters. Their association was eventually named the European Economic Community (EEC) and is also referred to as the Common Market.

As more countries joined the EEC, the association began to consider other goals in addition to purely economic ones. In 1993 the organization became the European Union (EU). Member nations agreed to cooperate on immigration, law enforcement, and foreign policy issues. By 2001 the EU had 15 members, and 13 southern and eastern European countries were applying for membership.

6. Which question would a good summary of this passage help answer?

   (1) What does *Common Market* mean?
   (2) Which treaty established the EU?
   (3) How did the EU develop into more than an economic association?
   (4) Why wasn't England an original member of the EU?
   (5) Why have several eastern European nations been invited to join the EU?

7. Which statement about the European Union is a hasty generalization?

   (1) European nations make up the membership.
   (2) Former communist countries may become members.
   (3) Membership in the EU is likely to increase in the coming years.
   (4) Members talk about economic issues.
   (5) Members never disagree about policy.

Civics and Government

Civics is the branch of political science that deals with the rights and duties of citizens. Government refers to the system of laws and the political bodies that make it possible for a nation, a state, or a community to function. As a citizen or a resident of the United States, civics and government affect your daily life. Learning about civics and government can help you understand how our country operates.

When did you last vote in an election?

_____

Write two ways state and local government affect your daily life.

_____

_____

Thinking About Civics and Government

You may not realize how much you already know about civics and government. Think of news reports that you have seen or heard. What did they tell you about the workings of your community and the nation as a whole?

Check the box for each fact that you already know.

☐ The U.S. system of government is a representative democracy based on the Constitution.

☐ The Bill of Rights guarantees Americans freedom of speech.

☐ The national government is divided into three branches: the executive branch, the legislative branch, and the judicial branch.

☐ The Senate and the House of Representatives are the legislative branch of the national government.

☐ In the United States, you must be at least eighteen years old to vote.

☐ Taxes pay for services that the government provides.

Write two other facts that you know about civics and government.

_____

_____

Previewing the Unit

In this unit, you will learn:

- how local governments deal with community problems
- how the concept of checks and balances is part of our government
- how the government protects the rights of citizens
- what responsibilities citizens have
- how Americans choose their leaders
- how a political campaign is conducted
- how the government gets and uses money for the benefit of the people

LESSON 13

State and Local Governments

State and Local Governments

Vocabulary

Constitution

federal government

ordinance

hazardous waste

landfill

groundwater

aquifer

recycling

composting

After the Revolutionary War, the loyalty of many Americans was mainly to the state in which they lived. Creating a nation of these separate states led to many questions. What form should the national government take? What powers would the national government have over its citizens? What matters could state and local governments decide for themselves?

The answers to these questions were not easily decided. Some disputes about the powers of the national, state, and local governments arise even today. For the most part, however, government works best when federal, state, and local officials cooperate for the good of all Americans.

Relate to the Topic

This lesson is about ways that state and local governments get rid of trash. Do you recycle cans, plastic, glass, newspapers, or paper? Why or why not?

_____

_____

_____

_____

Reading Strategy

PREVIEWING A POLITICAL CARTOON   A political cartoon can help you better understand ideas. Not only can a political cartoon give information about a topic, it also expresses an opinion about that topic. Look at the cartoon on page 110. Then answer the questions.

1. Based on the cartoon, what do you think the lesson will be about?

_____

Hint: Which words and art details catch your attention first?

2. Who does the man represent? _____
Hint: How does what the man is saying relate to what he is doing?

Check your answers on page 241.   UNIT 3 CIVICS AND GOVERNMENT

Taking Care of Everyday Needs

The **Constitution** is the basic law for American citizens. It describes the parts of the government and spells out the powers that belong to each part. These powers are shared between smaller, regional governments and a central, national government. The national government is in Washington, D.C. It is called the **federal government.** The regional governments are all over the nation. They are in states, cities, towns, counties, and villages and are called state and local governments.

The Constitution lists which powers the federal government has and which powers it cannot have. The Constitution also lists powers that state governments have and cannot have. However, many of the powers of state and local governments are not listed in the Constitution. If the Constitution does not ban the states from having a certain power, and it does not give the same power *only* to the federal government, then that power belongs to the states. States, for example, decide how old you must be to get a driver's license. This age varies from state to state.

Handling Trash

Many powers of state and local governments deal with the basic services people need every day. Local government, in particular, affects the quality of life. Cities and counties, for example, pave streets, treat and supply water, manage law enforcement and fire protection, and collect trash.

Today local governments face a trash crisis. Since 1960, the amount of trash people produce has increased dramatically. The Environmental Protection Agency estimates that Americans throw away 232 million tons of trash each year.

Local governments have four choices in getting rid of this trash. They can burn it, bury it, compost it, or recycle it. But first they must sort it. Glass, metal, and other solid materials are separated from garbage, which decays by itself. Most local governments have **ordinances,** or laws, that require people to separate hazardous wastes from the rest of their trash. **Hazardous wastes** are those items that harm the environment. They include old batteries, motor oil, and certain kinds of paint.

Some counties and towns have furnaces that burn trash. It is burned under carefully controlled conditions. Burning reduces the volume of some trash by 90 percent, leaving only ash. The ash is then buried.

Most trash is not burned but buried in landfills. A **landfill** is a plot of land that is reserved for trash. It is often in areas away from neighborhoods. Trash is buried in the landfill between thin layers of soil. The United States had 8,000 landfills in 1988. Today more than 6,000 of them are closed. Many were older landfills that closed because they were full. Other older landfills closed because they became dangerous. As garbage decays, it forms poisons that can seep into the soil. The poisons pollute **groundwater,** which is an underground source of water. Groundwater feeds wells, springs, ponds, and **aquifers.** About half of the country's drinking water comes from groundwater.

Taking Responsibility

In many states, state and local government officials have worked together to solve their trash problems. They looked at all their options. As a result, they have passed laws that encourage recycling.

Recycling is reusing trash for the same or new purposes. To be used again, most recyclable trash must be processed into a new form. Some places require people to separate recyclable materials, such as aluminum, from their trash. Towns may get people to recycle by establishing "pay-as-you-throw" programs—charging people for trash pickup by the volume or weight of their garbage. The more people throw out, the more they pay. Communities with these programs have seen a decrease in the amount of trash and an increase in recycling.

by Don Landgren; *The Landmark;* Holden, Mass. Reprinted with permission.

Reading a Political Cartoon   A political cartoon expresses an opinion on an issue. The cartoonist uses exaggerated drawings and symbols to express his or her views. It is important to know what the symbols mean and understand why they are used. What idea is the cartoonist expressing by having the man toss the globe as shown?

   a.   By not recycling, the man can have more fun.

   b.   By not recycling, the man is sacrificing the planet.

Some communities practice composting. **Composting** is letting plants and food waste decay on their own. These materials are then turned into rich soil. Almost 4,000 communities have set up leaf-and-yard-waste compost centers.

Some states have laws that set requirements for new landfills. Towns and cities can no longer build their landfills near aquifers or lakes. The new landfills are also designed to be safer. The pits are lined with layers of sand, plastic, and clay. These linings prevent poisons, formed as trash decays, from oozing into the ground outside the pits. Also, pumps remove dangerous liquids from decaying trash. Many communities are cleaning up old landfills. When landfills are full, some local governments recycle the land and build golf courses and parks there.

The table below shows how some states have disposed of their trash. Each one (with its local governments) has made different decisions. Keep in mind that some states have more land available for landfills than others. Most landfills in the eastern half of the United States are full or will be within a few years. These states are more densely populated. A place that is densely populated has many people living within a square mile. Most land in these states is already in use.

Trash Disposal Methods for Selected States

	California	Florida	Indiana	Maine	Minnesota	New Jersey	New York	Texas	Utah
Landfilled	57%	56%	61%	21%	35%	45%	46%	65%	90%
Recycled	42%	28%	35%	40%	42%	38%	42%	35%	5%
Burned	1%	16%	4%	39%	23%	17%	12%	<1%	5%

Zero Waste

Recycling has been increasing since the 1980s, and today 32 percent of all waste is recycled nationwide. High costs allow local governments to recycle only a fraction of their trash. Even though new technology has helped lower the costs of recycling and burning trash, landfills are still the cheapest form of trash disposal. In general, it costs approximately twice as much to burn trash as to bury it and approximately three times as much to recycle it.

Some trash experts suggest that manufacturers should work harder to design their products with trash disposal in mind. These experts want companies to create ways for customers to reuse, recycle, or compost products and packaging. They hope to see the day when "zero waste"—in which all materials are either reused or returned safely to the environment—becomes not just a goal but a reality.

Finding the Implied Main Idea   The topic sentence of a paragraph tells the main idea of the paragraph. Sometimes a paragraph has no topic sentence. So the main idea is not stated, but it is implied. The reader must determine the main idea from the details in the paragraph. Reread the first paragraph under the heading "Zero Waste." Which sentence best describes the main idea of the paragraph?

a.   Recycling is an expensive way for local governments to dispose of trash.

b.   More local governments are recycling trash than ever before.

Thinking About the Article

Practice Vocabulary

The words below are in the passage in bold type. Study the way each word is used. Then complete each sentence by writing the correct word.

| **Constitution** | **ordinances** | **hazardous wastes** |
| **landfill** | **groundwater** | **recycling** |

1. A _____ is likely to be located away from densely populated areas.

2. Some local governments have _____ that require people to separate their trash.

3. Some states have fewer than a dozen curbside programs for

   _____; other states have hundreds of such programs.

4. Old landfills may leak poisons into the _____, polluting water supplies.

5. The _____ lists the powers of the federal government.

6. _____ include old batteries, motor oil, and certain kinds of paint.

Understand the Article

Write the answer to each question.

7. Why do American citizens pay taxes more than once?

   _____

   _____

8. What are the four ways that local governments dispose of trash?

   _____

   _____

9. What are two reasons that landfills have been closing?

   _____

   _____

10. How are recycling and composting different?

    _____

    _____

Apply Your Skills

Circle the number of the best answer for each question.

11. Look at the cartoon on page 110. Which opinion does it express?
    (1) Americans are too lazy to recycle.
    (2) Americans should clean up their homes.
    (3) Americans' trash smells.
    (4) The United States needs more landfills.
    (5) Americans should recycle tires, sinks, and newspapers.

12. Reread the second paragraph under the heading "Taking Responsibility" on page 110. Which sentence states the paragraph's implied main idea?
    (1) Most Americans refuse to recycle.
    (2) Individuals and all levels of government must deal with the trash crisis.
    (3) Recycling is the answer to the trash crisis.
    (4) Getting cash refunds is a popular way to recycle.
    (5) Local governments have set up different ways to get people to recycle.

13. Some cities now charge people for trash pickup according to how much trash they produce. Which opinion does the success of these programs support?
    (1) Only individuals can end the trash crisis.
    (2) People take local government's basic services for granted.
    (3) People care about trash when it hits their pocketbooks.
    (4) Nobody wants his or her trash picked up.
    (5) The trash crisis is the government's problem.

Connect with the Article

Write your answer to each question.

14. Based on the table on page 111, what general statement can you make about the ways state and local governments dispose of trash?

    _____

    _____

    _____

15. What are you doing now to help your community dispose of trash? What more could you do?

    _____

    _____

    _____

The Constitution of the United States

Vocabulary

legislative branch

executive branch

judicial branch

separation of powers

checks and balances

veto

bill

override

impeach

appeal

judicial review

federal deficit

In 1748 French writer Baron de Montesquieu wrote a book praising Great Britain's government. In the book he explained that the British balanced the power of government among three branches. Parliament made the laws. The courts interpreted the laws. And the monarch and his or her ministers carried out the laws. Under such a system, Montesquieu wrote, "power should be a check to power."

Montesquieu's ideas became popular in Britain's American colonies. Many Americans agreed that government should be divided into branches. Later, they used Montesquieu's ideas when they wrote the Constitution.

Relate to the Topic

This lesson is about the way that the Constitution divides the government's power among three branches. Recall the last time you heard that Congress, the President, or the Supreme Court had taken action. What was the action, which branch of government took this action, and what did you think of it?

_____

_____

_____

Reading Strategy

SKIMMING A DIAGRAM Diagrams can be an excellent way to present detailed information in social studies materials. Turn to page 116 and look at the diagram. Then answer the questions.

1. What is the main topic of the diagram? _____
   Hint: Look at the title.

2. How does the diagram relate to the topic of the lesson? _____

   _____

   Hint: What words are in both the diagram title and the lesson headings?

Check your answers on page 242.　　**UNIT 3 CIVICS AND GOVERNMENT**

Separation of Powers

In the United States, three branches of the federal government share power. Each branch has a specific job. The **legislative branch** makes laws. The **executive branch** carries out laws. The **judicial branch** decides what the laws mean. The Constitution spells out each branch's powers. The three branches work together to govern the nation.

Because each branch has responsibility for one key job of government, no one branch can become too powerful. This idea is called **separation of powers.** The writers of the Constitution also gave each branch ways to make sure the other two branches do not act beyond their power. Each branch has a certain amount of authority over the other branches. This balances the power among them and makes them equal partners in running the government. This idea is called **checks and balances.** The writers of the Constitution were the first to form a government that combined these two ideas.

Checks and Balances in the Executive and Legislative Branches

The President and Vice President lead the executive branch of the federal government. They make sure that the laws Congress passes are carried out. This branch is the only one in charge of enforcing laws. It has many departments to help. For example, the Labor Department enforces laws about workers, and the Interior Department carries out laws that deal with the use of the nation's natural resources.

The executive branch has powers that check the legislative branch. For example, the President may **veto,** or reject, bills. A **bill** is a proposed law. Without a President's support and signature, a bill usually dies.

The executive branch also has a power that checks the judicial branch. The President appoints Supreme Court justices and other federal judges. Presidential appointees often share the President's views. Still, judges have a duty to be impartial and to relate their rulings to an interpretation of the Constitution.

Congress is the legislative branch of the federal government. This legislature is made up of two houses, the House of Representatives and the Senate. American voters elect the members of each house. Together both houses of Congress make laws. This branch is the only one in charge of making laws.

The legislative branch has powers that check the executive branch. Although the President may veto a bill, the Constitution allows Congress to vote on the bill again. If two-thirds of both houses vote in favor of the bill, it becomes law. This action is called an **override** of the veto. The Constitution also gives Congress the power to approve government spending. To check the President, Congress can deny funds to pay for the President's favorite programs. The legislative branch can check the judicial branch, too. It must approve the President's appointments and has the power to impeach judges. To **impeach** means to accuse someone of misconduct. If the House of Representatives impeaches a judge, the Senate may remove the judge from office.

Reading a Diagram A **diagram** shows how a system works. Look at the diagram below. Follow the arrows from each branch of government and read what checks it has over the other branches. Which branch determines if a law is constitutional?

      a.   legislative branch   b.   executive branch   c.   judicial branch

The System of Checks and Balances

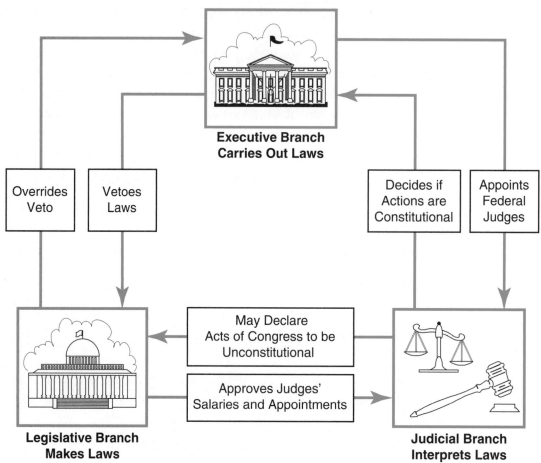

Checks by the Judicial Branch

    The judicial branch of the federal government makes certain that the government follows the Constitution. At the head of the judicial branch is the Supreme Court. It has many lower courts to help it. If citizens object to a decision made in a federal court, they can **appeal,** or bring the case to another federal court called the appeals court. If citizens are unsatisfied with the appeals court's ruling, they can go to the Supreme Court.

    The judicial branch checks both the legislative and executive branches in a similar way. It uses its power of **judicial review.** This means the Supreme Court and lower federal courts can determine whether a law passed by Congress follows the Constitution. If the Court rules that a law is unconstitutional, the executive branch stops enforcing the law.

A Case Study in Checks and Balances

Government officials are sometimes frustrated with checks and balances. The following example is a case in which the judiciary checked both the executive and legislative branches. It shows the system of checks and balances in action.

In 1997 Congress passed the line-item veto law. Before this law, the President could reject only an entire spending bill or tax bill. The President could not accept some parts of the bill and reject others. The line-item veto law allowed the President to veto only specific parts of a bill.

Surprisingly, Congress was in favor of this law, which gave the President more power. Lawmakers thought the law would be a good way to control wasteful spending. They hoped it would encourage presidents to lower the huge **federal deficit.** This is the amount of money the government has to borrow each year. Congress knew that governors in 44 of the 50 states had line-item veto power. Governors who had used this power had some success in limiting spending in their state budgets.

Other people thought that giving the President a line-item veto was a bad idea. They said that the Constitution gave the power to control spending to Congress, not to the President. They believed the line-item veto weakened the separation of powers between these two branches of government.

When the new law took effect, President Bill Clinton praised it as "a powerful tool to protect taxpayers." Many presidents before him had wanted more power to curb government spending. Members of the executive branch saw the passage of the law as their victory.

In 1998 the Supreme Court ruled that the line-item veto law was unconstitutional. In the written decision, the justices quoted George Washington, who wrote that a president cannot change the text of a bill by Congress. In addition, the Constitution allows a president to veto a bill, but it does not say if the President can veto only parts of it. The Court decided that Congress could not give this power to the executive branch.

President Clinton was unhappy about the Supreme Court's decision. "The decision is a defeat for all Americans," he said. "It deprives the President of a valuable tool for eliminating waste in the federal budget."

Senators who favored the line-item veto were also unhappy with the decision. Usually Congress combines many kinds of spending in one bill. These unhappy senators threatened to include only one type of spending in each bill. If lawmakers used this method, the President would have to sign or veto thousands of spending bills each year.

Distinguishing Fact from Opinion A **fact** states something that can be proved. An **opinion** expresses what a person or group thinks or believes. Which statement is a fact?

   a. The Constitution's writers gave the executive branch the power to veto bills.

   b. The judicial branch is the most powerful branch of government.

Thinking About the Article

Practice Vocabulary

The words below are in the passage in bold type. Study the way each word is used. Then complete each sentence by writing the correct word.

legislative branch	**executive branch**	**judicial branch**
checks and balances	**separation of powers**	**bill**

1. Determining whether the federal government acts according to the Constitution is the main job of the _____.

2. A(n) _____ does not usually become a law until the President signs it.

3. The _____ includes many departments that help enforce laws.

4. The writers of the Constitution used the idea of _____ by creating three branches of government to run the United States.

5. The Constitution gave the _____ control over government spending.

6. The idea that each branch of government has a certain amount of power over the other branches is called _____.

Understand the Article

Write the answer to each question.

7. What is an example of a check that the President has on Congress?

   _____

8. What is a check that the Supreme Court has on the executive branch?

   _____

9. Why did the President and some people in Congress favor the line-item veto?

   _____

   _____

10. Why did the Supreme Court declare the line-item veto law to be unconstitutional?

    _____

    _____

Apply Your Skills

Circle the number of the best answer for each question.

11. Look at the checks and balances diagram on page 116. Which fact is supported by the information in the diagram?
    (1) The legislative branch is the most powerful because Congress makes laws.
    (2) Each branch of government checks the power of the other branches.
    (3) The veto power gives the President great power over Congress.
    (4) The Supreme Court has lower federal courts to help it interpret laws.
    (5) Congress is made up of the Senate and the House of Representatives.

12. What opinion did President Clinton hold about the line-item veto?
    (1) Presidents had been trying since the 1870s to gain the line-item veto.
    (2) President George Washington would have supported the line-item veto.
    (3) Putting each government expense in a separate bill would overload the President.
    (4) Some governors had the power to veto specific lines in a spending bill.
    (5) The line-item veto was a powerful tool to protect taxpayers.

13. According to the Supreme Court, how did the line-item veto disrupt the balance of power among the branches of the federal government?
    (1) It gave power to state governors that the executive branch should have.
    (2) It gave power to the executive branch that the state governors should have.
    (3) It gave power to Congress that the executive branch should have.
    (4) It gave too much power over Congress to the executive branch.
    (5) It did a poor job of limiting government spending.

Connect with the Article

Write your answer to each question.

14. How is the idea of separation of powers different from the idea of checks and balances?

_____

_____

15. Do you think it is in your best interest for the President to have a line-item veto? Explain your answer.

_____

_____

Rights and Responsibilities

Rights and Responsibilities

Vocabulary

amendment

Bill of Rights

justice

due process

warrant

indict

What do you think Andrew Jackson, the seventh President of the United States, meant by this statement? "Every good citizen makes his country's honor his own, and cherishes it not only as precious but as sacred. He is willing to risk his life in its defense and is conscious that he gains protection while he gives it."

Jackson's words speak of the double nature of citizenship. As citizens, we appreciate what our country gives us. We also respond by giving of our time and talents to our country.

Relate to the Topic

This lesson is about some of the basic rights and freedoms that Americans enjoy—and what is expected of Americans in return. What do you think you should expect of your country? What should it expect of you?

_____

_____

_____

Reading Strategy

RELATING TO WHAT YOU KNOW   To make sense of informational reading, compare the facts with what you have read or experienced. Read the first paragraph under the heading "Guarantees of Freedom and Justice" on page 121. Then answer the questions.

1. What do you already know about the First Amendment?

   _____

   _____

   Hint: When or where might you have heard the term First Amendment?

2. When have you experienced the freedoms that the paragraph names?

   _____

   _____

   Hint: Think about the amendment's focus on communication.

Making Freedom Work

After the Constitution was written in 1787, several states were reluctant to approve it. They wanted the document to say that the federal government would protect certain rights of citizens. With these rights Americans would truly be free.

Many of the Constitution's framers saw no need for such a list. Most state constitutions already gave these rights to their citizens. Some of the states, however, pressured the government. In 1789, in the first session of Congress, James Madison of Virginia introduced 17 amendments to the Constitution. An **amendment** is an addition or change. These amendments included the list of rights that many people had wanted to see in the Constitution. By 1791 the states had approved ten of the amendments that Madison had suggested. These first ten amendments to the Constitution are called the **Bill of Rights.**

Guarantees of Freedom and Justice

The Bill of Rights protects the freedom of Americans. The First Amendment is the main guarantee of personal freedoms. This amendment protects Americans' right to speak and write about their beliefs and opinions. It also allows them to gather and associate with people of their choice and to worship, or not worship, freely.

Several of the other amendments in the Bill of Rights guarantee **justice,** or fair and equal treatment under the law. These amendments grant due process to a person who is accused of crime. **Due process** is the set of steps that law enforcement personnel and the courts must follow to protect the rights of the accused. It includes the right to be represented by a lawyer (Sixth Amendment) and the right to a trial by jury (Seventh Amendment).

Three other amendments in the Bill of Rights describe additional rights and protections related to due process. The Fourth Amendment prohibits police and other government agents from searching a person's body, house, car, or other belongings without good reason. Law enforcement personnel must obtain a **warrant**—a legal permit from a court, before they can conduct a search. According to the Fifth Amendment, a person cannot be tried for a crime unless **indicted,** or formally charged. This amendment also says that a person cannot be tried twice for the same crime and cannot be forced to testify against himself or herself. According to the Eighth Amendment, a person who is found guilty of a crime cannot be punished in a cruel or unusual way.

The protections that we have as Americans are important, but they also are open to interpretation. The Supreme Court often is asked to decide whether the rights guaranteed by the Bill of Rights apply to specific situations.

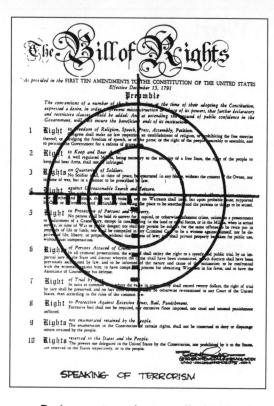

Other matters regarding American rights are part of our public debate. For example, the Second Amendment names "the right of the people to keep and bear arms" as key to "a well-regulated militia." Should citizens who are not in the military be allowed to own guns? Should a person need a permit to own a gun? People on opposing sides of the issue interpret the Second Amendment differently.

There are limits on the guarantees provided in the Bill of Rights. For instance, the First Amendment gives people the right to hold parades. In practice, however, they must get a permit before they can parade on city streets. Similarly, a person cannot use freedom of speech to yell "fire" in a theater just to see what happens.

Perhaps at no time are limits on rights and freedoms of greater concern than during war or other national emergency. Many Americans are willing to make some sacrifices for the sake of national security. Still, they are cautious. They know that if they allow some rights and freedoms to be compromised in a time of crisis, it may not be easy to get them back when the crisis has passed.

Interpreting Political Cartoons An artist who creates a political cartoon uses symbols and words to express an opinion. A political cartoon may not need many words to express an opinion. Which opinion is expressed in the cartoon above?

   a.   The desire for national security may put the Bill of Rights in danger.
   b.   The Bill of Rights is dangerous and out of date.

With Rights Come Responsibilities

Guaranteed rights are part of our American heritage. Another part of that heritage is the responsibility to support the United States. Just how can we do that?

One answer—perhaps the most important answer—is by participating in government. Before elections, for example, responsible citizens inform themselves about the issues and candidates. Some people work on candidates' campaigns or help educate the public about issues that they consider important. They even may run for public office themselves. Then, on election day, they vote.

Another way that American citizens act responsibly is by working to make their communities the best they can be. People who organize groups to clean up a park or who set up neighborhood watch groups to help the police keep the street safe are acting as responsible citizens. So are people who volunteer their time at libraries, senior centers, and charitable organizations. Indeed, the people who live in a community usually do the best job of improving that community.

Recently, some of the residents of Hartford, Connecticut, showed how volunteers can improve their communities. A group of people in the West End felt that their neighborhood needed a community center. At first, the idea was to provide a place for local teenagers to gather. Soon, however, residents realized that a neighborhood center could provide activities and classes for adults and seniors as well.

The people organized and began to plan. They knew that they would need popular support to make the West End Community Center a reality. Members of the West End Community Center Board took their case to the community. They signed up volunteer workers. They talked to businesses about supporting the center. They prepared plans that they would be able to show the city council. Early in 2002, when the city council was ready to decide about the center, the board printed the flyer below in both English and Spanish and distributed it to people in the neighborhood.

West End Community Center

This is it! If you want a Community Center, come down to City Hall and tell City Council.

Monday, March 11 at 7:30PM
at City Hall, 550 Main Street
Public Hearing for the City Council.

The City Council will be deciding whether to give the West End money to buy 461 Farmington Avenue (Mark E. Salomone building, big white building with the columns next to Subway)

If you want to see the plans before Monday, Call or come to the West End Community Center Board meeting on Friday, March 8 at 6PM at Shepherd Park, 170 Sisson Avenue

---

The West End Community Center Board's campaign worked. The city council approved $450,000 for the project. Soon after, the Board began the process of buying a building and raising funds to support the operation of the center.

Understanding Persuasive Information Writing that is **persuasive** encourages you to have a certain opinion or to take a certain action. Reread the information in the flyer above. What is the flyer trying to persuade people to think or do?

   a. to believe that a community center would be good for the West End
   b. to speak in support of the community center at the public hearing

Check your answer on page 242. **123**

Thinking About the Article

Practice Vocabulary

The words below are in the passage in bold type. Study the way each word is used. Then complete each sentence by writing the correct word.

amendment	Bill of Rights	justice
due process	warrant	indicted

1. The _____ guarantees freedom of religion to Americans.

2. A police officer cannot search your home without first obtaining a(n) _____.

3. _____ exists when people receive fair and equal treatment under the law.

4. A(n) _____ is an addition or other change to an existing legal document.

5. _____ is the set of steps that the police and court officials follow to protect the rights of people accused of crimes.

6. A person must be _____ for a crime before his or her case can go to trial.

Understand the Article

Write the answer to each question.

7. What are two freedoms guaranteed in the First Amendment?

_____

_____

8. What is one way that Americans can participate in government?

_____

_____

9. How did people in Hartford, Connecticut, plan to make the West End neighborhood a better place to live?

_____

_____

_____

Apply Your Skills

Circle the number of the best answer for each question.

10. Look at the cartoon on page 122. Which statement best summarizes the cartoon's main idea?
    (1) Some people hate the Constitution of the United States.
    (2) Attacking guaranteed rights is as much a danger as terrorism.
    (3) Free speech is the most important freedom named in the Bill of Rights.
    (4) The Bill of Rights requires people to get a permit for holding a parade.
    (5) The Bill of Rights encourages limits upon gun ownership.

11. Imagine that a jury finds a man not guilty of murder. Years later, new evidence suggests that he may have committed the crime after all. Which part of the Bill of Rights makes it impossible for him to be tried again?
    (1) the First Amendment
    (2) the Fourth Amendment
    (3) the Fifth Amendment
    (4) the Seventh Amendment
    (5) the Eighth Amendment

12. Look again at the flyer on page 123. How does the flyer try to persuade readers to take action quickly?
    (1) by describing what the City Council will be doing
    (2) by telling people what to do at the public hearing
    (3) by explaining where the meeting will be held
    (4) by identifying the people who support the community center
    (5) by saying "This is it!" and giving the meeting date and time

Connect with the Article

Write your answer to each question.

13. Why is due process important to Americans?

    _____

    _____

14. Think about your community. How could you help make it a better place?

    _____

    _____

LESSON 16

Elections

Vocabulary

politics

political party

nominate

candidate

campaign

primary election

general election

media

political action committee

soft money

Each year American voters go to the polls and choose their representatives in government. Every four years Americans elect the President of the United States. Every two years they elect members in the House of Representatives and one-third of the U.S. Senate. Voters also choose state governors, city mayors, local judges and sheriffs, and many other government leaders.

People vote for or against issues as well as candidates on election day. They may vote to approve the local school budget or a new tax for enlarging the public library. By voting, people directly decide important matters of government.

Relate to the Topic

This lesson is about the election process and what it takes to run for political office. When was the last election held in your community? Write something that was decided in that election.

_____

_____

_____

Reading Strategy

SKIMMING BOLDFACED WORDS   You can get an overview of article by skimming it and looking for boldfaced words—words that appear in dark type. These are words of special importance to the topic. Skim the article that begins on page 127. Look for boldfaced words. Then answer the questions below.

1.   List two boldfaced words in the lesson that refer to groups of people.

_____

Hint: Look for nouns, not verbs.

2.   What do the boldfaced words you listed have in common?

_____

Hint: Think about the overall topic of the lesson.

Check your answers on page 243.   **UNIT 3 CIVICS AND GOVERNMENT**

The Election Process

The right to vote is one of the most important rights of a citizen. It is a right that many groups of Americans have worked hard to win. Only white men who owned land could vote in the early 1800s. Women could not vote in national elections until 1920. Native Americans did not vote until 1924. African Americans could not vote in some Southern states until the 1960s. And young people did not gain the right to vote until 1971.

American Voters

Americans must meet certain requirements to vote. Voters must be citizens and at least 18 years old. Most Americans are citizens because they were born in the United States. Others came to this country, studied English and U.S. history, and became citizens. Voters also must have lived in a state a certain length of time before they can vote. Most states require people to live there at least 30 days before they are eligible to vote. Other state laws also bar certain people from voting. No state allows people who are in a mental institution to vote. Most states will not allow people convicted of serious crimes to vote. Some states disqualify homeless persons.

Voters learn about **politics,** or the ideas and actions of government, at a very young age. As children, they hear their parents talk about issues and leaders. In time the children form opinions. About two of every three Americans have the same political beliefs as their parents. Often they express these beliefs by joining a political party. A **political party** is a group that **nominates,** or chooses, candidates. A **candidate** is a person who runs for public office. People in the same political party often share the same views on one or more issues. If their party's candidate wins the election, the members of the party assume that the candidate will promote their political goals.

The Democratic and Republican parties are the major American political parties. Almost every election has candidates from one or both of these parties. Other political parties have fewer members. These parties often have too little support to run candidates for every political office.

Supporting Conclusions To draw a conclusion, you must identify which facts about a subject are important. Then you judge or decide what the facts tell you about the subject. The judgment you make after examining facts is called a conclusion. The facts on the subject should support your conclusion.

Reread the first paragraph under the heading "American Voters." One conclusion you might draw is that not all voters are American born. Which fact in the paragraph supports that conclusion?

a. Most states require people to live there at least thirty days before they can vote.

b. Others came to this country, studied English and U.S. history, and became citizens.

Check your answer on page 243.

Persuading the Voters

Before an election, a candidate takes part in a series of events called a **campaign.** The goal of the campaign is to persuade people to vote for the candidate. If several members of a political party want to run for the same office, the party chooses its candidate by committee, convention, or a **primary election.** This is an election in which voters choose the party's candidate for the office.

In a presidential election year, many states hold primary elections in the spring. In the summer the delegates, who were selected in the primary, attend the party's national convention. There they nominate the party's candidate for President in the **general election** in the fall. Because of this process, a presidential campaign can last for many months. Candidates must first campaign within their party to get the nomination. Then, if they are successful at the national convention, they must campaign for all the voters' support in the general election.

Many Americans learn about election candidates and issues from the media. The **media** include radio, television, newspapers, and magazines. Reporters present news stories and other information about a campaign. The people who run a campaign also use the media. They run ads to persuade people to vote a certain way. Television has become the key means of gaining support for candidates. To be successful, candidates must get their point across in television ads and compete for the American voters' attention.

The media are on hand to cover campaign events.

UNIT 3 CIVICS AND GOVERNMENT

Political ad writers use the same methods to win votes that advertisers use to sell products. In recent years many political ad writers have taken a negative approach. They want their candidate's opponents to look like poor choices. Their ads often reveal only some of the facts and may mislead voters.

Advertising is not the only way television presents political information. News programs analyze campaign issues and candidates. Candidates participate in televised debates. Some appear as guests on talk shows. Elections even provide rich material for television comedians. Young people, in particular, often learn about politics while laughing at televised skits and stand-up routines.

Distinguishing Fact from Opinion Political ads mix opinions with facts. They do this in order to help the candidate put forth the best image he or she can.

Circle the letter of the opinion below.

a. Our candidate is the best person to speak for our state's concerns.

b. Our candidate has supported children's rights in her work as a defense attorney.

c. Our candidate has worked in the governor's office for 10 years.

Financing Campaigns

Campaigns today are expensive. Running a TV ad just once can cost hundreds of thousands of dollars.

Raising money has become an important task of political parties. Some money comes from individuals. However, most of it comes from **political action committees** (PACs). Special interest groups, such as the American Association of Retired Persons and the National Rifle Association, set up PACs. The PACs give money to candidates who share their political beliefs about certain issues. PACs also do a good job of getting members of special interest groups to vote. Election experts know that PACs can help a candidate win. PACs also may help defeat candidates who oppose their views.

In the 1970s Americans became concerned about the high cost of running for office. Many worried that the people were losing political power to wealthy persons and PACs whose donations candidates needed to get elected. So in 1974 congress passed a law limiting the amount of money a person or a PAC could give to a candidate.

The PACs soon found a loophole in the law. It placed no limits on **soft money**— donations made to a state or local political party instead of to a specific candidate. The party could then legally turn this money over to the candidate. Congress finally closed this loophole in 2002 by passing the Bipartisan Campaign Reform Act. This law severely limits the collection and use of soft money. It is likely, however, that some candidates and PACs will look for loopholes in this law, too.

Check your answer on page 243.   **129**

Thinking About the Article

Practice Vocabulary

The words below are in the passage in bold type. Study the way each word is used. Then complete each sentence by writing the correct word.

politics   political party   campaign   primary election

general election   media   political action committees

1. Television advertising is an important way that candidates communicate with voters during a _____.

2. Candidates use all kinds of _____ to communicate with the American voters.

3. Special interest groups called _____ support candidates who promote political beliefs similar to their own.

4. The family is a major influence on Americans' attitudes toward

    _____.

5. The Democratic candidate who wins the _____ in the spring runs against the Republican candidate in November.

6. Democrats belong to the same _____.

7. In the United States a _____ is held in November.

Understand the Article

Write the answer to each question.

8. What three qualifications must an American meet to vote?

    _____

    _____

9. Why might a candidate's political campaign last for many months?

    _____

    _____

10. What is one way elections have changed since George Washington was President?

    _____

    _____

Apply Your Skills

Circle the number of the best answer for each question.

11. Which of the following examples <u>best</u> supports the conclusion that the media sometimes take sides in political campaigns?
    (1) A newspaper article describes both sides of a campaign issue.
    (2) A television network broadcasts a debate between candidates.
    (3) A radio announcer points out factual errors in political ads.
    (4) A magazine includes information about only one candidate for senator.
    (5) A newspaper runs political ads about all the candidates for mayor.

12. Why is a special interest group most likely to form a PAC?
    (1) to give money to the candidates who need it the most
    (2) to support candidates who share the group's views
    (3) to run political ads that present all views on the issues
    (4) to encourage people to stay home instead of voting
    (5) to support all the candidates running for office

13. Which of the following statements is a fact, rather than an opinion, about financing political campaigns?
    (1) The high cost of running for political office is a major problem in American politics.
    (2) Setting up a PAC is the fairest and most effective way to raise money for political campaigns.
    (3) It is unfair that wealthy candidate have an advantage over less wealthy candidates in financing political campaigns.
    (4) The high cost of political campaigns has raised concerns among many Americans.
    (5) More Americans should support proposals for new campaign finance reform laws.

Connect with the Article

Write your answer to each question.

14. Do you think television ads are a wise use of a candidate's campaign funds? Explain your answer.

    _____

15. Most campaign finance laws have failed to hold down the cost of presidential campaigns. What two changes would you make if you were in charge of campaign spending?

    _____

    _____

Paying for Government

Vocabulary

revenue

income tax

progressive tax

flat tax

sales tax

property tax

excise tax

entitlement

budget

Before the Revolutionary War, Great Britain demanded payment of all sorts of taxes from the American colonists. The colonists were furious that they were required to pay taxes levied by the British Parliament, in which they had no voice. "No taxation without representation" became a rallying cry of the war.

After the war, the new leaders of the country gave Americans a strong voice in government. But they asked themselves if all Americans should decide about taxes spent in only one part of the country. The leaders agreed that people who lived in different parts of the country should decide on their own taxes. Thus, each level of government—national, state, and local—shares the power to tax.

Relate to the Topic

What taxes are you aware of paying now? What taxes do you expect to pay in the future?

_____

_____

_____

Reading Strategy

PREVIEWING GRAPHS   Graphs can present statistical information well—sometimes more clearly than words can. Turn to the circle graphs on page 134. Think about how they can help you prepare to read the lesson. Then answer the questions.

1. How are the two graphs related? _____

_____

Hint: Read the title and headings for both graph.

2. Based on the graphs, what do you think the lesson will discuss?

_____

Hint: Think about why the graphs might be shown.

Check your answers on page 244.   **UNIT 3 CIVICS AND GOVERNMENT**

Where Do Our Taxes Go?

You probably pay taxes each and every day. For example, the total amount you pay for most items is higher than the posted price because you also pay sales tax. Also, the amount of your paycheck is less than you earned because you pay income tax.

What are taxes, and who decides how much you have to pay? In general, a tax is a contribution that a government requires you to make. Governments use tax **revenue,** or money collected as income, to pay for their cost of operating and to provide services for their citizens.

Since ancient times, governments have collected taxes of various kinds. Today people use money to pay taxes, but that has not always been the case. In earlier times, for example, some people paid taxes by giving their government part of their harvest or by working on government projects.

How We Pay Taxes

Income taxes—taxes on earnings—are an important source of government revenues in the United States. Individuals pay personal income taxes, and businesses pay corporate income taxes. The federal government collects the largest share of the personal income taxes levied—some $1.1 trillion in 2001. However, the majority of Americans also pay state income taxes. In some places, people pay local income taxes as well.

How income tax should be calculated is a matter of debate. The federal income tax system is a **progressive tax.** This means that the more money a person earns, the higher the tax rate. In other words, the tax takes a larger percentage of the income of wealthy people than of less-wealthy people. That seems fair to many people. However, some people think that a flat tax is more just. Under a **flat tax,** everyone pays the same percentage regardless of income. Some states levy income taxes at a flat rate.

Most workers pay income tax with each paycheck they receive. A certain amount is automatically deducted from their pay. That way, they do not have to pay their taxes in one large lump sum, and the government receives a flow of revenue throughout the year. Social Security and Medicare taxes are also deducted from most workers' paychecks. These taxes help pay for pensions and healthcare for retired workers.

Another major source of tax revenue is **sales taxes,** or taxes on purchases. Sales taxes are levied in most states, with the individual state governments setting the rate. Local governments may tack on an additional sales tax, or they may choose not to tax certain items. For example, in many places, some food purchases are not taxed.

Property taxes, or taxes on the value of what one owns, are a third source of tax revenue. Real estate—land and the buildings on it—is the main source of property taxes. Property taxes also include taxes on automobiles and business equipment. Most property taxes are state or local taxes.

Excise taxes are taxes on specific items, especially items that the federal, state, and/or local government wants to control. Taxes on cigarettes, alcohol, and gasoline are among the most common excise taxes. If you look at a telephone bill, you will notice that excise taxes are also placed on telephone service.

How Tax Revenue Is Used

How does the government spend your money? The answer depends on whether you are talking about the federal government, the state government, or the local government. The federal government's single largest expense is Social Security. Other major expenses are Medicare, Medicaid (a cost that is shared with state governments), and national defense.

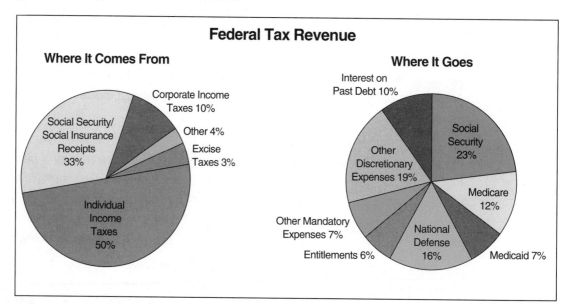

Federal Tax Revenue

Where It Comes From
- Corporate Income Taxes 10%
- Social Security/Social Insurance Receipts 33%
- Other 4%
- Excise Taxes 3%
- Individual Income Taxes 50%

Where It Goes
- Interest on Past Debt 10%
- Social Security 23%
- Other Discretionary Expenses 19%
- Medicare 12%
- Other Mandatory Expenses 7%
- National Defense 16%
- Entitlements 6%
- Medicaid 7%

Using Two Circle Graphs A **circle graph** is good for showing parts of a whole. You can learn much by studying two related circle graphs. Study the circle graphs above. Then answer the questions.

1. From which source did the federal government get ten percent of its revenue?
   a. corporate income taxes
   b. excise taxes

2. For which expense did the federal government spend ten percent of its revenue?
   a. Medicare
   b. interest payments

The federal government funds many **entitlements,** or programs for people who meet certain requirements. Federal entitlements include the food stamp program and pensions for armed forces veterans. Other expenses include aid to foreign countries and interest payments on money the government has borrowed.

A chief expense of state governments is education. Education accounts for more than one-third of the money that many states spend each year. The justice and prison systems take a major share of state funds as well. So do a variety of health care and social programs known as health and human services.

The largest expense of most local governments is public safety, the services that protect people and property. Police and fire departments are included in this category. Among other expenses are community services, which may include snow removal and a local library system, and capital improvements such as upgrades to the community's streets, parks, and utilities.

At each level of government, the amount to be spent is determined by a **budget,** or spending plan. Unexpected events can create budget problems. Unusually heavy snows, for example, may require a city to spend more on plowing snow than budgeted. Less tax revenue may be collected when a weak economy cuts into the earnings of individuals and businesses.

A weak economy caused serious budget problems in California. That state is home to many businesses that develop computers, computer software, and other technological products. Throughout the 1990s, these businesses were extremely successful. They produced a great deal of tax revenue for the state. In turn, the state increased its spending. More money flowed to California's schools, for example. State employees received raises, and state parks lowered entrance fees.

Then the economy suddenly changed. Many high-tech businesses closed. Others had to lay off employees and limit production. As a result, California saw the largest drop in revenue since the Great Depression of the 1930s. In 2002 the state faced a gap between revenue and expenses of more than $23 billion. To help make up the difference, the state increased the sales tax and delayed some planned spending. Will these changes work? Many economists are cautious. They say that it will take years of careful money management and an improving economy to put California's state finances back on track.

Recognizing the Adequacy of Facts As you read informational materials, consider the **adequacy** of the facts—that is, whether there is enough information to prove a point. Reread the next-to-last paragraph above about California. For which statement does that paragraph provide adequate facts?

    a.   In the 1980s, state employees were appealing to the government for pay raises.

    b.   In the 1990s, the state government expected good economic times to continue.

Thinking About the Article

Practice Vocabulary

The words below are in the passage in bold type. Study the way each word is used. Then complete each sentence by writing the correct word.

revenue	income taxes	progressive tax
flat tax	excise tax	entitlements

1. The tax on alcohol is an example of a(n) _____.

2. The food stamp program is one of the _____ provided by the federal government.

3. Corporate taxes are one source of _____ for government programs.

4. _____ come from the wages of workers.

5. Under a(n) _____, all people pay the same percentage of their income as taxes.

6. Under a(n) _____, the tax rate varies according to a person's income.

Understand the Article

Write the answer to each question.

7. Why do governments collect taxes?

_____

_____

_____

_____

8. Name two main expenses of (a) the federal government, (b) state governments, and (c) local governments.

(a) _____

(b) _____

(c) _____

Apply Your Skills

Circle the number of the best answer for each question.

9. Look at the circle graphs on page 134. From highest to lowest, what are the federal government's three greatest sources of tax revenue?
   (1) excise taxes, social security/social insurance taxes, corporate income taxes
   (2) personal income taxes, social security/social insurance taxes, corporate income taxes
   (3) corporate income taxes, excise taxes, personal income taxes
   (4) social security/social insurance taxes, excise taxes, corporate income taxes
   (5) corporate income taxes, social security/social insurance taxes, personal income taxes

10. Based on the circle graph, which of the following costs the federal government more money than national defense?
    (1) Social Security
    (2) Medicare
    (3) Medicaid
    (4) interest on past debts
    (5) entitlement programs

11. Reread the information under "How We Pay Taxes" on pages 133 and 134. Which statement does the information support?
    (1) State and local governments have the highest tax rates.
    (2) Individual states decide which kinds of taxes to levy.
    (3) Without property taxes, there would be no entitlement programs.
    (4) Sales taxes and excise taxes are progressive taxes.
    (5) The Supreme Court once declared income taxes unconstitutional.

Connect with the Article

Write your answer to each question.

12. Why do states compete to attract businesses that are considering relocating? Relate your answer to what you have learned about government and taxes.

_____

_____

13. If you could choose between a flat tax and a progressive tax on your income, which would you choose? Why?

_____

_____

Civics at Work

Service: Community Worker

Some Careers in Community Service

Food Bank Worker
collects and distributes food and other products to community residents

Community Outreach Worker
helps local residents organize for their rights or against unfair or discriminatory practices

Shelter Coordinator
oversees providing shelter, clothing, food, and counseling to the homeless and to victims of domestic violence

They may work for environmental groups, political organizations, social service agencies, or neighborhood and grassroots organizations. Who are they? They're community workers. Community service work is usually challenging, but it is also rewarding. There is often a lot of work to do, and the hours can be unpredictable. But if you care about the well-being of your community, then this may be the type of job for you.

A broad range of community service work exists. Some workers help clients obtain basic services such as housing assistance, job placement, medical care, and child care. Others may focus their efforts on community safety or environmental protection. Still other community workers may help residents speak up for their personal and political rights.

Community workers must be familiar with the laws and rules affecting the work they perform. They need to be good listeners and speakers, and to be able to put their ideas and the ideas of others into writing.

Look at the Some Careers in Community Service chart.

- Do any of the careers interest you? If so, which ones?

- What information would you need to find out more about those careers? On a separate piece of paper, write some questions that you would like answered. You can find more information about those careers in the *Occupational Outlook Handbook* at your local library or online.

Read the material below. Then answer the questions.

MEMO

To: Evan, Project LINK Director

From: Anita, Community Outreach Worker

Re: Election Efforts

Last Thursday evening I was distributing election flyers at Stone Elementary School. I was asked to leave the site by the school's principal and a police officer. When I asked them why, they gave no explanation. They grabbed me by my elbows and escorted me to my car.

I know by now you have heard about this incident. I would like you to know that I followed all the laws that you explained to me. I stood more than 15 feet from the school's entrance. I did not give a flyer to anyone under the age of 18. I did not force anyone to take a flyer.

This troubles me. I know that the First Amendment to the Constitution guarantees me the right to freedom of speech. I think this action violates my rights. Please let me know what I can do about this situation.

1. What was Anita's assignment for Thursday evening?
   (1) to guard the entrance of Stone Elementary School
   (2) to help the principal at Stone Elementary School
   (3) to distribute election flyers at Stone Elementary School
   (4) to get arrested by the police at Stone Elementary School
   (5) to make sure no one under age 18 entered the school

2. Which of the following is a right guaranteed Anita by the First Amendment?
   (1) voting, if she is at least 18 years old
   (2) giving flyers about the election to interested adults
   (3) refusing to let police search her car unless they show a warrant
   (4) receiving an explanation of the reason for her arrest
   (5) having her case tried in court before a judge and jury

3. Why is it likely that Anita stood more than 15 feet from the entrance of the school?
   (1) She was able to talk to more people before they entered the school.
   (2) She was nervous that the principal would make her leave.
   (3) The local law specified she must be that distance.
   (4) The First Amendment requires her to stand that distance.
   (5) The principal and the police told her to stand that far away.

Unit 3 Review
Civics and Government

The Miranda Decision

In March 1963 a man kidnapped and raped a young girl. Ten days later the police arrested Ernesto Miranda. After police questioned Miranda alone for two hours, he confessed to the crime. Prosecutors used Miranda's confession as evidence against him at the trial. The jury found Miranda guilty. In 1966 the Supreme Court overturned, or set aside, Miranda's conviction. The justices believed police had violated Miranda's constitutional rights. Police had not told Miranda that, as a suspect in a crime, he had the right to talk to a lawyer before they questioned him. This Supreme Court ruling is called the Miranda Decision.

As a result of the Court's ruling, police must tell people they arrest about three of their constitutional rights: First, people have the right to remain silent. Second, anything they choose to say can be used against them in court. Third, they have the right to have a lawyer present while police question them. These rights are known as the Miranda rights.

In 1986 another case about suspects' rights reached the Supreme Court. The New York City police chased a man suspected of rape into a store. When the officers checked to see if the man had a weapon, they found an empty holster. When police asked him where his gun was, the suspect told them. After police found the gun, they read the suspect his Miranda rights. The gun and the man's statement were used as evidence against him. The Supreme Court decided that "public safety outweighs the need for the rule protecting the Fifth Amendment's privilege against self-incrimination."

Write the answers to the question.

1. What are two ways the two cases described in the article are alike?

_____

_____

Circle the number of the best answer for each question.

2. Which conclusion is the best one to draw from the facts in the article?
   (1) The Supreme Court can reverse its decisions after time has passed.
   (2) When suspects threaten public safety, their rights are not fully protected.
   (3) The Supreme Court does not side with criminals.
   (4) Reading Miranda rights makes it harder for police to make arrests.
   (5) The three Miranda rights that police read have been changed.

City Government

Two Plans of Mayor-City Council Government

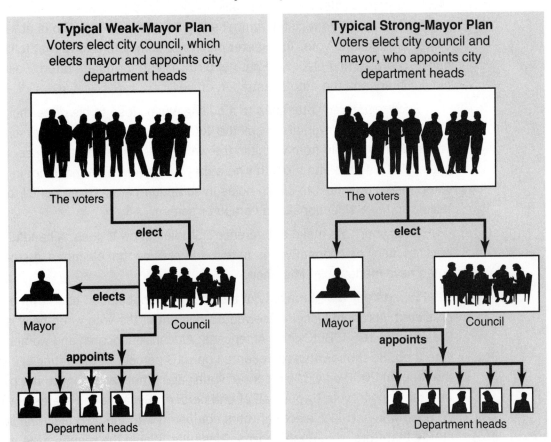

Typical Weak-Mayor Plan
Voters elect city council, which elects mayor and appoints city department heads

The voters
elect
Mayor ← elects — Council
appoints
Department heads

Typical Strong-Mayor Plan
Voters elect city council and mayor, who appoints city department heads

The voters
elect
Mayor   Council
appoints
Department heads

Circle the number of the best answer for each question.

3. Which statement is supported by information in the diagram?
   (1) Voters must go to the polls only for the strong-mayor plan.
   (2) A weak mayor can reject decisions that the city council makes.
   (3) The voters choose the mayor in the weak-mayor plan.
   (4) The mayor has no direct voter support in the strong-mayor plan.
   (5) The council appoints department heads in the weak-mayor plan.

4. Which idea about local government does the diagram imply most clearly?
   (1) The power of voters is greatest in the strong-mayor plan.
   (2) The council approves all mayoral decisions in the weak-mayor plan.
   (3) The council must approve the strong-mayor's choices for department heads.
   (4) Local government is weakest when voters elect both the council and mayor.
   (5) Local government is most representative when most voters stay away from the polls.

Voting Makes a Difference

Just before elections, the ads appear. "Don't forget to vote!" "Every vote counts." Many registered voters go to the polls on election day. However, many people who are eligible to vote fail to register. Almost every American citizen who is at least 18 years of age is eligible to vote. To **register** means to complete a form that tells the voter's name, address, and place and date of birth. These forms are often available at the public library and the auto registration office.

Each registered voter goes to a polling place close to his or her home on election day. There, election workers check the voter list to make sure the person is registered. This prevents people from voting in the wrong place or more than once. In some polling places, voters step into a booth where they pull levers on a machine. In other places, voters use a punchpin to punch holes in computer cards, use a pencil to mark a paper ballot, or make selections on a computer screen.

Does your vote make a difference? Studies show it does. A handful of votes decides many elections. Even in nationwide presidential elections, a small number of votes have made a big difference.

Experts say that a majority of the voting-age population has never elected a president. Abraham Lincoln received 55 percent of the vote when he was reelected President in 1864. But Native Americans, African Americans, and women could not vote then. So those votes represented only 13 percent of the voting-age population at the time. In 2000 only 51 percent of voting-age Americans went to the polls. Al Gore won the popular vote by one-half of one percent. Because the states in which George W. Bush won had 271 electoral votes compared with the 266 electoral votes in the states that Gore won, Bush became President. Would the results have been different if all eligible voters had taken time to vote? No one will ever know.

Write the answer to each question.

5. Where can an eligible voter go to register to vote?

_____

6. Why is a person's date of birth important on the voter's registration form?

_____

Circle the number of the best answer for the question.

7. Which statement does the article support?
   (1) If you pay taxes, you must register to vote.
   (2) Registering is a way of helping people vote.
   (3) Most people register to vote.
   (4) More people would vote if they registered.
   (5) Votes can make a difference in all kinds of elections.

The Right to Privacy

Write the answer to each question.

8. What does the man on the left with the beard represent?

_____

9. The drawing on the right is of Bill Gates, the head of a major computer software company. What does he represent in the cartoon?

_____

Circle the number of the best answer for the question.

10. What does the cartoon imply about Americans' right to privacy in the world today?
    (1) Americans have little privacy because they are just numbers to government and big business.
    (2) Protecting the right to privacy is challenging because computers make information easily available.
    (3) The right to privacy is threatened because criminals can get information about Americans.
    (4) The right to privacy is guaranteed because the federal government and big business promise not to abuse this right.
    (5) Americans' right to privacy is safeguarded under the Constitution.

Social Studies Extension

Attend a meeting of your local city council, county commission, or school board. List all the topics the officials discuss and circle those that lead to a decision by the group.

Mini-Test Unit 3

This is a 15-minute practice test. After 15 minutes, mark the last number you finished. Then complete the test and check your answers. If most of your answers were correct but you did not finish, try to work faster next time.

Directions: Choose the one best answer to each question.

Questions 1 and 2 refer to the following information.

During George Washington's first term as President, the government imposed an excise tax on whiskey. Whiskey makers felt that the tax was an attack on their liberty. In 1794 the Whiskey Rebellion began. There were riots, and some federal tax agents were tarred and feathered. The President called out troops to stop the protests. When two rioters were convicted of treason, however, he pardoned them.

1. Which information best supports the conclusion that the Whiskey Rebellion was a violent protest against the U.S. government?

    (1) Washington taxed whiskey.
    (2) Rebels assaulted federal workers.
    (3) The revolt did not last long.
    (4) The whiskey tax was removed.
    (5) Two rioters were pardoned.

2. Which of these government actions is most similar to the government action that led to the Whiskey Rebellion?

    (1) lowering excise taxes
    (2) taxing corporate income
    (3) taxing the sale of cigarettes
    (4) changing to a flat tax
    (5) getting rid of income tax

Question 3 refers to the following photograph.

3. The people in the photograph are exercising a right that is protected by the Constitution. Which of the following would involve exercising the same right?

    (1) members of a jury listening to a case in court
    (2) demonstrators protesting U.S. involvement in a war
    (3) worshippers attending an interfaith prayer service
    (4) people of all races registering to vote in an election
    (5) eighteen-year-olds voting for the first time

Questions 4 and 5 refer to the following quotation from the Declaration of Independence.

"The history of the present King of Great Britain is a history of repeated injuries and usurpations, all having in direct object the establishment of an absolute Tyranny over these States. To prove this, let Facts be submitted to a candid world.

He has refused his Assent to Laws, the most wholesome and necessary. . . .

He has forbidden his Governors to pass laws of immediate and pressing importance, unless suspended in their operation till his Assent should be obtained. . . ."

4. Based on the quotation, which statement is a fact rather than an opinion?

  (1) The king is a tyrant.
  (2) Representative government is good.
  (3) The colonists would make better laws than the British king.
  (4) The powers that the king wants should belong to colonial governments.
  (5) The king has restricted the powers of colonial governors.

5. For which statement does the quotation provide adequate factual support?

  (1) Some colonists were very disappointed with the King of Great Britain.
  (2) The king wanted to give up his American colonies.
  (3) The king imposed unfair taxes upon the American colonists.
  (4) The king's actions were based on hatred of the American colonists.
  (5) Other governments refused to help the Americans win independence.

Questions 6 and 7 refer to the following information and political cartoon.

Politicians can run positive or negative campaigns. In positive campaigns, politicians focus on their own qualifications and accomplishments. In negative campaigns, they focus on attacking their opponents.

6. Which of the following ideas is implied by this cartoon?

  (1) Americans watch too much television.
  (2) There should be more political ads on television.
  (3) During election season, attack ads insult television viewers.
  (4) Many people who run for public office have low moral standards.
  (5) People who watch television are like pigs.

7. What is the cartoonist trying to persuade people to do?

  (1) stop eating pork and pork products
  (2) to not watch campaign ads
  (3) urge television networks to have more family-friendly shows
  (4) be ashamed of the nastiness of negative political campaigns
  (5) to spend less time watching television

UNIT 4

Economics

Economics

Have you ever bought something that you wanted but didn't really need? Do you make rent or car payments? These are examples of individual choices that involve money. **Economics** is the study of how people satisfy their wants and needs by making choices about how to use limited resources.

Would you describe yourself as a good money manager? A cost-conscious shopper? A saver? Explain.

_____

_____

Economics

Thinking About Economics

You may be surprised to see how much you already know about economics. Think of news reports that you have seen on television, for example. How many of those reports involve information about money? In what other ways does television keep you thinking about your economic choices? Think about what you know about economics from daily life.

Check the box for each fact that you already know.

- ☐ When there is a sudden demand for a product, the price of that product usually rises.
- ☐ Two of the largest monthly expenses for an average American family are food and housing.
- ☐ Smart shoppers consider the quality of an item as well as its price.
- ☐ Today many jobs require the ability to use computers or other technology.
- ☐ Restaurant workers, sales clerks, and nurses are examples of people who work in service industries.
- ☐ A country's government wants businesses to export more goods than are imported from other countries.

Write one economic decision that you make at least once each week and one that you make only once or twice each year.

_____

_____

Previewing the Unit

In this unit, you will learn:

- how a free enterprise system works
- what kinds of decisions help you use your money wisely
- how supply and demand affect prices
- what the job market is like in the United States today
- how the United States interacts with other countries in economic matters

Lesson 18	Free Enterprise
Lesson 19	Money Management
Lesson 20	Supply and Demand
Lesson 21	The Changing Nature of Work
Lesson 22	The Global Economy

Free Enterprise

Vocabulary

free enterprise
  system

consumer

market

incentive

demand

efficiency

corporation

cooperative

Each day in the United States, people choose how they will spend the money they have earned. For example, some people travel several miles to buy groceries from a supersized grocery-hardware-clothing store. Others decide to shop at a supermarket in their neighborhood. Factors such as price, convenience, and good service influence their decisions.

Businesses make economic decisions, too. They note which products are selling well and which are not. They study which supplier offers the lowest prices, the best quality, and the fastest delivery. Americans are free to buy, and American businesses are free to sell, what they want.

Relate to the Topic

This lesson uses farming to explain how the economy in the United States works. Think back to your childhood. Recall two specific food products or toys that your parents bought for you. Are those items still available? Why do you think that they are—or are not—for sale today?

_____

_____

_____

_____

Reading Strategy

PREVIEWING LINE GRAPHS   A line graph can show changes in a situation. Previewing line graphs can help you understand important information in a passage. Look at the line graphs on pages 150 and 151. Then answer the questions.

1. What general topic are both line graphs about? _____
   Hint: Look for words that appear in both graph titles.

2. What specific types of changes do you expect to see on each graph?

   _____

   _____

   Hint: Look at the titles and at vertical scales.

Check your answers on page 245.

How Free Enterprise Works

The United States has an economic system called the **free enterprise system.** In this type of economy, **consumers,** or buyers, buy products and services from privately owned businesses. Producers determine the kinds, the amounts, and the prices of goods based on what consumers want to buy. In other words, Americans make economic choices based on opportunities in the market. A **market** means several related things. It could be a place where producers sell to sellers. It could be a place where people who buy products from producers sell to consumers. It can also mean all the potential customers for a particular product or service. For example, consumers of agricultural products make up a market. Farming is a good example of how free enterprise works in the United States.

Farming for a Market

How do farmers decide what crops to grow? How do they decide what animals to raise? How do farmers know how much to produce? Farmers try to find answers to these questions by watching consumers. For example, American consumers today are buying more cheese than they did in the past. In 2000 the average American consumed 30.5 pounds of cheese. That figure is up from 28.39 pounds per person in 1998 and 27.3 pounds per person in 1995. It is about twice as much cheese as Americans consumed in 1975. An increase in pizza sales and sales of frozen dinners with cheese contributed to the rise. Over the years, stores have also ordered more cheese. As a result, dairy farmers raised more cows, whose milk was used to make more cheese.

Farmers have an **incentive,** or good reason, to produce the kinds of goods people want. Farmers want to make as much money as possible. By looking at what consumers buy, farmers learn what to produce and how much.

The amount of goods or services consumers are willing to buy at a certain price at a given time is called **demand.** If people prefer potatoes over beets, then demand is higher for potatoes. This gives farmers an incentive to grow potatoes. As a result, more farmers grow potatoes than beets.

An incentive for the consumer is price. The price of a product helps to determine how many people will buy it. Fewer people can afford high-priced goods. But if the price is low, more people can buy the goods.

Making Inferences It is important to look for main ideas and details as you read. Sometimes you can use that information to figure out things that are not actually stated. This is called making an **inference.** Reread the first paragraph under the heading "Farming for a Market." Which inference can you make from details in the paragraph?

a. The market determines what products are produced.

b. Consumers will pay any price for cheese.

How Competition Leads to Efficiency

Farmers sell their goods in a market where there is competition from other farmers. Because many buyers and sellers are in the market, no one buyer or seller sets the price. In a competitive market, sellers have an incentive to keep prices low. Suppose one farmer's price for corn is higher than another farmer's price. The consumer will buy the corn at the lower price. So a farmer has to sell at the lowest possible price. But the price must not be so low that the farmer cannot recover the costs of growing the corn, such as supplies, equipment, and labor. Each farmer wants a price that allows him or her to make some money after paying expenses.

A competitive market requires efficiency. **Efficiency** means that the time, energy, and money put into a job results in a great deal of production without much waste. Over the years American farmers have become more efficient. In the 1850s one farmer produced enough food to feed five people. About 50 percent of Americans were farmers. In 2000, however, the average farmer fed 139 people. Only 0.8 percent of Americans today make their living as farmers.

So few farmers can produce so much food because of technology, which includes the tools and methods used to increase production. Today farmers use more machines. They also have special seeds, fertilizers, and weed killers. As a result, it takes fewer farmers to produce a larger food supply.

The graph on page 151 shows that farms today are larger than they were in the past. But as the graph below shows, there are fewer farms. Many farms are now owned by corporations rather than by individuals. A **corporation** is a business that stockholders own. Each stockholder shares in the profits and the risks of the business. Since a corporation may consist of many people, it can raise large sums of money. Today large amounts of money and skill are needed to run a farm.

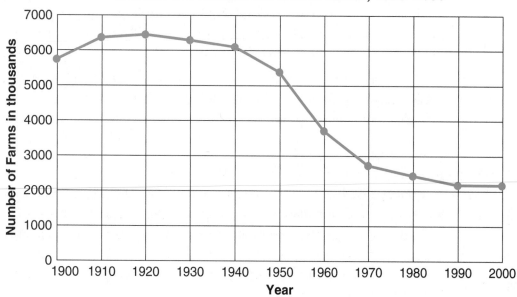

Number of Farms in the United States, 1900–2000

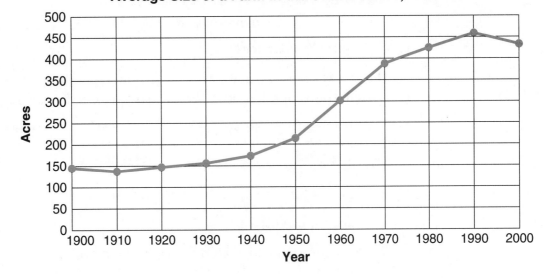

Average Size of a Farm in the United States, 1900–2000

Comparing Line Graphs A line graph usually shows changes over time. A change may be an increase or a decrease. Look at the line graphs on page 150 and above. They show changes in the number and average size of U.S. farms over 100 years. During different periods farms changed in different ways. How did farms change overall between 1900 and 2000?

  a.   The number of farms stayed the same while the size of farms decreased.

  b.   The number of farms decreased while the size of farms increased.

How Competition Affects Farmers and Consumers

Competition among farmers benefits consumers in many ways. In 1900 the average American family spent more than 45 percent of its income on food. They ate nearly every meal at home. Today the average family spends only about 12 percent of its income on food. More than 40 percent of the money in the food budget is spent on meals away from home. Competition has kept food prices down and given consumers more choices in how to spend their food money.

However, individual farmers have a hard time competing with large, corporate farms. As a result, some individual farmers have left the market. Others sign contracts with canneries, frozen-food companies, and other food processors before they plant their crops. These farmers know in advance how much they will get for their crop. Still other individual farmers join cooperatives. A **cooperative** is formed by people who join together to ensure the best price for their products. Many orange and grapefruit growers in California and Florida belong to cooperatives. Some cooperatives advertise to encourage consumers to buy their products. For example, beef and pork cooperatives use ads to convince consumers that beef and pork are part of a healthful diet.

 Check your answer on page 245.

Thinking About the Article

Practice Vocabulary

The words below are in the passage in bold type. Study the way each word is used. Then complete each sentence by writing the correct word.

free enterprise system	**market**	**consumers**
demand	**efficiency**	**cooperative**

1. An economy in which the buyers and sellers determine what goods are produced is called a(n) _____.

2. Someone who buys goods and services is a(n) _____.

3. A(n) _____ represents all the potential customers for a particular product or service.

4. If few people are buying a product, it has a low _____.

5. Members of a farm _____ work together to get the best price for their products.

6. Farms in the United States are known for their _____, because they produce more farm products with fewer farmers than in the past.

Understand the Article

Write the answer to each question.

7. Why do farmers experiment with new methods of farming?

_____

_____

8. What is one way consumers benefit from competition?

_____

_____

_____

9. What are the three definitions of market?

_____

_____

_____

Apply Your Skills

Circle the number of the best answer for each question.

10. Reread the third paragraph under "Farming for a Market" on page 149. Which statement might you infer from details in the paragraph?
    (1) Farmers earn more when they produce goods that are in demand.
    (2) The amount of goods consumers buy helps determine demand.
    (3) If people prefer potatoes over beets, then the demand is higher for potatoes.
    (4) Farmers have an incentive to grow potatoes.
    (5) More vegetable farmers grow potatoes than beets.

11. Look at the graphs on pages 150 and 151. What do the graphs suggest might be true by 2010?
    (1) Farms will be about the same size as in 2000, and there will be about the same number of them.
    (2) There will be more family-owned farms than in 2000.
    (3) Farms will be much larger than in 2000, and there will be fewer of them.
    (4) There will be fewer farms than in 2000, and individual families will own most of them.
    (5) Corporations will own almost all farms by 2010.

12. Read the first paragraph under "How Competition Affects Farmers and Consumers" on page 151. What can you infer based on the paragraph?
    (1) Competition has kept food prices down.
    (2) If there was less competition among farmers, food prices would be higher.
    (3) Competition gives consumers more choices in how to spend the money they budget for food.
    (4) Consumers eat out more often today than consumers did in 1900.
    (5) Consumers eat more chicken today than consumers did in 1900.

Connect with the Article

Write your answer to each question.

13. Why are products that are not readily available usually high in price? Why might such a product have a low price?

_____

14. How does competition among long-distance telephone companies help you choose which one to use?

_____

Check your answers on pages 245–246.

LESSON 19

Money Management

Some families have to guard every penny. They carefully keep track of expenses. They save money to reach their financial goals. Other families enjoy spending. They often give gifts. They may buy a bigger house when a new baby arrives. Some families are willing to take additional risks with their money. They like to invest if there seems to be a chance to make even more money.

What young people learn about money influences the role that money plays later in their lives. It helps determine how they spend money and what financial risks—if any—they take.

Vocabulary

budget

net income

fixed expense

flexible expense

opportunity cost

interest

annual percentage rate

Relate to the Topic

This lesson is about wise money management. Think about what you've just read about ways different families manage money. Name something you learned from your family about money management.

_____

_____

Reading Strategy

RELATING TO WHAT YOU KNOW   As you read informational material, compare the facts with what you already may have learned—from a book, for example, or from personal experience. Read the paragraph on page 155 that begins the article. Then answer the questions.

1. Of the people you know, whom would you call a money manager?

_____

_____

Hint: According to the paragraph, what does a money manager do?

2. What do you already know about borrowing money wisely?

_____

_____

Hint: Think about interest rates and monthly payments.

Getting the Most for the Money

Few people have as much money as they would like. To get the most out of what they earn, people must become money managers. This requires that they use their money wisely. People who manage their money well follow similar rules. First, they create and follow a spending plan. Second, they consider all the costs involved in a purchase before deciding to buy something. Third, they do not borrow money often. And last, if they <u>must</u> get a loan, they borrow carefully.

Follow a Plan

People who manage their money make a budget. A **budget** is a detailed spending plan. It shows how much money comes in and goes out each month. To prepare a budget, first list your net income. **Net income** is money left after taxes are paid. It is also called take-home pay. Then list all expenses, or money that is owed. Start with **fixed expenses,** which are payments that stay the same each month. Rent and car payments are fixed expenses. Next list expenses that vary from month to month. This kind of expense is called a **flexible expense.** Clothing is a flexible expense.

The chart below is an example of a budget. The amounts the family planned to spend in a month are in the left-hand column. The amounts actually spent are in the right-hand column. A budget contains categories of expenses. Utilities generally include electricity, natural gas, water, sewer, and trash removal. Transportation may include gasoline, bus fare, and an emergency auto repair fund.

Budget for the Rivera Family
Net Monthly Income $3,200

Fixed Expenses	Planned	Actual
Home mortgage	$760	$760
Car payment	$280	$280
Insurance	$110	$110
Flexible Expenses		
Utilities	$205	$205
Transportation	$320	$320
Food	$440	$475
Credit card payments	$250	$250
Health Care	$180	$200
Clothing	$170	$170
Entertainment	$180	$140
Savings	$150	$125
Other	$155	$165
Total	$3,200	$3,200

Fixed expenses are usually easy to budget. However, sometimes fixed expenses are due only a few times a year and are forgotten until the bill comes in the mail. Property taxes are an example of this type of periodic expense. It is important to set aside money each month for periodic expenses. Then these bills can be paid when they are due.

Flexible expenses are harder to budget. The best way is to make a prediction. Base your prediction on how much was spent in these categories in the past months or years.

A budget helps people decide what they can and cannot afford. They see how each purchase could affect other things they want or need. They may find places where they can cut costs.

Many people are surprised when they prepare a budget. They see how much money they spend on things they do not really need. Some people give up smoking, drinking alcohol, or expensive entertainment after they realize how much income these activities use up.

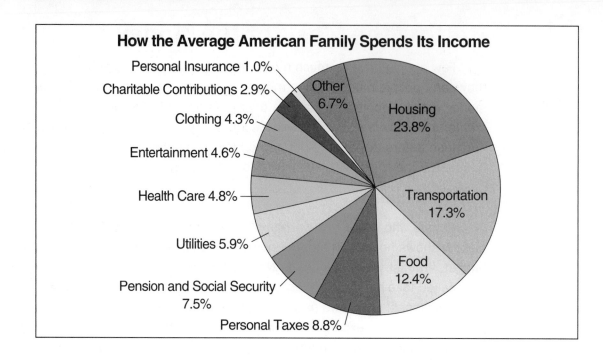

Reading a Circle Graph A circle graph is used to compare parts to a whole and to each other. Circle graphs are sometimes called pie charts. Each section of the graph looks like a slice of a pie. The sections can be compared to one another or to the whole amount. The larger the section, the greater the amount. Often a circle graph is presented using percents. The whole circle is always 100 percent. Look at the circle graph above. It shows the percent of income the average family spends on various goods and services. What expense takes up the largest percentage of the average family's income?

a. transportation   b. housing

Consider the Costs

It is important to look at all the costs involved before deciding on a purchase. The cost of a new pair of shoes is not just the price of the shoes. There is also an opportunity cost. **Opportunity cost** is the cost of choosing one thing over another. For example, as a result of buying shoes, the shopper may have less money for a new winter coat. Sometimes opportunity cost is called a trade-off. In making choices, a person knows that he or she gives up one thing in order to get something of greater value. Good money managers know what the results of most of their buying decisions will be.

Once the shopper decides to buy the shoes, he or she must decide how much to spend. A smart shopper makes this choice by asking what will be gained by buying a good pair of shoes rather than a pair of lesser quality. A smart shopper is willing to substitute one thing for another. The shopper may choose an inexpensive pair of shoes to save money. Or the shopper may choose a better brand that will last longer. Comparing prices of the same pair of shoes at several stores also may save money.

The Riveras' budget allows only $170 a month for clothing, including shoes. Mr. Rivera needs work boots that cost $130. Mrs. Rivera wants to buy shoes for a party. To stay within the family's budget, the pair she chooses should cost no more than $40. If she chooses to spend $75 on a fancy pair of shoes, the opportunity cost of the shoes is that the family must spend less on something else to stay within the budget. For example, they might decide to reduce their entertainment expenses by renting videos rather than going to the movie theater.

Identifying Cause and Effect Every event has at least one cause and one effect. The cause is why something happened. The effect is what happened as a result of the cause. Words like *because, reason,* and *since* suggest a cause. Such words or phrases as *as a result, cost,* and *for this reason* signal effects. Reread the paragraphs under the heading "Consider the Costs." What would be an effect of ignoring opportunity cost when deciding to buy something?

   a.   The purchase would cost more than the budget allows.
   b.   The family might have no money for something else it wants or needs.

Careful Borrowing

People do not always have enough cash on hand to pay for the things they want or need. They may decide to borrow the money now and pay it back later. Borrowing money can be more expensive than combining the price of the item and the opportunity cost. The loan's **interest,** or the fee for borrowing the money, must be considered, too.

Some experts suggest that a person should borrow no more than one-fifth of his or her net income. In other words, a person who takes home $20,000 a year should limit debts to $4,000. Borrowing includes anything bought on a payment plan, paid for with a credit card, charged at local stores, or borrowed from a bank.

Knowing the cost of borrowing helps people get the most for their money. Interest rates can vary greatly. One study of new-car loans showed that some lenders charged ten percent more interest than others. Many loans had hidden costs. In some cases, borrowers had to pay a fee just to apply for the loan. In other cases, they had to pay extra money if payments were late. Some lenders charged a penalty if borrowers paid off their loans early.

A smart borrower never signs a loan agreement without reading and understanding the contract. By law, lenders have to tell people what a loan will cost. Borrowers have a right to know the interest rate on the loan. A borrower also needs to know the annual percentage rate. The **annual percentage rate,** or APR, is the percent of interest a lender charges per year for the money that is borrowed. By knowing the APR, borrowers can compare loans.

People who are good money managers take charge of their finances. They know what they spend their money on and how much they spend. They not only take advantage of opportunities, but they also make the most of those opportunities.

Thinking About the Article

Practice Vocabulary

The words below are in the passage in bold type. Study the way each word is used. Then complete each sentence by writing the correct word.

budget   **fixed expense**   **net income**   **flexible expense**

interest   **opportunity cost**   **annual percentage rate**

1. The _____ of buying a new car is that a family may have to wait another year to go on vacation to Disney World.

2. Take-home pay is often called _____.

3. Unfortunately the rate of _____ that banks give for saving money is not as high as the rate they charge for lending money.

4. Before taking a loan, the borrower should know its

   _____, or the amount of interest a lender charges each year.

5. An example of a(n) _____ is a mortgage payment.

6. The first step in managing money is setting up a(n)

   _____.

7. A grocery bill is an example of a(n) _____.

Understand the Article

Write the answer to each question.

8. What are two benefits of following a budget?

   _____

9. What costs should someone consider before borrowing money to buy a used car that costs $7,000?

   _____

10. What are four rules that help people become better money managers?

    _____

    _____

    _____

    _____

Apply Your Skills

Circle the number of the best answer for each question.

11. Look at the chart of the Riveras' budget on page 155. They spent more on health care than they budgeted. Which was one effect?
    (1) They made smaller credit card payments.
    (2) Their housing and insurance expenses decreased.
    (3) They had less money to put into savings.
    (4) They spent less on "Other" expenses.
    (5) They had to sell their car.

12. How might the Riveras cause a decrease in their fixed expenses every month?
    (1) They might move to a more expensive house.
    (2) They could pay off their credit card debt.
    (3) They could switch to less expensive insurance.
    (4) They might eat all their meals at home.
    (5) They could cut their monthly savings.

13. What does the circle graph on page 156 show about the average American family's spending habits?
    (1) It spends more on taxes than anything else.
    (2) It spends one-half its income on housing and food.
    (3) It spends about the same on transportation as it does on clothing.
    (4) It spends the least on entertainment.
    (5) It spends less on health care than it does on electricity, gas, telephone, and other utilities.

Connect with the Article

Write your answer to each question.

14. Why do you think some lenders charge a fee if a loan is paid off early?

    _____

    _____

15. People often buy things on the spur of the moment. This means they make the purchase without planning. What was the last item that you bought on the spur of the moment? What was the opportunity cost for this type of purchase? Explain your answer.

    _____

    _____

    _____

Supply and Demand

A weekend trip to the video store can be frustrating. Family members plan to watch a movie they missed in the theater. They scan the shelves and see the title, but they find the case empty. "Why didn't the store order enough of these?" they wonder.

Stocking the right number of movies is not easy. A store owner may expect demand for a new video or DVD to be high—but how high? The owner wants to order enough copies to satisfy customers, but not so many that unrented copies sit on the shelves. When copies are not rented, the store loses money. This is an example of an economic choice that results in making money or losing it.

Vocabulary

supply

estimate

profit

elastic demand

inelastic demand

elastic supply

inelastic supply

scarce

Relate to the Topic

This lesson discusses the economic laws of supply and demand. List the last item that was marked so low you bought an extra one. Was that item a want or a need? Then list an item that you refused to buy because the price was too high. Was that item a want or a need?

Did buy _____   Did not buy _____

Want or need _____   Want or need _____

Reading Strategy

PREVIEWING A TABLE   Tables present information. They can also help you prepare to read an accompanying article. Look at the table on page 162. Consider why that information might be given. Then answer the questions.

1.   What information in this table is related to economics?

_____

Hint: Look at the first and fifth columns.

2.   How might this table relate to the article title, "Supply and Demand"?

_____

Hint: Look at the subheadings and skim the article.

It's All in the Cards

Two things determine the price of goods. One is the consumers' demand for the goods. The other is the **supply,** or the amount of goods and services sellers offer at certain prices at a given time. People who study the market economy look closely at how supply and demand affect each other.

A Changing Market

Ideally sellers would supply the same amount of goods and services that the consumers will buy. But just like the owner of the video store, business owners can only **estimate** how much to order or produce. Sometimes they are right, and sometimes they are wrong. Considering the past and their business knowledge, sellers learn to predict what and how much to sell. Stadium vendors predict how many fans a team will draw so they can order enough hot dogs. And grocery store owners predict how much candy corn to order for Halloween.

More sellers enter a market when prices are high. They have seen the success of other businesses and want to make money selling the goods, too. Sellers usually increase production when prices are high. That is what generally happens with baseball cards.

Young people have been collecting baseball cards for decades. A photo of a baseball player appears on the front of each card. On the back are facts about the player. In the past, young people traded cards with friends to get a favorite player or a set of all the players on their favorite team. Some young card traders kept collecting cards even after they had grown up. Today, in fact, more than half of all card collectors are adults.

Card collectors sometimes **profit,** or make money, by selling cards at prices higher than what they paid for them. Old baseball cards, especially, can earn an amazing profit. For example, a person who paid one cent for a Yogi Berra card many years later sold that card for $6,000! The value of some old baseball cards shows how supply and demand affect each other.

A Matter of Supply and Demand

How a price change affects supply or demand is called elasticity. The supply and demand of certain products are either elastic or inelastic. An **elastic demand** means that a change in price affects the number of people who will buy the product. When steak goes up in price, for example, fewer people buy it. When the price drops, people buy more. A product has an **inelastic demand** if a price change does not affect the number of people who buy it. Products with an inelastic demand are generally things that are always needed. When the price changes for bread and milk, for example, shoppers still buy about the same amount. Because they need the product, its demand stays about the same despite a price change.

An **elastic supply** means that sellers can increase the supply of a product that has increased in price. Sports-card producers tend to increase supplies when cards are selling at high prices. This means the supply of new baseball cards is elastic.

Supply and Demand

On the other hand, an **inelastic supply** is limited. The supply of older baseball cards is inelastic. The supply cannot increase regardless of what happens to the price. For example, Topps, a sports-card producer, made a certain number of rookie baseball cards for Mark McGwire in 1985. At the beginning of the 1998 baseball season, that card was worth $30. Later that year, after McGwire broke Roger Maris's home-run record, the card's value rose to $200. However, when Barry Bonds broke McGwire's record three years later, the value of McGwire's rookie card dropped to $80—the demand for McGwire's card had declined.

The law of supply says that if prices are high, suppliers will make more products for the market. If prices are low, they will cut back production. Prices go up if the demand is greater than the supply. So prices for old baseball cards are generally high. Below are recent values for some baseball cards in near-perfect condition.

Reading a Table A table organizes information in columns and rows. The title tells what kind of information is in the table. Look at the table below. For example, to find the 2002 value of a 1951 Willie Mays rookie card, read down the column under the heading "Player." When you come to *Willie Mays*, read across the row to the column labeled *Mid-2002*. The Willie Mays card is valued at $3,000. Which of the two Mickey Mantle baseball cards has a higher value?

   a.   the Topps edition   b. the Bowman edition

A Honus Wagner baseball card in near perfect condition sold for $1.265 million in 2000.

Baseball Cards for Investment				RC = Rookie Card
Player	**Card Year**	**Card Producer**	**Card No.**	**Mid-2002 Value**
Mantle, Mickey	1951 RC	Bowman	253	$8,500.00
Mays, Willie	1951 RC	Bowman	305	$3,000.00
Mantle, Mickey	1952	Topps	311	$18,000.00
Aaron, Hank	1954 RC	Topps	128	$1,500.00
Ryan, Nolan	1968 RC	Topps	177	$700.00
Clemente, Roberto	1973	Topps	50	$50.00
Clemens, Roger	1984 RC	Fleer Update	U27	$200.00
Clemens, Roger	1985	Donruss	273	$30.00
McGuire, Mark	1985 RC	Topps	401	$80.00
Bonds, Barry	1987 RC	Topps	320	$10.00
Sosa, Sammy	1990 RC	Upper Deck	17	$8.00
Jeter, Derek	1993 RC	SP	279	$120.00
Rodriguez, Alex	1994 RC	Fleer Update	86	$40.00
Wood, Kerry	1997 RC	Bowman	196	$5.00
McGwire, Mark	1998	Fleer	25	$2.50
McGwire, Mark	1998	Leaf	171	$12.00
Suzuki, Ichiro	2001 RC	Upper Deck	271	$20.00
Bonds, Barry	2001	Donruss Classics	2	$5.00
Jeter, Derek	2002	Topps	75	$1.50
Sosa, Sammy	2002	Upper Deck	301	$1.25

Barry Bonds' rookie card has likely increased in value since his record-breaking season.

The Mickey Mantle 1951 rookie baseball card is scarce, and people are willing to pay a lot of money to get it. **Scarce** means that the demand for the item is much greater than the supply. People will pay even more money for cards that are extremely rare.

Scarcity and Price

In 2000 a baseball card of Honus Wagner sold at auction for $1.265 million. Wagner was a popular shortstop for the Pittsburgh Pirates in the early 1900s. Why is his card so valuable? In the early 1900s, tobacco companies distributed baseball cards. They printed cards of Honus Wagner. Wagner did not want to encourage tobacco use, so he refused to let the company distribute his card. Today less than 75 Wagner cards are known to exist. Their scarcity makes them rare. The few that are in excellent condition are rarer still. It was one of these cards that sold for $1.265 million.

A controversial purchase shows what can happen when a rare card becomes one of a kind. A 13-year-old boy bought a 1968 Nolan Ryan rookie baseball card for $12 at a store. The card was worth $1,200, but the store clerk did not read the price correctly. The store had a big sign that read "All sales final," but the store owner took the boy to court anyway. He wanted the other $1,188 from the boy.

During the trial, the boy told the judge that he had already traded the Ryan card. He had traded it for two cards that were worth about $2,200. The judge ordered that the Nolan Ryan card be brought to court as evidence.

Predicting Outcomes Trying to figure out what will happen next is called **predicting outcomes.** As you read, try to guess something based on what you have read so far. Use what you already know from past experiences to help make predictions. Reread the paragraphs above. How do you think the court case affected the value of the Nolan Ryan card?

a. The value of the card increased.
b. The value of the card went down.

The new owner agreed to bring the card to court. But he asked that the court's "Exhibit 1" sticker remain on the card after the case was settled. The card, with the sticker, could be worth as much as $3,000. The trial and the sticker made the card one-of-a-kind, so it has increased in value.

Today many collectors continue to buy cards, hoping to find a rare one and strike it rich. Critics doubt that anyone will get rich from cards produced in the last few years. They say the supply of new cards is far too great. They point out that in 1951, only two major companies, Topps and Bowman, made baseball cards. Today there are several companies. Many of them produce more than one series of baseball cards.

Other baseball-card experts disagree with this idea. They believe that baseball cards will never lose value. One trader said, "As long as there are baseball fans, there will be baseball cards, and those cards will be worth something."

Thinking About the Article

Practice Vocabulary

The words below are in the passage in bold type. Study the way each word is used. Then complete each sentence by writing the correct word.

inelastic demand   **elastic demand**   **supply**   **profit**

elastic supply   **inelastic supply**   **scarce**

1. Mickey Mantle's baseball cards are an example of a(n)

   _____.

2. A collector who sells a rare baseball card is likely to

   _____.

3. If the amount of a product increases when its price goes up, the

   product has a(n) _____.

4. When the supply of a product is very low, the product is considered

   _____.

5. Products and services with a(n) _____ are generally
   necessities.

6. Fewer people buy a product with a(n) _____ when
   its price goes up.

7. A seller increases the _____ of a product when its
   price goes up.

Understand the Article

Write the answer to each question.

8. How does decreased demand for a product often affect its price?

   _____

9. Why is the word *elastic* used to describe products with a changing
   supply or demand?

   _____

10. Why do necessities such as milk and dish soap have an inelastic
    demand?

    _____

Apply Your Skills

Circle the number of the best answer for each question.

11. Reread page 163. Which prediction would the information in the paragraphs support?
    (1) There is only one 1968 Nolan Ryan rookie card marked "Exhibit 1."
    (2) The "Exhibit 1" sticker on the card will lower the card's value.
    (3) The store owner received his $1,188 from the boy.
    (4) The new owner of the Ryan card will make a profit.
    (5) The boy was put in jail for trading the card.

12. Look at the table on page 162. Which best explains why the two Roger Clemens cards have different values?
    (1) Clemens had a better year in 1984 than 1985.
    (2) The demand for the 1985 Clemens card may increase over time.
    (3) The demand for a Clemens card increased from 1984 to 1985.
    (4) Clemens was traded to another team after the 1984 season.
    (5) Clemens' Fleer card is in shorter supply than his Donruss card.

13. Based on information in the article and table, whose card would likely be worth the least a year from now?
    (1) Hank Aaron
    (2) Yogi Berra
    (3) Mickey Mantle
    (4) Nolan Ryan
    (5) Ichiro Suzuki

Connect with the Article

Write your answer to each question.

14. How do supply and demand cause companies that make a product to enter or leave a market?

    _____

    _____

    _____

15. Would you advise someone to invest his or her money in baseball cards? Explain your answer.

    _____

    _____

    _____

The Changing Nature of Work

Vocabulary

work ethic

quality circle

job rotation

service industry

bachelor's degree

apprenticeship

internship

job shadowing

mentoring

Most early Americans worked as farmers. Decades later, many of the nation's farmers left farming for jobs in factories. In both instances they worked with their hands, and needed little formal education or training.

The U.S. economy is no longer dominated by agriculture or manufacturing. Because of modern technology, our economy has become increasingly centered around the creation and distribution of information. So, more and more jobs are requiring formal education or training. Most of the highest-paying jobs call for skilled, trained workers in business and the service industry. Since this trend is likely to continue, workers today must learn more in order to earn more.

Relate to the Topic

This lesson is about today's job market and how people must prepare to enter it. Think about the kind of work that you would like to do. What training do you think you will need to get a job in that field?

_____

_____

_____

Reading Strategy

RELATING TO WHAT YOU KNOW One way to understand new information is to compare it with your personal experiences. Skim the section on page 167 called "Jobs Today." Then answer the questions.

1. What jobs do you know of that require the use of modern technology?

   _____

   _____

   Hint: Think of people you know who use a computer at work.

2. What industries seem to be growing fastest in your community?

   _____

   _____

   Hint: What kinds of jobs seem to be most available near where you live?

Check your answers on page 247.

UNIT 4 ECONOMICS

Work in the Twenty-first Century

Work is a foundation stone of our society. But the American workplace has changed. New kinds of work skills and the ability to adapt to change are the tickets to success for workers in the 2000s.

Jobs Today

In the early 1900s, most Americans worked at unskilled jobs in farming and manufacturing, which required only manual labor. Today machines do most farm work. Computer-operated robots assist in manufacturing. Many workers who used to be on the assembly line now have been retrained. Some perform sophisticated tasks with computers. Modern technology is here to stay.

Many jobs require technological literacy. For example, a job may require that a person has a lot of experience with computers. Most jobs in the United States today use technologies that process information. They demand specialized education and training. Workers in the best-paying jobs are those who are comfortable with technology. For example, medical workers must know how to use computerized health aids. Mechanics must know how to use computerized tools.

Yet the new workplace demands more than technological skills. Workers must be able to follow directions and work with a team or as a team leader. It also requires personal skills. Having a strong **work ethic** is important. Workers with a strong work ethic come to work on time, act responsibly, and use common sense in making judgments.

Workers must also be flexible. They must adapt to new ways of doing things as technology changes everyday tasks in a particular job. Many industries have adopted high-performance work systems. These programs aim for efficiency through quality circles and job rotations. **Quality circles** are groups of employees who monitor the quality of a product or service they produce or perform. **Job rotation** means workers learn different jobs so that they can step in to help other workers when the need arises.

Learning to Earn

The U.S. Bureau of Labor Statistics predicts that job growth in coming years will be highest in service industries. Education, banking, medicine, hotels, restaurants, and theme parks are all **service industries.**

One of the fastest-growing service industries is health care. The generation born between 1945 and 1960 make up a large part of the American population. Today they are aging and need more medical care. To cut expenses, many people today use outpatient facilities, nursing homes, and home health care rather than hospitals. Personal and home care aides are already in great demand. They care for the aging and people recovering from surgery and other serious health conditions.

Other quickly growing service industries include desktop publishing and education. Desktop publishers use personal computers to create reports, presentations, advertisements, magazines, and books. The greatest need for teachers is in the field of special education. School districts are also looking for bilingual teachers and people who can teach science and math.

The Bureau of Labor Statistics has identified fields of work and specific occupations in which job opportunities are likely to increase in the near future. Many of those jobs require a **bachelor's degree,** which is a four-year college education. Such jobs include computer engineers, social workers, and database administrators. These are already among the better-paying jobs. That connection—more education resulting in higher pay—is likely to continue.

Education does not necessarily mean college, however. A number of occupations do not require a bachelor's degree, yet offer higher-than-average earnings. These include nurses, mechanics, carpenters, and various kinds of technicians. These careers require on-the-job training, advanced training in a technical or vocational school, or apprenticeships. An **apprenticeship** is a period of training that includes specialized classroom work as well as on-the-job training. All of these continuing education opportunities help workers prepare for more challenging and better-paying occupations.

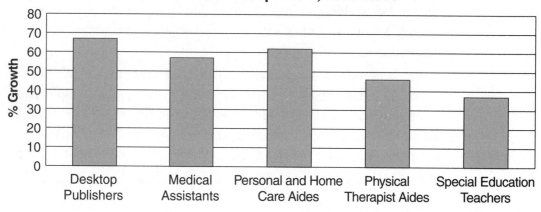

Estimated Growth in Employment in Some Service Occupations, 2000–2010

Reading a Bar Graph A bar graph is often used to make comparisons. The title tells what information is presented in the graph. The labels along the side and bottom of the graph tell the key categories of information. Look at the bar graph above. Each bar shows the estimated percent of growth from 2000 to 2010. Which job shows the highest estimated growth for that period? Circle the letter.

a.   medical assistant

b.   desktop publisher

c.   physical therapy aide

Choosing a Career

To determine which career is for you, consider your interests and abilities. You can identify these by recalling past successes. You can ask for observations and suggestions from friends, family, and teachers. They may see you differently than you see yourself. School guidance departments and career development centers offer skills and interest inventories or lists of questions that reveal your strong points. These can help you narrow down the many possibilities for your future work.

Once you have decided what you want to do, you must prepare for the career of your choice. Preparing for a rewarding career may include technical courses, on-the-job training, or a four-year college degree. Some programs combine work and learning. In school-to-work programs, for example, students study in a classroom for part of the day and then work on a job for another part of the day. These programs give students the basic academic and workplace skills to succeed at work and in advanced education. Career exploration may also include internships, job shadowing, or mentoring.

Drawing Conclusions You draw a conclusion by reading for the main idea. You also read for details that lead to a conclusion. These details are called supporting statements. Reread the paragraphs under "Choosing a Career."

1. Which conclusion is supported by details in the first paragraph?
   a. I should choose my career based on how much schooling it requires.
   b. My career should be in a field that I find interesting.

2. Which conclusion is supported by details in the second paragraph?
   a. I can prepare for a career in one or more of a variety of ways.
   b. Going to college for four years is the only pathway to a career.

Temporary assignments at a job or company that interests you are called **internships.** These assignments can last for a few months or a year. Often an internship can lead to a permanent job.

Spending time with someone who has a job in which you are interested is called **job shadowing.** The person you are shadowing introduces you to the people, the equipment, and the skills that it takes to do the job. You see what spending time working in the actual job setting is like. Job shadowing may last several hours or a full day.

Teaching what is important in a job or career by example or discussion is called **mentoring.** The teacher is called a mentor. Mentors allow you to observe. They give advice on how to go about achieving the career goals you have set. A mentor can also provide references to people who make hiring decisions.

Internships, job shadowing, mentoring, or school-to-work programs reinforce what is taught in classes and offer you a variety of career options. All these things increase your chances of being valued and hired by employers.

Thinking About the Article

Practice Vocabulary

The words below are in the passage in bold type. Study the way each word is used. Then complete each sentence by writing the correct word.

work ethic   service industries   bachelor's degree

apprenticeship   internship   job shadowing   mentoring

1. A person can earn a(n) _____ at a college or university.

2. A(n) _____ is a temporary work assignment.

3. A(n) _____ consists of on-the-job training and classroom work.

4. _____ employ people who meet the needs of other people.

5. Employers appreciate workers who have a strong _____.

6. _____ helps you learn from a professional's experience.

7. _____ may take several hours or a full day.

Understand the Article

Write the answer to each question.

8. What kinds of service jobs are projected to grow most quickly in the next decade?

   _____

9. What kinds of skills do most jobs today require?

   _____

10. How can workers best prepare for today's higher-paying careers?

    _____

    _____

11. What is job rotation?

    _____

    _____

Apply Your Skills

Circle the number of the best answer for each question.

12. Based on the article, what conclusion can you draw about the way to find a good job?
    (1) Get education or training in a field that interests you.
    (2) Get a job where you know someone.
    (3) Look at the newspaper's classified ads to find a career.
    (4) Ask your relatives for a job.
    (5) Check to see what the hourly wage is before you consider any job.

13. Look again at the bar graph on page 168. Which statement does the information in the graph support?
    (1) There will be little demand for manufacturing workers in 2010.
    (2) Jobs in medicine always grow faster than jobs involving computers.
    (3) Between 2000 and 2010, the growth in jobs for physical therapist aides and for personal and home care aides will be about equal.
    (4) Between 2000 and 2010, the need for special education teachers will grow, but not as quickly as the need for desktop publishers.
    (5) Between 2000 and 2010, there will be more jobs for medical assistants but fewer jobs for veterinary assistants.

14. Which detail supports the conclusion that technological literacy is more important than manual ability in high-paying jobs?
    (1) In the early 1900s, many Americans worked at unskilled jobs in farming and manufacturing.
    (2) Workers of the future must be able to follow directions.
    (3) Many jobs in the United States today use technologies that process information.
    (4) Workers learn different jobs so that they can step in to help other workers.
    (5) Groups of employees monitor the quality of a product or service they produce or perform.

Connect with the Article

Write your answers to each question.

15. Why do you think a good work ethic is important to employers?

    _____

16. What three subjects or skills would you include if you put together your own school-to-work program for achieving your career goals?

    _____

    _____

The Global Economy

The Global Economy

Nations have traded with one another since ancient times. In the past, though, each nation was mostly self-sufficient. In other words, the nation could produce enough goods and services for its own people. When nations did trade, they tended to trade only with their allies. Trading often was a friendly gesture made when two countries began working together on other governmental policies.

Today the world has changed. Most countries have opened their markets to goods and services from many other countries. Consumers from all over the world contribute to the supply and demand for these goods and services. As a result, trade among countries has increased dramatically.

Relate to the Topic

This lesson is about the global economy and how it affects the American economy. Think of products that you recently purchased. Which ones were made in another country?

_____

_____

_____

_____

Reading Strategy

SKIMMING A DOUBLE LINE GRAPH   Line graphs often show change over time. A double line graph shows how two things change. Look at the double line graph on page 174. Then answer the questions below.

1. What is the subject of the graph? _____
   Hint: Look at the graph's title.

2. Why are there two kinds of lines on the graph? _____

   _____

   Hint: Look at the legend, the box within the graph.

Vocabulary

interdependent

protectionist

tariff

quota

trade deficit

free trade

bloc

currency

Check your answers on page 248.

UNIT 4 ECONOMICS

The World's Interdependent Economy

Borders, distance, and different languages were once barriers to trade. But because of telecommunications technology, companies on opposite sides of the globe can work together. Nations' economies have become linked to one another because companies in many countries do so much business together. Nations today are **interdependent.** This means they depend on one another to be successful. The marketplace created by the many business transactions among nations is called the global economy. Because nations are interdependent, what happens in one country's economy affects economies in many other countries.

International Trade

Huge amounts of goods and services are traded among nations every day. Companies that need a natural resource, such as iron or phosphate, may import that resource from another country. The companies then make their products and export them to the world. For example, American plastics companies import oil from the Middle East. They make computer parts, which they then export for sale to the rest of the world. By importing raw materials, a nation with limited natural resources can produce more than it otherwise could.

The United States imports such resources as aluminum, rubber, tin, and graphite from other countries. It also imports energy resources used to build and run machines. And many consumer goods—from cocoa to cars—come from other countries.

Imported products are important because they give consumers a wider variety of goods at what often are lower prices. These products also affect American producers. American businesses are forced to keep their costs down and the quality of goods high to stay competitive in the American market.

International trade also increases the number of places a country can sell its goods. If one country cannot or will not buy a particular product, another one may. As a result, wealth and goods are spread over a larger part of the globe than ever before. Producers in each country, however, must sell enough of their goods to earn enough money to buy the products they need.

International trade increases the demand for goods, which leads to greater production and more use of raw materials and labor. If more people want to buy American products, for example, American companies will need to make more. Consequently, more Americans will have jobs at these companies.

Competition from international trade can force a country's businesses to become more efficient. The businesses develop new and better ways of doing things. Competition from international trade also can drive a company out of business if it does not keep up with other companies making similar products.

American companies export many products. Machinery, chemicals, grains, and beef are just a few. Exports generate money that companies need to succeed. Successful businesses make the American economy strong.

International Trade Policies

Political and economic matters can make trade between nations complex. When problems arise, nations sometimes create a protectionist trade policy. Governments that have a **protectionist** trade policy place limits on imports to ensure the success of their own nation's businesses.

Some of the protectionist trade barriers that nations set up are high **tariffs,** or taxes on imported goods. The tariff is added to the selling price of the imported item. American consumers then compare the cost of the imported product to the cost of an American-made product. Often they choose the less expensive American-made product. Another barrier is setting quotas. A **quota** limits the amount of goods a country can import.

When one country places a trade barrier on products, other countries often respond with their own protectionist measures. In 2002, for example, the United States placed tariffs on imported steel to help protect American steel producers. Several steel-producing countries objected to this move. Some threatened to raise tariffs on goods that they imported from the United States.

When a country buys more imports than it sells exports, the country has a **trade deficit.** When nations have a trade deficit, they are more eager to protect their own share of the world market.

During the 1800s and 1900s, the United States took many protectionist actions against other countries. Beginning in the 1990s, however, former communist nations began to build new economies. Some economies were modeled after the United States economy. More and more American companies were ready to do business in other countries. As a result, many governments abandoned protectionist actions in favor of free trade. **Free trade** means that no legal or political barriers stop a country from importing and exporting goods. To encourage free trade, the United States and other countries formed trade **blocs.**

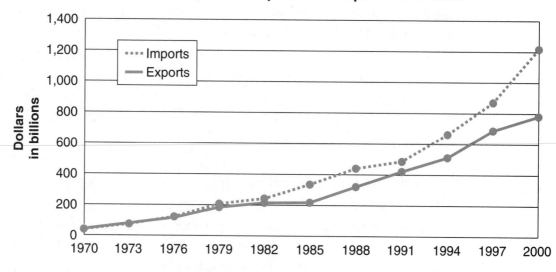

United States Imports and Exports 1970–2000

Reading a Double Line Graph One way to compare information and show change over a period of time is with a double line graph. On the graph on page 174, the dotted line represents imports and the solid line represents exports. During the time period shown on the graph, which has risen more?

    a. exports   b. imports

Some trade blocs are regional. In North America the United States, Canada, and Mexico have the North American Free Trade Agreement (NAFTA). In Europe, countries have joined to create a regional economic market called the European Union. In 2002 most members of the European Union began using a **currency,** or kind of money, called the euro. The euro makes trade among its members easier than ever.

Impact on the United States Economy

From the 1950s to the 1970s, the United States had the strongest economy in the world. But then things began to change. American goods were too expensive for other nations to buy. At the same time, imported goods like cars, cameras, and clothes became cheaper for Americans to buy. In addition, American industries had to buy huge amounts of imported oil and other energy resources. As a result, other countries built strong economies. Their trade with the United States grew rapidly.

These developments were both good and bad for Americans. Increased international trade meant they could choose cheaper goods and services. But the success of imports also put pressure on American companies to lower their prices. Many chose to cut expenses by firing workers. Some businesses even moved to other countries where people worked for very low wages.

In the United States, unions and labor laws require many companies to pay fairly high wages with benefits. In some poorer countries, people work for pennies a day. Some Americans have mixed feelings about this situation. They like the idea of low-priced, imported goods but dislike the fact that the workers are terribly underpaid.

The interdependent global economy has brought many economic benefits to the United States. But it has presented problems for American workers. For example, in recent years Asia has suffered an economic decline. At first Asia's trouble was good for the United States—televisions and other electronic goods got cheaper. But because Asia couldn't afford imports, American farmers and manufacturers suffered. Sometimes when factory owners threaten to shut down, workers agree to pay cuts or benefit cuts. When plants do close, skilled workers must find jobs elsewhere. They often have to take jobs that pay lower wages.

Supporting Conclusions You draw conclusions by reading for the main idea and for details that support the conclusion. Which statement supports this conclusion: "An interdependent global economy has advantages and disadvantages"?

    a. Many U.S. businesses moved to where people worked for very low wages.

    b. From the 1950s to the 1970s, the U.S. had the world's strongest economy.

Thinking About the Article

Practice Vocabulary

The words below are in the passages in bold type. Study the way each word is used. Then complete each sentence by writing the correct word.

| interdependent | free trade | quota | tariff |
| protectionist | trade deficit | currency | |

1. _____ means no barriers to trading with other countries.

2. Most nations have their own _____, or money.

3. A country with a(n) _____ trade policy limits imports.

4. Nations that are trading partners have a(n) _____ relationship.

5. A tax placed on imports is called a(n) _____.

6. Countries create a(n) _____ by importing more than they export.

7. A country has set a(n) _____ when it allows only a certain number of imports from a particular country.

Understand the Article

Write the answer to each question.

8. Why is a global economy an interdependent economy?

_____

9. How does international trade force businesses to become more efficient?

_____

_____

10. In what two ways does an increase in international trade help a nation's economy?

_____

_____

11. What are two trade barriers that a nation with a protectionist trade policy might build against another country?

_____

Apply Your Skills

Circle the number of the best answer for each question.

12. Look at the line graph on page 174. Which of the following best describes the growth of imports and exports in the United States from 1970 to 2000?
    (1) sharp increases in imports and decreases in exports
    (2) sharper decreases in imports than exports
    (3) increases in imports and exports
    (4) sharper increases in imports than exports
    (5) decreases in exports and increases in imports

13. Look again at the graph on page 174. After 1982, in which year did U.S. imports and exports come the closest to being equal?
    (1) 1988
    (2) 1991
    (3) 1994
    (4) 1997
    (5) 2000

14. Which statement supports the conclusion that the global economy brings many benefits to the American economy?
    (1) The United States sometimes places tariffs on imports.
    (2) Union workers may accept lower wages if owners threaten to shut the factory down.
    (3) American consumers can choose from a variety of goods.
    (4) Imports became less expensive than American-made goods.
    (5) Imports help nations with limited natural resources produce more.

Connect with the Article

Write your answer to each question.

15. Protectionist policies discourage international trade and free trade encourages it. Why is this true?

    _____

    _____

16. Would you choose to buy a Japanese-made automobile at a cost of $18,000 or an American-made automobile, of equivalent size and features, at a cost of $22,000? Explain your answer.

    _____

    _____

    _____

Economics at Work

Horticulture: Flower Shop Manager

Some Careers in Horticulture

Garden Planner uses knowledge of green plants and flowers to plan gardens for individuals and companies

Garden Center Worker takes care of plants, assists customers, stocks supplies

Groundskeeper cares for flowers, grass, trees, and shrubs in public and private settings

Landscape Worker plants flowers, shrubs, and trees according to design plans

Lawn Service Worker tends lawns flower beds, and shrubs

Do you like working with plants and flowers? You may enjoy managing a flower shop. However, being a florist involves more than customer service and arranging flowers. It also requires a good understanding of the economics of running a store.

Flower shop managers are responsible for ordering and maintaining cut flowers and green plants. They must be aware of the best sources for economically priced flowers. They must also know what prices to charge for the flowers so that they can make money while competing with other stores.

A major part of each day is spent ordering, caring for, and arranging cut flowers. Managers must be familiar with each type of plant and be able to recommend plant and bouquet selections to their customers.

Look at the Some Careers in Horticulture chart.

- Do any of the careers interest you? If so, which ones?
- What information would you need to know more about those careers? On a separate piece of paper, write some questions that you would like answered. You can find more information about those careers in the *Occupational Outlook Handbook* at your local library or online.

Use the material below to answer the questions that follow.

Maria is a floral shop manager. She reviewed all the invoices from the past year and recorded the highest and lowest prices she paid for the best-selling flowers. In general, the law of supply and demand dictates that flowers cost more when they are out of season and in scarce supply. Maria made a table of information from the invoices.

Flower	Highest Price Paid	Lowest Price Paid
Calla lily	$2.50 per stem	$1.20 per stem
Carnation	$5.35 per bunch	$1.25 per bunch
Delphinium	$7.95 per bunch	$4.95 per bunch
Hyacinth	$3.95 per bulb	$1.25 per bulb
Poppy	$6.25 per bunch	$2.25 per bunch
Tulip	$2.25 per stem	$0.65 per stem

1. Below is a list of prices Maria paid for each flower. Determine if each flower was purchased in season or out of season. Circle the correct answer.

Calla lily—$1.25 per stem	in season	out of season
Carnation—$5.19 per bunch	in season	out of season
Delphinium—$6.95 per bunch	in season	out of season
Hyacinth—$3.45 per bulb	in season	out of season
Poppy—$2.55 per bunch	in season	out of season
Tulip—$0.72 per stem	in season	out of season

2. Which of the following prices indicates that the plant is out of season?
   (1) Tulip—$0.70 per stem
   (2) Calla lily—$2.25 per stem
   (3) Delphinium—$5.25 per bunch
   (4) Carnation—$1.75 per bunch
   (5) Poppy—$2.75 per bunch

3. Have you ever noticed how certain items are more expensive during certain times of the year? You may be aware of this when you go grocery shopping or when you buy certain types of clothing. Use a separate piece of paper to describe at least one seasonal pricing difference that you've encountered.

Unit 4 Review Economics

Increasing Demand

Producers of goods and services are always looking for ways to increase demand. When consumers want to buy more products and services, producers and sellers are able to make higher profits. One way to increase demand is to find new uses for products. New uses for a product attract new customers. Farm products are a good example. In recent years scientists have found ways to increase the demand for many crops. Take corn, for example.

For years, people bought corn as a food product. Today, however, corn is used to make everything from paint to diapers. In some cases, corn is a good substitute for oil in making paint. It is an ingredient in coatings for wood and metal. Adding a small amount of cornstarch to plastic can help protect the environment. Ordinarily plastic does not decompose or break down. It lasts forever—unless a small amount of cornstarch is added during the plastic-making process. Then the plastic will decompose. As a result, cornstarch is an additive to such products as disposable diapers and plastic bags.

No one is sure how many other products could be improved with a little corn. But scientists continually research the possibilities. As the demand grows, farmers have more reasons to grow corn.

Circle the number of the best answer for each question.

1. According to the article, which of the following would be most likely to encourage the new uses of corn?
   (1) people who like to eat corn
   (2) people who use corn as animal feed
   (3) gasoline producers
   (4) wheat farmers
   (5) people concerned about the environment

2. Which of the following is the best conclusion that can be drawn from the passage?
   (1) Demand for corn is likely to increase.
   (2) Demand for corn is likely to decrease.
   (3) The supply of corn is likely to stay the same.
   (4) The supply of corn is likely to decrease.
   (5) Supply and demand will stay the same.

A Wedding Budget

Josh and Jennifer Lee's Wedding Expenses			
Expense	Planned	Actual	Percentage of Actual Amount Spent
Clothing	$1,600	$1,670	12%
Wedding rings	450	650	5%
Wedding stationary	350	335	2%
Limousine rental	500	560	4%
Chapel Fee	200	200	1%
Flowers	1,250	1,225	9%
Reception	7,050	6,975	50%
Wedding photographs	1,500	1,140	10%
Wedding video	250	250	2%
Music	250	450	3%
Other	350	275	2%
Total	13,750	13,730	100%

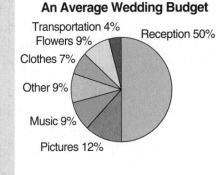

An Average Wedding Budget

Transportation 4%
Flowers 9%
Clothes 7%
Other 9%
Music 9%
Pictures 12%
Reception 50%

Write the answer to each question.

3. What makes up the largest percentage of an average wedding budget?

_____

4. Did the Lees spend the average amount on that item? Explain.

_____

_____

Circle the number of the best answer for the question.

5. Which of the following is <u>best</u> supported by the graph and the table?
   (1) The Lees spent less on music than they had planned.
   (2) The Lees spent about an average amount on flowers, but less than average on music.
   (3) For both the average wedding budget and for the Lee's wedding budget, flowers and pictures account for 15 percent of the total expense.
   (4) Wedding flowers cost too much money.
   (5) Although transportation is the smallest average expense, it was the Lees' second-largest expense.

   Go on to the next page.

Deceptive Selling

Almost everyone has been the victim of deceptive selling methods. Perhaps you paid too much for an item. Maybe the product you bought was not worth as much as you thought it was. Smart shoppers learn to be cautious. They watch for one or more of the following selling practices.

Special Pricing.   A seller offers a product at a "special low price." The seller tells the customer to buy now because the price will go up soon. However in many cases, the "special" price is actually higher than the price of the same item at other stores.

Bait and Switch.   An ad offers an item at a very low price. When customers go to buy that item, they are told that the item is an inferior product. The seller then suggests switching to a more expensive model of the same item. The seller may also tell buyers that the advertised item is "out of stock." The seller then urges the customer to buy the more expensive model that just happens to be "in stock."

Chain Referrals.   Customers are told that if they buy a product and then refer other customers, they will receive a gift or a reduced price. Often the price of the product, even with the gift or discount, is higher than the price of the same item at other stores.

Write the answer to each question.

6. An ad offers a deal on a TV. When the customer goes to buy the item, the seller says it is out of stock. The seller notes that a more expensive model is in stock. Which sales method is the seller using?

   _____

7. A seller tells the buyer that the price of a compact disc player will go up next month. There will never be a better time to buy than now. Which sales method is the seller using?

   _____

Circle the number of the best answer for the question.

8. Which of the following statements is supported by the article?
   (1) All sellers are dishonest.
   (2) Let the buyer beware.
   (3) If a deal sounds good, buy the item.
   (4) Never check prices in other stores.
   (5) Don't buy an item if you don't need it.

Opportunities in the Work Force

Top 15 Fastest-Growing Occupations, 2000–2010
(Numbers in thousands of jobs)

Occupation	Number of expected jobs in 2010	Expected % change 2000–2010	Education and training catagory
• Computer software engineers, applications	760	100%	Bachelor's degree
• Computer support specialists	996	97%	Associate degree
• Computer software engineers, systems software	601	90%	Bachelor's degree
• Network and computer systems administrators	416	82%	Bachelor's degree
• Network systems and data communications analysts	211	77%	Bachelor's degree
• Desktop publishers	63	67%	Postsecondary vocational award
• Database administrators	176	66%	Bachelor's degree
• Personal and home care aides	672	62%	Short-term on-the-job training
• Computer systems analysts	689	60%	Bachelor's degree
• Medical assistants	516	57%	Moderate-term on-the-job training
• Social and human service assistants	418	54%	Moderate-term on-the-job
• Physician assistants	89	53%	Bachelor's degree
• Medical records and health information technicians	202	49%	Associate degree
• Computer and information systems managers	463	48%	Bachelor's or higher degree, plus work experience
• Home health aides	907	47%	Short-term on-the-job

Write the answer to each question.

9. Which occupation group is expected to have the fastest growth by 2010?

_____

10. What education or training do medical assistants need?

_____

Circle the number of the best answer.

11. Which conclusion does the information in the table best support?
    (1) Database administrators will have the greatest choice of jobs.
    (2) Physician assistants will have the greatest choice of jobs.
    (3) Occupations expected to have high growth will have the most jobs.
    (4) Skills for most computer occupations can be learned on the job.
    (5) The fastest growing jobs generally require education beyond high school.

Social Studies Extension

Look at the circle graph on page 156 to review the spending of the average American family. Over the next two weeks, write down all that you and your family spend in each of these categories. Then calculate the percentage of your total spending that fell in each category. How similar are your results to those shown on page 156?

Mini-Test Unit 4

This is a 15-minute practice test. After 15 minutes, mark the last number you finished. Then complete the test and check your answers. If most of your answers were correct but you did not finish, try to work faster next time.

Directions: Choose the one best answer to each question.

<u>Questions 1 and 2</u> refer to the following information.

A wise shopper often thinks about unit price—the cost of an item in terms of its unit of measurement. For example, a unit price for a bag of apples might be the price per pound.

In the past, consumers had to figure out unit prices themselves. Today, most supermarkets post the unit price along with the item's price on the item's shelf display.

1. What do you infer is the reason supermarket owners post unit prices?

    (1) to help shoppers compare the value of similar items
    (2) to advertise the highest quality items
    (3) to announce price changes
    (4) to keep shoppers from buying items they cannot afford
    (5) to encourage shoppers to save as much money as possible

2. Based on the passage, in which situation would unit pricing most likely be used?

    (1) deciding whether to buy tickets for a concert
    (2) deciding which brand of corn flakes is the better buy
    (3) choosing between a used car and a new car
    (4) choosing between two sweaters
    (5) figuring the cost of a family vacation

<u>Question 3</u> refers to the following line graph.

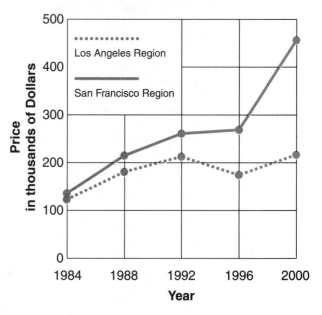

Average Price of a Single-Family Home, 1984–2000

3. Which of the following is a valid conclusion based on the graph?

    (1) Prices of homes rose steadily in both San Francisco and Los Angeles between 1984 and 2000.
    (2) Prices of homes declined steadily in both San Francisco and Los Angeles between 1984 and 2000.
    (3) Between 1984 and 1992, home prices in both San Francisco and Los Angeles rose and then fell.
    (4) Between 1992 and 1996, homes in San Francisco and in Los Angeles gained little or no value.
    (5) Between 1996 and 2000 prices of homes rose faster in Los Angeles than in San Francisco.

Questions 4 and 5 refer to the following table.

How We Pay—and May Pay Tomorrow

Method of Payment (Partial Listing)	Billions of Transactions		Percent of Transactions	
	1999	2005	1999	2005
Personal Checks	29.4	23.8	27.9	17.6
Money Orders	1.2	1.4	1.1	1.1
Credit Cards	18.4	23.2	17.4	17.2
Debit Cards	6.4	18.4	6.1	13.6
Cash	46.6	58.6	44.2	43.4

4. Which information best supports the conclusion that cash and personal checks will continue to be very popular ways to pay for purchases?

(1) The use of debit cards will decline between 1999 and 2005.

(2) There will be more transactions of all kinds in 2005 than in 1999.

(3) Many more transactions are made with checks than with money orders.

(4) Credit cards and checks will be used almost equally in 2005.

(5) As in 1999, cash and checks will be used for most purchases in 2005.

5. Based on the information in the table, which view do most Americans likely hold?

(1) Use credit for small purchases before using it for major purchases.

(2) It is unwise to buy on impulse.

(3) It is better to pay cash for purchases than to borrow money.

(4) Credit should be used only for emergency purchases.

(5) Carrying paper money is risky.

Questions 6 and 7 refer to the following information.

When stock analysts talk about a bear market, are they giving you good news? What about a bull market? These "animal" terms have important meanings.

In a bear market, stock prices go down. The drop isn't sudden, as in a crash; rather, investors expect stock prices to decline and to stay low. A bear market, which may last for many months, reflects a generally slow economy.

A bull market is just the opposite—stock prices are going up, and experts predict that the trend will last for a while. A bull market indicates a growing economy and a good chance for investors to profit.

6. Why are these animal names appropriate for the stock markets conditions they refer to?

(1) Bears are furry and bulls are not.

(2) Bears are wild animals and bulls are domesticated animals.

(3) Bears have sluggish periods and bulls sometimes charge or stampede.

(4) Bears hunt and bulls graze.

(5) Bear skins have higher value than bull hides do.

7. Which of the following is most likely to lead to a bear market?

(1) growth in the amount of exports

(2) poor earnings predictions from major companies

(3) a high demand for a new product

(4) stockholders buying more stock instead of selling the stock they have

(5) an increase in the number of first-time homebuyers

 Check your answers on page 249.

UNIT 5

Geography

Geography

Geography

Earth has many remarkable places. **Geography** is the study of our planet's places and the people who live in them. Geographical study includes a place's physical features, such as weather, land, animals, plants, and minerals. Geography also includes a study of a place's cultural features—the people's customs and the ways they make their living.

How does the place in which you live differ from the picture above?

_____

How do the jobs of people who live in the Arctic differ from jobs in your area?

_____

Thinking About Geography

You already may know more about geography than you realize. Travel or nature programs on television can get you thinking about Earth's lands and peoples. News stories, too, can remind you that people constantly interact with their environments.

Check the box for each fact that you already know.

☐ Oceans are among Earth's most prominent features, covering about two-thirds of the planet's surface.

☐ Frequently, what people eat reflects the climate in which they live.

☐ Wind and water can change the environment of an area by carrying away soil.

☐ The presence or absence of mountains affects the weather in a place.

☐ Using rivers for transportation is an example of how people interact with the environment.

☐ Overpopulation and pollution threaten the environment in many parts of the world.

Write two other facts that you know about geography.

_____

_____

Previewing the Unit

In this unit, you will learn:

● how one group of people have adapted to life in a harsh environment

● why there are different climates in different parts of the world

● what actions people have taken in response to an environmental disaster

● how various countries are working to protect a valuable resource—productive land

Lesson 23	People and Regions
Lesson 24	Climatic Regions
Lesson 25	Rescuing an Environment
Lesson 26	Taking Care of Resources

LESSON
23

People and Regions

People and Regions

Vocabulary

region

vegetation

tree line

climate

tundra

In 1993 Canada arranged to give the Inuit people their own territory in the Canadian Arctic. The Inuit are the native people of northern Canada. They now own and control the land and mineral wealth of the new territory of Nunavut.

Nunavut is a huge territory. It covers 20 percent of Canada, including two-thirds of the Canadian coastline.

Relate to the Topic

This lesson is about the Arctic and the Native Americans who live there. Think about the place where you live.

In what part of your state do you live? _____

What makes your neighborhood different from a neighborhood nearby?

_____

_____

_____

Reading Strategy

PREVIEWING A MAP   Like many other visual aids, maps can give you a general idea about the content of material before you begin reading. Look at the map on page 189. Then answer the questions.

1. What part of the world will the lesson discuss? _____

    _____

    Hint: Look at the title.

2. Why might this region be a difficult place to live?

    _____

    _____

    Hint: Study the labels on the map.

188

Check your answers on pages 249–250.

UNIT 5 GEOGRAPHY

The Arctic

Located around the North Pole, the Arctic is one of Earth's unique regions. A **region** is an area that differs in one or more ways from the areas around it. Physical features, such as mountains or plants, may set the region apart. The culture of the people or the way they make their living also may set a region apart. Few regions have real borders that mark where one region ends and another begins.

Vegetation and Climate

Vegetation can define a region. **Vegetation** is the plants that grow naturally in an area. The Arctic region, however, is often defined by the plants that cannot grow there. It is the land north of the tree line. The **tree line** marks where temperatures become too cold for trees to grow.

The Arctic region can also be defined by its climate. **Climate** is the general weather of a region over a long time. The climate of the Arctic includes short summers and long, very cold winters. The Arctic region is surrounded by a line called the 50° summer isotherm. This line marks the area in which the average temperature of the warmest month is less than 50° F (10° C).

Permanent snow and ice cover the North Pole and the land along the Arctic Ocean. Algae and other plants that thrive on rocks may grow in this part of the Arctic. The rest of the region is **tundra.** This treeless stretch of land has only a thin layer of soil above the frozen earth. Herbs, vines, mosses, wildflowers, and small shrubs grow on the tundra during the Arctic summer.

The Arctic Region

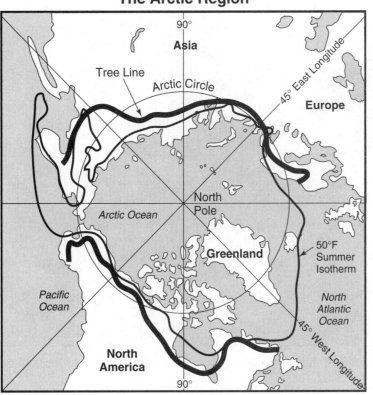

Reading a Map Maps use symbols to tell about places. Symbols can be lines, dots, colors, or pictures. Study the map on page 189. In what continent is the tree line farthest from the North Pole?

    a.   North America

    b.   Europe

The Early Inuit

The Arctic region spans North America, Europe, and Asia. In North America, the Arctic region lies in northern and western Alaska and northernmost Canada. Native Americans who live in the Arctic region are called the Inuit, a word that means "the real people."

The Inuit were once called Eskimos. They are descended from Asian whale hunters who came to Alaska. They moved east to Canada and Greenland in about A.D. 1000.

The Arctic climate is too harsh for farming. So, the Inuit relied on fishing and hunting for food. Most settled along the coastlines, where they hunted seals, walrus, and whales. Others traveled in small groups made up of several families and lived in camps. In the spring, they fished, hunted caribou, and gathered berries. In the winter, they hunted whales and seals and trapped birds. They traveled on foot or by boat during the short summer and by dog team during the rest of the year.

The Inuit depended on animals for other needs, too. They used animal hides and bones to build shelters, boats, and sleds. They also dressed in layers of seal skins and caribou hides. The layers trapped warm air near the body. The outer layer generally had fur for greater warmth.

Native Americans in Canada's Arctic region today combine modern ways with traditional ones.

The Inuit had a very rich culture. The people generally chose their best hunter as their leader. However, they made decisions through group discussion. And they used storytelling and singing, rather than writing, as their main ways of communicating.

Over time, part of the Arctic came under Canadian control. From the 1950s through the 1970s, Inuit children attended Canadian schools during the fall and winter. They learned their lessons in English and French. The children forgot not only their Inuit language but also the Inuit way of life.

The Canadian Inuit Today

Today there are more than 100,000 Inuit. Most live in Alaska, Canada, Greenland, and Russia. The Inuit in Canada still hunt and fish, but most of them also earn wages. They need cash to buy tools, rifles, and snowmobiles. So, many Inuit work at mining camps or on oil rigs. They also earn cash by selling furs or native arts and crafts.

The Inuit have struggled to keep their traditions. Inuit leaders have looked at the schools their children attend and have suggested changes to the government. Today the schools teach native languages and customs to Inuit students.

In 1987 the Inuit of Alaska, Canada, and Greenland joined forces to protect the Inuit way of life. Their leaders organized an annual Inuit conference. They discussed wildlife rights and land claims. They agreed that the Arctic region should be "used for peace and environmentally safe purposes." This cooperation gives the Inuit political power to help hold on to their way of life.

The majority of Canadian Inuit live in the northeastern part of the country. Their families have lived and hunted there for nearly a thousand years. Until recently, however, the Inuit did not own the land. So Canada's Inuit began demanding control of their hunting grounds. In 1993 the Inuit and the Canadian government agreed to form a new territory that the Inuit began governing in April 1999. The Inuit named the territory Nunavut, which means "our land." They own the mineral rights in some parts of the land and also earn a share of the profits from oil and mineral development in other parts.

Finding the Main Idea One way to make sure you understand what you read is to find the main idea of each paragraph. A paragraph is a group of sentences about one main idea or topic. The main idea usually is stated in one sentence, called a topic sentence. The topic sentence makes a general statement that sums up all the details in the other sentences of the paragraph. Reread the paragraph that begins "In 1987." Note that the first sentence is the topic sentence and states the main idea of the paragraph.

What is the topic sentence of the first paragraph under "The Canadian Inuit Today"? Circle the letter of the correct answer.

a. The Inuit in Canada still hunt and fish, but most of them also earn wages.

b. They also earn cash by selling furs or native arts and crafts.

Check your answer on page 250.

Thinking About the Article

Practice Vocabulary

The words below are in the passage in bold type. Study the way each word is used. Then complete each sentence by writing the correct word.

region   **vegetation**   **tree line**

climate   **tundra**

1. The _____ is land on which few plants grow.

2. Bitter cold temperatures and very short summers make up the Arctic

   _____.

3. _____ that grows in warm and wet places differs greatly from what grows in warm and dry places.

4. In North America trees grow in the area south of the

   _____.

5. A _____ may be defined by its natural features, climate, plant and animal life, or people.

Understand the Article

Write the answers to the following.

6. Describe the climate and vegetation of the Arctic region.

   _____

   _____

   _____

7. Describe the early Inuit way of life. How did they get food? What were their clothes like? How did they get from place to place?

   _____

   _____

   _____

8. List three ways the Inuit worked together to save their way of life.

   _____

   _____

   _____

Apply Your Skills

Circle the number of the best answer for each question.

9. Review the map and paragraphs on page 189. According to this information, which of the following statements is true?
   (1) The Arctic region is defined only by the Arctic Circle.
   (2) The 50° summer isotherm marks where trees will grow.
   (3) The tundra in Europe is flatter than the tundra in North America.
   (4) Europe has more arctic land than Asia.
   (5) Greenland lies entirely within the Arctic region.

10. Read the paragraph on page 190 that begins "The Arctic climate." What is the main idea of this paragraph?
    (1) The Inuit met their needs by fishing and hunting.
    (2) The Inuit traveled from place to place.
    (3) The Inuit did not farm.
    (4) The Inuit lived in a cold climate.
    (5) The Inuit ate berries.

Connect with the Article

Write your answer to each question.

11. What do you think was the most valuable thing the Inuit gained by working together? Why?

    _____

    _____

    _____

12. A few decades ago, Inuit children went to school far from their homes. Imagine that children in your family or children you know had to go to a school in another country for six months of the year. What changes might you expect to see in their behavior when they returned? Think about language, dress, and sense of closeness to you and your family.

    _____

    _____

    _____

    _____

    _____

LESSON 24

Climatic Regions

Vocabulary

equator

latitude

tropics

current

parallels

longitude

meridians

precipitation

elevation

From your window, the day looks sunny. So you step outside without a hat or an umbrella. Before you walk two blocks, though, you hear a rumble of thunder. Rain starts to fall—first as a drop or two, but then in sheets.

Weather can change in just minutes. A region's climate, on the other hand, changes more slowly. Factors such as sun, rain, and wind determine climate.

Relate to the Topic

This lesson is about climate and factors that determine climate. If you could live in any part of the world, where would you choose? Describe the climate there.

_____

_____

What is the climate like where you live now?

_____

_____

Reading Strategy

USING TITLES AND HEADINGS TO ASK QUESTIONS   One way to get the most out of your reading is to look at titles and headings. They can help you plan your reading and review what you have read. Skim the headings in the article that begins on page 195. Then answer the questions.

1. What is one question you could ask about the article as a whole.

_____

   Hint: What word appears in the title and several headings?

2. Write a question that you could ask about all of the headings.

_____

   Hint: What word in the title relates to factors?

Check your answers on page 250.   UNIT 5 GEOGRAPHY

Factors Determining Climate

Earth has many different climates. One factor that influences a region's climate is its location on Earth, especially its distance from the equator. The **equator** is an imaginary line that circles Earth exactly halfway between the North Pole and the South Pole. Nearby mountain ranges or large bodies of water also affect climate. The kinds of winds that blow across the region make a difference, too.

The Equator and Climate

All year round, places along the equator receive direct rays from the sun. Direct sunlight is very strong. As a result, temperatures near the equator are usually warm. Places away from the equator, on the other hand, receive slanted rays from the sun. In other words, the sun's rays strike Earth at an angle. This indirect sunlight is weaker than direct sunlight. As a result, temperatures far from the equator are generally cooler than those near the equator.

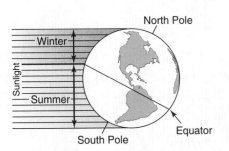

This diagram shows winter north of the equator. Notice that the Sun's rays hit Earth at more of an angle in the Northern Hemisphere.

The amount of sunlight a place gets depends on its distance from the equator. This distance is measured with lines of **latitude.** Lines of latitude run east and west like the equator.

The lines of latitude farthest from the equator lie near the North Pole or South Pole. Places along these lines get less sunlight than other places on Earth. They get no sunlight for part of the year and slanting rays for the rest of the year. As a result, the polar regions are cold all year and have short summers.

Earth is tilted slightly. The tilt of the Earth affects how sunlight strikes the Earth. The northernmost line of latitude that receives almost direct rays from the sun is called the Tropic of Cancer. The southernmost line of latitude that receives almost direct rays from the sun is called the Tropic of Capricorn. The region between these two lines of latitude is called the **tropics.** Most places in the tropics have warm temperatures year-round.

Between the tropics and the two polar regions are the middle latitudes. These two regions have temperate climates. Temperatures there are cooler than those in the tropics but warmer than those at the poles. Temperatures in the middle latitudes vary from place to place and from season to season.

Identifying Details A paragraph is a group of sentences about one main idea. **Details,** or small pieces of information, explain or support the main idea. The main idea in the first paragraph under the heading "The Equator and Climate" is "The location of a place determines the amount of sunlight it receives."

Reread the first paragraph under the heading "The Equator and Climate." Which of the following details from the paragraph supports its main idea?

   a.   Lines of latitude run east and west.

   b.   Places along the equator receive direct rays from the sun all year round.

Check your answer on page 250.   195

Water and Wind

Latitude explains why Alaska is colder than Florida. However, latitude does not explain why winters in southern Alaska are often warmer than winters in Montana. What is the reason? Southern Alaska borders the Pacific Ocean, and Montana lies inland.

Oceans and large lakes help keep temperatures mild. These large bodies of water do not gain or lose heat as quickly as land areas do. In summer, ocean water stays cold long after the land has grown warm. Large bodies of water also hold the summer's heat as the land cools in fall. The temperature of water affects the air above it. After winds blow over the water, they cool the land in summer and warm the land in winter. As a result, places near an ocean or a large lake often have milder temperatures than places far from large bodies of water.

Another fact helps explain why the climate in southern Alaska is mild. A warm ocean current flows along Alaska's coast. A **current** is like a river in the ocean. Some ocean currents carry warm water, while others are very cold. Without the warm current, the ocean along the coast of southern Alaska would be frozen all winter.

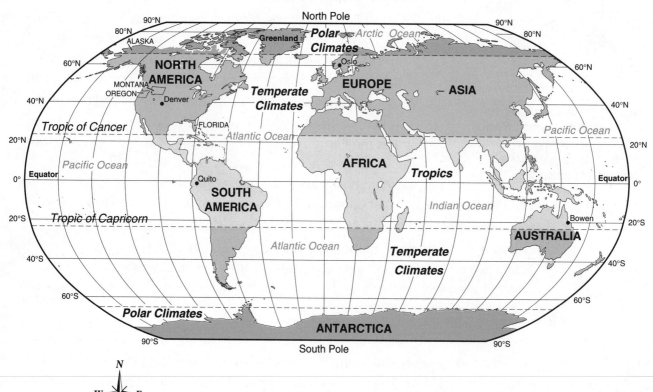

Latitude and Climate

Using Latitude Many maps have two sets of lines. These lines cross each other to form a grid. You can use this grid to locate places on a map of Earth. Lines of latitude, called **parallels,** measure distances from the equator in degrees. The equator lies at 0° latitude. All other parallels lie either north or south of the equator, and are labeled N or S. Lines of **longitude,** or **meridians,** reach from pole to pole. These lines measure distances from the Prime Meridian in degrees. The Prime Meridian lies at 0° longitude. All other meridians lie east or west of the Prime Meridian and are labeled E or W.

Look at the map on page 196 to answer the following questions.

1. Which city lies closest to 40° N latitude?
   a. Denver   b. Oslo

2. Which city shown on the map is outside the tropics?
   a. Bowen   b. Quito   c. Oslo

Montana and other places surrounded by land and far from large bodies of water have a continental climate. Places with continental climates have cold winters and hot summers. Even the amount of **precipitation**—rain or snow—follows a pattern. Cities such as Des Moines, Iowa, have a continental climate. They get more snow than New York City and other places on the northeastern coast.

Mountains and Climate

Mountains also affect climate. The most important factor in a mountain climate is elevation. **Elevation** is the height of the land, and it affects both temperature and precipitation. This is because air cools as it rises. Temperatures at the top of a mountain are much colder than at the bottom of the mountain. As a result, some mountains along the equator are snowcapped all year long.

Mountains affect temperatures in other places, too. For example, mountains in the western United States block mild winds from the Pacific Ocean. So the moist, mild ocean air never reaches Montana and other places that lie east of the mountains. These places have colder winters and hotter summers than places along the Pacific coast.

Mountains also influence precipitation. In Oregon, for example, mountains line the coast. Moist winds from the Pacific Ocean rise up the western slopes of the mountains. As the air rises, it cools. Cold air cannot hold as much moisture as warm air. So clouds form and rain falls on the western side of the mountains. When the air reaches the eastern side of the mountains, it has dropped all its moisture and is dry. So the east side of Oregon's mountains gets very little rain.

Many factors—latitude, winds, elevation, and nearness to mountains and large bodies of water—determine the climate of a place. Climate determines how people live. It influences their choice of food, housing, and clothing.

Thinking About the Article

Practice Vocabulary

The words below are in the passage in bold type. Study the way each word is used. Then complete each sentence by writing the correct word.

equator	latitude	current
longitude	precipitation	elevation

1. The sun's rays shine directly on places along the

   _____ year-round.

2. A warm ocean _____ can give places located along a northern coastline a fairly mild climate.

3. _____ may fall to Earth as rain or snow.

4. The factor that determines the climate of polar regions is

   _____.

5. A mountaintop is colder than the foot of the mountain because of

   _____.

6. The Prime Meridian is the starting point on a map for measuring

   _____.

Understand the Article

Write the answer to each question.

7. What are three factors that affect the climate of a place?

   _____

8. How would you describe the climate in the tropics? Middle-latitude areas? Polar regions?

   _____

   _____

9. How do oceans keep land temperatures mild in both summer and winter?

   _____

   _____

Apply Your Skills

Circle the number of the best answer for each question.

10. Which of the following details supports the main idea that latitude affects climate in the tropics?
    (1) The tropics lie close to the poles.
    (2) Winds from the ocean bring moist air to places in the tropics.
    (3) Rain usually falls on the windy side of a mountain.
    (4) Warm ocean currents keep water from freezing in winter.
    (5) The tropics receive almost direct rays from the sun.

11. Look at the map on page 196 to determine which of these lines of latitude lies in the tropics.
    (1) 90° S latitude
    (2) 60° N latitude
    (3) 40° S latitude
    (4) 10° N latitude
    (5) 60° S latitude

12. Which two continents does the equator pass through?
    (1) North America and Europe
    (2) South America and Africa
    (3) Australia and Asia
    (4) Africa and Asia
    (5) South America and Australia

Connect with the Article

Write your answer to each question.

13. The Rocky Mountains cover the western third of Montana. Do you think the western or the eastern part of the state gets more precipitation each year? Explain your answer.

    _____

    _____

    _____

14. On the map on page 196, find the approximate location of your home state. Use climate words from this article to write a sentence that describes the climate in your area.

    _____

    _____

    _____

LESSON 25

Rescuing an Environment

Vocabulary

sound

environment

glacier

iceberg

crude oil

March 24, 1989, was the date of the worst oil spill in North America. Along the southeastern coast of Alaska, a huge oil tanker ran off course and struck a reef. The tanker's bottom tore open. Almost 11 million gallons of oil spilled into the sea.

Many people rushed to clean up the oil spill. They worked to help save the wildlife along Alaska's coast.

Relate to the Topic

This lesson is about how people rescued Alaska's southern coast from an oil spill. Smaller but similar problems with pollution can affect everyone's surroundings. What could you do to improve a garbage-strewn park in your neighborhood?

_____

_____

_____

_____

Reading Strategy

RELATING TO WHAT YOU KNOW Understanding facts in informational material is easier if you compare those facts with what you have previously read or experienced. Read the first three paragraphs on page 201. Then answer the questions.

1. Does this description of Alaska's environment match what you already know about it?

    _____

    _____

    Hint: When you hear the word Alaska, what picture comes to mind?

2. What do you already know about the way that oil is transported?

    _____

    _____

    Hint: What have you learned about oil by watching the news?

Oil Spill in Alaska

The oil spill took place in Prince William Sound. A **sound** is a long, wide inlet from the ocean. Prince William Sound, which is off the Gulf of Alaska, has a marine, or sea, environment. An **environment** is all of the living and nonliving things that make up a place's surroundings. People, fish, seaweed, and other animals and plants are the living parts of the environment of Prince William Sound. The nonliving parts are soil, rocks, water, and glaciers that line the coast. A **glacier** is an enormous mass of ice that moves slowly over land.

Every part of an environment is closely tied to all its other parts. Sea otters, for example, depend on fish and birds for food. Seal meat and fish are important to Native Alaskans' diet. Many people of the Prince William Sound area fish for a living. Others work in the tourist business. Thousands of tourists visit parks, forests, and wildlife refuges near the sound.

Some people who live along the sound work in the oil industry. They store and ship oil. The Alaskan pipeline carries oil from Alaska's Arctic region to Valdez. This is a port on Prince William Sound. Oil tankers come to Valdez each month to carry Alaskan oil to other parts of the United States.

Using a Glossary or Dictionary When you read the sections in this book, you will come across words in bold type. You can find their meanings in the glossary at the back of this book. You may also come across other words that you do not understand. Look in a dictionary to find the meaning of each word. Then, on the lines below, write the definition that best fits the use of the word in the article.

_____

_____

_____

_____

Disaster in Prince William Sound

On Thursday evening, March 23, 1989, an oil tanker called the _Exxon Valdez_ left port and headed for California. Shortly after midnight, the tanker turned sharply to avoid a dangerous iceberg. An **iceberg** is a huge block of floating ice that has broken off from a glacier.

The tanker missed the iceberg but ran over a reef. The smell of untreated oil, called **crude oil,** filled the air. The ship was leaking. By dawn on March 24, a thick oily film, called an oil slick, covered six square miles of the surface of Prince William Sound. By early evening, about ten million gallons of oil had spilled. The oil slick stretched over more than 18 square miles.

Check your answer on page 251. **201**

The slick continued to spread. Wind and water carried the oil farther into the sound. Then a storm hit just four days after the spill, carrying the oil into tiny inlets and coves along the shore. After the storm, the oil slick covered 500 square miles. The oil spill traveled southwest with the ocean currents, polluting more than 1,200 miles of Alaskan coastline.

The spill claimed the lives of 1,000 sea otters. It also killed 100,000 birds, including about 150 bald eagles. People who fished for a living wondered if the oil would harm the salmon, herring, and other fish they depended on.

The Cleanup

No one had ever cleaned up an oil spill as large as this one. So no one knew exactly what to do. The Exxon Corporation sent about 11,000 workers to help. It owned the *Exxon Valdez.* The company that managed the Alaskan pipeline also took some responsibility for the cleanup. The state of Alaska, the U.S. Coast Guard, and several U.S. government agencies helped, too. But it was not always clear who was in charge.

The cleanup crews tried many ways to remove the spilled oil. Some tried to skim the oil from the water. They transferred it to other ships. The workers needed special equipment, but it was slow to arrive.

Some experts wanted to spray the oil with chemicals. These chemicals act much like a detergent. But the company did not have enough chemicals to treat the whole spill. Besides, state and federal officials were slow to permit the spraying. By the time everybody was ready to act, it was too late. In the end, cleanup crews recovered less than ten percent of the oil.

Exxon Valdez Oil Spill

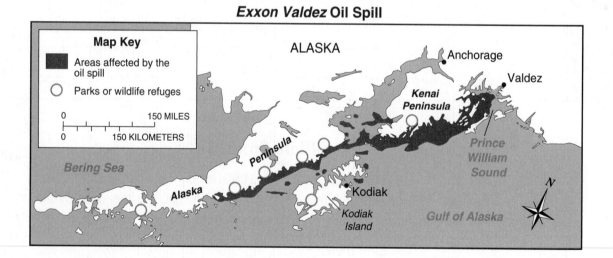

Map Key

▪ Areas affected by the oil spill

○ Parks or wildlife refuges

0 — 150 MILES
0 — 150 KILOMETERS

ALASKA

Anchorage

Valdez

Kenai Peninsula

Prince William Sound

Bering Sea

Peninsula

Alaska

Kodiak

Kodiak Island

Gulf of Alaska

N

Meanwhile, workers attacked the spill on the beaches. Some crews tried to blast the oil from rocks. Others sprayed the beaches with hot water and fertilizer. The fertilizer encouraged the growth of bacteria that eat oil.

Some of the cleanup methods worked, while others did more damage than the oil. The hot water killed some wildlife. It also sent oil deep into the gravel beaches, where it was unreachable, but still harmful to the environment. The bacteria ate up the oil on some beaches. But the fertilizer killed seaweed, a plant important to the region's environment. Workers rescued some of the many fish, birds, and animals. They also protected some fish hatcheries. But later on, some wildlife died after eating fish or animals that were poisoned by the spill.

Drawing Conclusions Recall the last time you listened to someone talk about a problem. Did you make judgments about how the problem started? Or get ideas about how to fix the problem? Or guess how people might react to it? If you did any of these things, you were drawing a conclusion. You based your conclusion on the facts as you understood them.

Reread the paragraphs on pages 202–203 that are under the heading "The Cleanup." From the information presented, what conclusion can you draw about why the oil spill was difficult to clean up? Write your conclusion on the lines below.

_____

_____

The Effects of the Oil Spill

Just after the oil spill, many people believed that wildlife would never return to Prince William Sound. Yet less than a year later, the air and water were clear again. Fish and whales that had survived the spill returned to the sound in the spring as they always had. Plants began to grow again.

The environment had changed, however. By spring of 1991, many groups of sea birds had not recovered from the spill. Scientists said it would take from 20 to 70 years for the birds to build up their numbers to the population levels before the spill. Injuries to other wildlife were just beginning to show. Studies showed that oil still at the bottom of the sound continued to harm the sea life.

In 1994 a federal court jury ordered the Exxon Corporation to pay $5 billion to Alaskans who earned their living fishing. Native American companies and Alaskan cities also shared this award. In a separate settlement, the United States and Alaskan governments won $900 million. To administer that money, state and federal officials formed the *Exxon Valdez* Oil Spill Trustee Council, with headquarters in Anchorage. This group uses the settlement money to restore natural resources and the activities that depend on these resources, such as commercial fishing and tourism. The council monitors and evaluates restoration activities and meets several times a year to report on the progress of recovery efforts.

Check your answer on page 251. **203**

Thinking About the Article

Practice Vocabulary

The words below are in the passage in bold type. Study the way each word is used. Then complete each sentence by writing the correct word.

sound   **environment**   **glacier**

iceberg   **crude oil**

1. A(n) _____ is an inlet of the ocean.

2. A nearby body of water has a strong influence on the surroundings in a marine _____ .

3. A(n) _____ is formed when snow and ice accumulate on land over a long period of time.

4. Tar and gasoline are two products that come from

   _____ .

5. A(n) _____ poses dangers to ocean liners and other ships traveling in northern waters.

Understand the Article

Write the answer to each question.

6. Describe how the accident in Prince William Sound occurred.

   _____

   _____

   _____

7. What caused the oil spill to travel so far from the accident site?

   _____

   _____

8. What happened to the environment around Prince William Sound as a result of the oil spill?

   _____

   _____

   _____

Apply Your Skills

Circle the number of the best answer for each question.

9. Which of the following dictionary definitions for *sound* gives the meaning used in the article and shown on the map?
   (1) anything that can be heard
   (2) a long narrow channel connecting large bodies of water
   (3) a long inlet of the ocean
   (4) energy in the form of pressure waves
   (5) an air-filled bladder in a fish's body

10. The spring after the oil spill, plants sprouted, whales returned, and salmon catches were high. Based on this information and what you read in the article, which conclusion might you draw about the cleanup?
    (1) Every part of the cleanup was a success.
    (2) The cleanup harmed more living things than it helped.
    (3) The water in the sound could no longer support life.
    (4) The cleanup removed all the oil in Prince William Sound.
    (5) The cleanup helped some living things in the environment.

Connect with the Article

Write your answer to each question.

11. Locate the wildlife refuges on the map on page 202. What problems might workers at hotels near these refuges have faced during the rest of 1989? Explain your answer.

    _____

    _____

    _____

12. The year after the oil spill, Congress created an oil-spill cleanup fund as a result of the *Exxon Valdez* accident. The money for the fund comes from taxes on crude oil. Do you think this tax affects the price you pay for oil products, such as gasoline? Explain your answer.

    _____

    _____

    _____

    _____

Taking Care of Resources

Vocabulary

topsoil

desertification

drought

overgrazing

displace

ecotourism

When you choose your activities, you may ask yourself, "Do I have enough money for this?" or "How much time will it take?" Money and time are two resources that are important to many people.

A resource is anything that people can use to satisfy their needs. Natural resources are essential materials supplied by nature. They include water, land on which plants can grow, and minerals. Natural resources support all of our activities. Without natural resources, life would be impossible. Therefore, preserving natural resources is a matter of vital importance to everyone.

Relate to the Topic

This lesson is about a global threat to productive land. Think back over the past 24 hours. List some things you ate that grew on or fed from the land.

_____

Why is it important to preserve productive land? _____

_____

_____

Reading Strategy

PREVIEWING A BAR GRAPH   Looking ahead at illustrations, such as bar graphs, can help you guide your reading. Look at the bar graph on page 208. Consider why this information might be given. Then answer the questions.

1. What is one word that you expect the lesson to explain? _____
   Hint: Study the title of the graph.

2. What three types of land usage do you expect you will learn about? _____

   _____

   _____

   Hint: Look at the legend to the graph.

Preserving Productive Land

With the gales came the dust. Sometimes it was so thick that it completely hid the sun. . . . At other times a cloud is seen to be approaching from a distance of many miles. Already it has the banked appearance of a cumulus cloud, but it is black instead of white, and it hangs low, seeming to hug the earth. . . . Birds fly in terror before the storm, and only those that are strong of wing may escape.

Where did these storms take place? In the African Sahara? Actually, this description came from a Kansas wheat farmer. He is talking about the Dust Bowl, a name given to parts of Texas, Oklahoma, Kansas, New Mexico, and Colorado in the 1930s. Winds raging across the Dust Bowl blew away the **topsoil**—the surface soil usually anchored down by plants. "Black blizzards" closed down roads and schools in many parts of the country. Some people even got sick and died from inhaling the dust.

The Dust Bowl was an example of **desertification,** or the turning of productive land into desert. But desertification was not a problem only of mid-twentieth-century America. According to the United Nations, in recent years desertification has affected more than a billion people in more than 110 countries.

Causes and Effects of Desertification

Although desertification is a complex process, two main factors contribute to it. One factor is **drought**—a long period of unusually dry weather in a region that normally receives rain. Drought is a natural factor in desertification. It results in not only lack of rain, but also the drying out of soil. Some droughts last for years. In most cases, however, droughts end. The rain returns, and the land becomes productive again—especially when people have taken care of it.

The other main factor in desertification is abuse of the land by people. One kind of abuse is **overgrazing.** This is the practice of letting too many animals feed on the grasses or of letting animals feed in one part of an area for too long. Cutting down too many trees and farming the land too heavily are other kinds of abuse. These are common practices in places where people are poor and depend on agriculture for their living. Abuse of the land ruins the ability of plants to hold topsoil in place.

Either drought or overgrazing can cause desertification. When both occur, the process speeds up. This is what happened in the Dust Bowl, when decades of overfarming were followed by drought. Thousands of family farms in the Dust Bowl and in nearby regions were ruined as a result.

Blowing dust troubles parts of the world that suffer from desertification. In addition, an increased amount of dust in the air makes it harder for raindrops to form, and lack of rain makes the situation even worse. Finally, dust can travel far enough to damage plants in areas that are not subject to either drought or abuse.

In such conditions, many people are **displaced,** or forced to leave their homes, because of the lack of food. Displaced people create a drain on resources wherever they settle.

Since the Dust Bowl, there have been other extreme cases of desertification. A disaster in the Sahel, a region of western Africa, focused the world's attention on the problem. The Sahel lies between the Sahara to the north and the savannah (tropical/subtropical grasslands) to the south. On average, less than eight inches of rain falls on the Sahel each year. Despite the dry conditions, people raised crops and herds there—often to the point of abusing the land. Between 1968 and 1974, the Sahel suffered a terrible drought. More than 200,000 people and millions of animals starved to death. Another drought brought more suffering to the region in the 1980s.

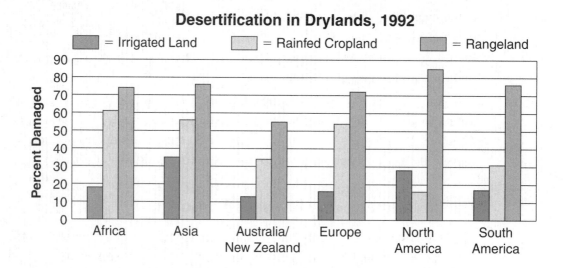

Desertification in Drylands, 1992

Reading a Triple Bar Graph Some bar graphs are used to compare information. The triple bar graph above is based on a 1992 study of the world's drylands— regions that can be productive even with little rainfall. The bar graph shows the percentage of drylands in various regions that are estimated to have been damaged by desertification. Use the graph's key to compare the bars.

1. Where has there been more damage to irrigated cropland than to rainfed cropland?
   a. in Asia
   b. in North America

2. Which continents have suffered similar percentages of damage to rainfed cropland?
   a. Australia and South America
   b. South America and Europe

Beating Back the Desert

The Sahel disaster prompted scientists to examine desertification in depth. Based on the information shown in the bar graph on the previous page, they concluded that desertification is a global problem. But it is a problem with solutions. Some methods of preserving land from desertification use state-of-the-art technology. For example, satellite pictures help scientists look for signs of desertification around the world. Many other techniques are more traditional. The United Nations has set up anti-desertification programs in many countries. It does much of its work at the local level, using methods that already are familiar to people or that can be taught easily.

For example, the United Nations encouraged farmers in Brazil to return to a traditional technique called "zero tillage." Using this technique, farmers do not plow their land, but drill seeds through existing plant cover. Zero tillage not only has reduced the loss of soil but has also produced larger corn and soybean harvests. The people of Zhangeldy, in Kazakhstan, also have worked with the UN to combat desertification. They have changed the way that they graze their sheep in order to help prevent overgrazing. With the help of the UN and the Zambia Alliance of Women, women in the community of Shantumbu, Zambia, have been exploring different ways of preserving and healing their damaged drylands. For example, instead of trying to raise crops there, they have turned to raising chickens and pigs for food and income. They are reducing their production of charcoal, which they formerly used for fuel and sold to people in nearby urban areas. Charcoal requires cutting down and burning trees. By reducing charcoal production, the people of Shantumbu are helping to save their forests. They are also promoting ecotourism in the region. **Ecotourism** is travel to areas of natural or ecological interest. The people of Shantumbu can earn money through ecotourism while preserving their local environment.

Recognizing Unstated Assumptions Information that you read is usually based on certain **assumptions,** or beliefs. For example, a writer discussing jogging may assume that his or her readers are interested in improving their health. Sometimes writers explain such assumptions. Other times the assumptions are left unstated. In the first paragraph on this page, what is an unstated assumption about change at the local level?

    a.   People who live in an area have the greatest motivation to improve that area.

    b.   Most people are suspicious of high-tech answers to local problems.

Governments can fight desertification on a national level. For example, China has experienced increasing sandstorms because of desertification. In 2002 the Chinese government announced a tree-planting program that would convert cropland to forests. If the program is successful, it should limit desertification dramatically. To succeed, however, the program needs funding of more than $1 billion a year as well as the support of farmers whose land will be taken. At both the national and local levels, stopping desertification is important—but it is not necessarily easy.

Thinking About the Article

Practice Vocabulary

The words below are in the passage in bold type. Study the way each word is used. Then complete each sentence by writing the correct word.

topsoil	**desertification**	**drought**
displaced	**overgrazing**	**ecotourism**

1. When _____ people find a place to settle, they face economic and social challenges in their new homes.

2. Herders who practice _____ can ruin the very pastures they need.

3. During the Dust Bowl, winds blew exposed _____ into "black blizzards" that disrupted people's lives.

4. Some ways of combating _____ include planting trees and adopting zero-tillage farming.

5. _____ can build the economy of a poor area and educate visitors about the environment.

6. Land that has suffered from a period of _____ can become productive again when rains return.

Understand the Article

Write the answer to each question.

7. What factors caused the Dust Bowl? _____

_____

_____

8. What event brought desertification to the world's attention?

_____

_____

_____

9. Name something that Brazilian farmers have done to preserve the land.

_____

_____

_____

Apply Your Skills

Circle the number of the best answer for each question.

10. Look at the bar graph on page 208. Which of the following statements about desertification does the information in the bar graph support?
    (1) Desertification has damaged more land in Australia than in Europe.
    (2) Rangeland has been managed and preserved best in Asia.
    (3) Irrigated land has suffered more damage than rainfed cropland.
    (4) Rangeland has suffered more damage than cropland.
    (5) Desertification happens fastest when drought strikes abused land.

11. How does drought differ from desertification?
    (1) Desertification refers to land; drought refers to the weather.
    (2) Both drought and desertification can ruin productive land.
    (3) Unlike desertification, drought does not affect the topsoil.
    (4) Land can be reclaimed from drought, but not from desertification.
    (5) Drought is the effect; desertification is the cause.

12. Reread the quotation and the first paragraph on page 207. What unstated assumption must the reader make to fully understand the paragraph?
    (1) The Dust Bowl was caused by desertification.
    (2) The Dust Bowl caused a great deal of damage to farms.
    (3) Black blizzards were raging dust storms.
    (4) Clouds of dust can be seen from miles away.
    (5) Airborne dust can cause severe health hazards.

Connect with the Article

Write your answer to each question.

13. What connection do you see between poverty and land abuse?

_____

_____

14. If you were trying to make the tree-planting program in China succeed, how would you gain the support of farmers who do not want to lose their cropland?

_____

_____

_____

Geography at Work

Transportation: Ticket Agent

Many people love to travel and to see new places or visit old favorites. Other people travel for business or personal reasons. Whether it's travel to a local or faraway spot, ticket agents help travelers get to their destinations on trains, subways or elevated rail cars. Ticket agents work for railroads or public transit systems. Because they have contact with customers, they should enjoy working with people.

Ticket agents help customers plan departure and arrival times, determine how long a trip will take, book reservations, and buy their tickets. Agents need to have good geography skills. They need to read maps, use tables and charts, and work with fare schedules. They must have a good understanding of directions and know where places are. Because they help customers set travel schedules, ticket agents must have good time measurement and arithmetic skills.

Look at the chart showing some of the careers in transportation.

- Do any of the careers interest you? If so, which ones?

- What information would you need to find out more about those careers? On a separate piece of paper, write some questions that you would like answered. You can find out more information about those careers in the *Occupational Outlook Handbook* at your local library or online.

Some Careers in Transportation

Transportation Ticket Agent makes reservations, sells tickets, and answers customers' questions

Station Agent assists travelers with special needs

Travel Clerk plans routes, calculates mileage, and answers questions

Passenger Rate Clerk sells tickets, plans special or chartered trips, works with customers

Rail ticket agents help customers plan their trips and make reservations. **Use the timetable and map below to fill in the spaces in the conversation that follows.**

Eastern Rail Line Timetable—Route: Washington, D.C., to New York, NY

Train	Washington, D.C. Departure Time	Baltimore Arrival/Departure Times	Philadelphia Arrival/Departure Times	New York
18	5:30 A.M.	6:15 A.M./6:20 A.M.	7:34 A.M./7:39 A.M.	8:59 A.M.
126	6:15 A.M.	7:00 A.M./7:05 A.M.	8:19 A.M./8:24 A.M.	9:44 A.M.
150	9:00 A.M.	9:45 A.M./9:50 A.M.	11:04 A.M./11:09 A.M.	12:29 P.M.
200	1:56 P.M.	3:41 P.M./3:46 P.M.	4:50 P.M./4:55 P.M.	6:15 P.M.

RAIL AGENT: "Good morning. This is the Eastern Rail Line. May I help you?"

CUSTOMER: "Yes. Do you have any trains leaving from the Washington, D.C., area that will get me into New York City by 12:30 p.m.?

RAIL AGENT: "We have _____ trains that arrive before 12:30 p.m. The train numbers are: _____ ; _____ ; and _____ ."

CUSTOMER: "I have an appointment at 12:45 p.m. in New York. Which train should I take?"

RAIL AGENT: "There is a train that arrives at _____ , but that will only leave you 16 minutes to get to your meeting. I recommend you take train number 126. It arrives in New York at _____ . It will give you plenty of time to get to your meeting."

CUSTOMER: "What is your first stop north of Washington, D.C.?"

RAIL AGENT: "_____ is the first stop north of Washington, D.C."

CUSTOMER: "That stop is closer to my house; I will catch the train there. Thank you. I'd like to buy my ticket now."

RAIL AGENT: "I will be happy to help you."

Check your answers on page 252.

Unit 5 Review
Geography

Robert E. Peary Reaches the North Pole

Explorer Robert E. Peary led many trips to the Arctic. The first was in 1891 when Peary explored northern Greenland and proved that it is an island. In 1898 he set out to find the North Pole. On that trip, Peary came within 390 miles of the pole, but hardships forced him to turn back.

In 1902 and from 1905 to 1906, Peary tried twice more to reach the pole. On the 1905–1906 trip, he came within 200 miles. This time, ice storms forced him to go home. However, Peary refused to give up. In 1908 he organized a fourth expedition, which included his assistant Matthew Henson and four Inuit. Finally, Peary succeeded. On April 6, 1909, his group reached the North Pole. They had traveled as far north as anyone can go on Earth.

For many years, some scientists thought that Peary had figured his location incorrectly and had not really reached the North Pole. In 1989 a group of explorers carefully studied Peary's notes and his log of compass readings. These proved Peary and his group were the first to reach the North Pole.

Circle the number of the best answer.

1. What is the main idea of this article?
   (1) Robert E. Peary was the only person ever to reach the North Pole.
   (2) Peary was the first person to prove that Greenland is an island.
   (3) Peary and his group were the first people to reach the North Pole.
   (4) Peary tried to reach the North Pole over almost a dozen years.
   (5) Some people doubted that Peary had reached the North Pole.

2. Study the map on page 215 and review the article. Based on the map and passage, which conclusion can you make about why Peary succeeded in 1909?
   (1) Peary followed the same route each time and eventually made it.
   (2) Peary followed a northerly route from the land that lay closest to the pole.
   (3) In 1909 Peary started in Greenland rather than in Canada.
   (4) Peary figured he could double his 1906 distance in 1909.
   (5) Peary followed a northerly route along the 70° W line of longitude.

Robert E. Peary Reaches the North Pole

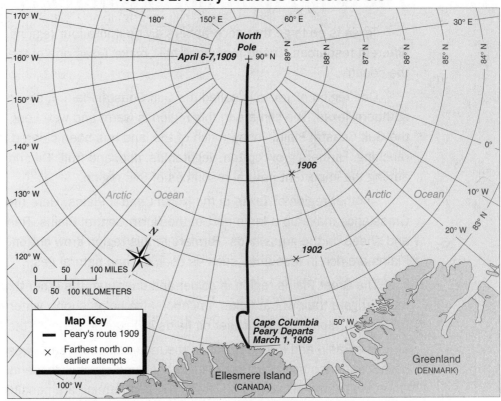

Write or circle the answer to each question.

3. Where did the ocean-going part of Robert E. Peary's final trip to the North Pole begin?

   _____

4. What latitude did Peary reach on his trip in 1902? _____

5. What latitude did Peary reach on his trip in 1906? _____

6. Which unstated assumption helps explain why it was so difficult for Peary to reach the North Pole?
   (1) The North Pole is too distant from land to be reached.
   (2) The North Pole is on the polar ice cap and is bitterly cold.
   (3) The North Pole was inhabited by unfriendly Inuit peoples.
   (4) The nearby nations did not want the explorers to reach the North Pole.
   (5) The expeditions did not have enough people and supplies.

The Geographic Regions of Texas

Texas is so large that geographers divide it into four regions. Each region has different resources. Those resources help make Texas one of the richest states in the country.

One region of Texas is called the Gulf Coastal Plain. It covers eastern and southern Texas. The climate in this region is warm and wet. Long ago forests covered the Gulf Coastal Plain. Today, much of the land has been cleared for farming and ranching. Farmers grow cotton, vegetables, rice, and fruit. Oil and natural gas are among the important natural resources of this region.

Another region of Texas is the North Central Plains. Here the climate is drier. Grasslands make up a large part of the North Central Plains. Ranchers graze cattle and sheep on the grasslands. Farmers in this region grow cotton. The North Central Plains are rich in resources such as coal, oil, and natural gas.

The Great Plains region is colder and drier than the other three regions. Farmers must irrigate their wheat fields. Irrigation also helps supply water to the ranchers of this region. Some of the richest oil fields in Texas lie beneath the Great Plains.

The Basin and Range region is the mountainous area in western Texas. Miners have found resources such as gold, copper, and silver in these mountains. Like the Great Plains, the climate is dry. Ranching and farming are possible only through the use of irrigation.

Circle the number of the best answer.

7. How do the farmers and ranchers of Texas use irrigation?
   (1) as a way to find rich oil fields
   (2) to help them find gold and silver
   (3) as a way to find natural gas deposits
   (4) to get water for their crops and animals
   (5) to get water from other regions

8. Someone who wants to go into ranching in Texas should settle in the North Central Plains. Which information best supports this conclusion?
   (1) Grassland covers much of the North Central Plains.
   (2) The North Central Plains is drier than the Gulf Coastal Plain.
   (3) The soil of the North Central Plains is not good for raising crops.
   (4) Coal and oil are two resources of the North Central Plains.
   (5) To varying extents, each region supports ranching activity.

Top Ten Cattle-Raising and Oil-Producing States

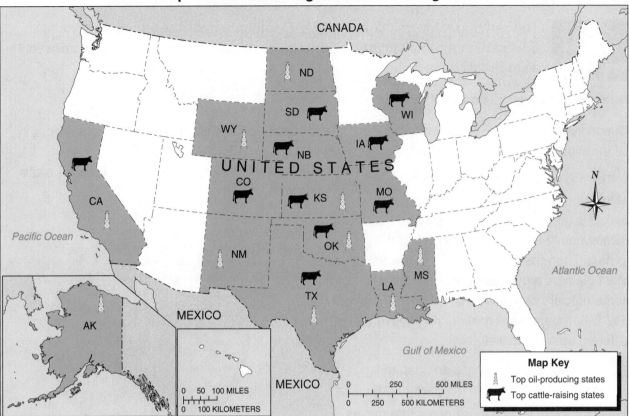

Write or circle the answer to each question.

9. How can you tell which states lead in cattle production?

_____

10. In addition to New Mexico, which states lead in oil production but not in cattle production?

_____

11. Which of the following can be determined from the map?
    (1) how much oil is produced in the top oil-producing states
    (2) how long Alaska has been one of the top oil-producing states
    (3) how many states are top producers of both oil and cattle
    (4) why the states that lead in both categories border each other
    (5) why no state in the Northeast leads in either category

Social Studies Extension

Borrow a videotape about the Arctic from your local library. As you watch the video, list the features that make the Arctic region special. Write down at least one new fact about the region that you learn from the video.

Mini-Test Unit 5

This is a 15-minute practice test. After 15 minutes, mark the last number you finished. Then complete the test and check your answers. If most of your answers were correct but you did not finish, try to work faster next time.

Directions: Choose the <u>one best answer</u> to each question.

Questions 1 and 2 refer to the following information.

The movement of glaciers shaped large parts of the Northern Hemisphere long ago. What makes a glacier move? Pressure and heat from friction cause the ice at the bottom of the glacier to melt. Then the glacier can slide downhill. Most glaciers move about one foot per day, but some glaciers can move more than 100 feet per day. Different parts of glaciers may move at different speeds as well.

1. Which of the following is an unstated assumption related to the paragraph?

    (1) A glacier is a mass of ice that moves over land.
    (2) The speed of glaciers can vary.
    (3) Africa probably was not shaped by the movement of glaciers.
    (4) Most glaciers do not move.
    (5) Glaciers no longer exist.

2. Which of the following <u>best</u> summarizes the main idea of the paragraph?

    The movement of glaciers is caused by

    (1) the chemical composition of the ice
    (2) melting at the bottom of the glacier and gravity
    (3) pressure changes at the glacier's surface
    (4) temperature changes at the glacier's surface
    (5) friction at the glacier's surface

Question 3 refers to the following circle graph.

Volume of Water in the Great Lakes

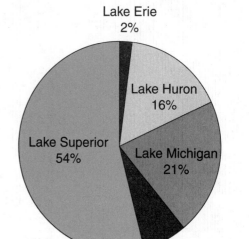

3. In terms of volume, Lake Superior is larger than all the other Great Lakes combined. Based on the graph, which of the following statements is both accurate and adequate to support this conclusion?

    Lake Superior

    (1) is smaller than Lake Michigan
    (2) is larger than Lake Erie
    (3) is larger than Lake Huron and Lake Ontario
    (4) has 2935 cubic miles of water
    (5) has 54% of the total volume of the Great Lakes

Questions 4 and 5 refer to the following information.

One of the major themes of geography is migration. Migration occurs when individuals or groups of people move from one place to another and resettle. Migration has two types of causes: push factors and pull factors.

Push factors force people to move. Drought, famine, and natural disaster are push factors. Other push factors are unemployment, war, and overpopulation.

Pull factors encourage people to move, but moving is a choice. When pull factors are at work, a different place seems to offer people better housing, better job opportunities, or an overall better standard of living.

4. Which of the following is the <u>best</u> conclusion about the nature of push factors?

When push factors exist,

(1) people are attracted to a different place
(2) people are happy about moving
(3) drought and famine kill many people
(4) moving is a matter of survival
(5) war is very likely to break out

5. Which of the following is an example of a pull factor?

(1) Kurds leaving Iraq during a civil war in the 1990s
(2) Jews escaping from anti-Semitism in Nazi Germany in the 1930s
(3) Irish families leaving Ireland during the potato famine in the 1840s
(4) Americans moving west to settle their own farms during the 1800s
(5) Africans traveling to North and South America as slaves in the 1700s

Questions 6 and 7 refer to the following bar graph.

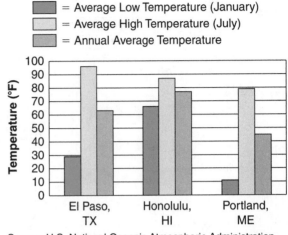

Average Temperatures in Selected U.S. Cities

Source: U.S. National Oceanic Atmospheric Administration

6. Based on the graph, where would you be most likely to use the same clothes all year?

(1) Portland, because its average high temperature is comfortable
(2) El Paso, because its average temperature is comfortable
(3) Honolulu, because its high and low temperatures are close
(4) all three cities, because their average temperatures are similar
(5) none of the cities, because they all have hot summers

7. Portland is farther north than Honolulu and El Paso. Based on the information on the graph, which generalization does this fact support?

In the United States,

(1) longitude has little to do with the weather
(2) latitude has little to do with the weather
(3) the farther north you go, the less the weather varies from season to season
(4) places in the north always have cold weather
(5) places in the north tend to be colder than places in the south

Posttest
Social Studies

Name: _____ Class: _____ Date: _____

1 ① ② ③ ④ ⑤   14 ① ② ③ ④ ⑤

2 ① ② ③ ④ ⑤   15 ① ② ③ ④ ⑤

3 ① ② ③ ④ ⑤   16 ① ② ③ ④ ⑤

4 ① ② ③ ④ ⑤   17 ① ② ③ ④ ⑤

5 ① ② ③ ④ ⑤   18 ① ② ③ ④ ⑤

6 ① ② ③ ④ ⑤   19 ① ② ③ ④ ⑤

7 ① ② ③ ④ ⑤   20 ① ② ③ ④ ⑤

8 ① ② ③ ④ ⑤   21 ① ② ③ ④ ⑤

9 ① ② ③ ④ ⑤   22 ① ② ③ ④ ⑤

10 ① ② ③ ④ ⑤   23 ① ② ③ ④ ⑤

11 ① ② ③ ④ ⑤   24 ① ② ③ ④ ⑤

12 ① ② ③ ④ ⑤   25 ① ② ③ ④ ⑤

13 ① ② ③ ④ ⑤

Directions

This is a 40-minute practice test. After 40 minutes, mark the last number you finished. Then complete the test and check your answers. If most of your answers were correct but you did not finish, try to work faster next time.

The PreGED Social Studies Posttest consists of multiple-choice questions that measure general social studies concepts. The questions are based on short readings and/or illustrations, including maps, graphs, charts, cartoons, or other figures. Study the information given and then answer the question(s) following it. Refer to the information as often as necessary in answering the questions.

Record your answers on the answer sheet on page 220, which you may photocopy. To record your answer, fill in the numbered circle on the answer sheet that corresponds to the answer you select for each question in the Posttest.

After you complete the Posttest, check your answers on pages 253–254. Then use the Posttest Evaluation Chart on page 231 to identify the social studies skills and content areas that you need to practice more. Fill in the numbered circle on the answer sheet that corresponds to the answer that you select for each test question.

EXAMPLE

The Declaration of Independence was drafted by Thomas Jefferson in which year?

(1) 1620
(2) 1700
(3) 1776
(4) 1789
(5) 1860

(On Answer Sheet)

①②●④⑤

The correct answer is "1776"; therefore, answer space 3 would be marked on the answer sheet.

If you do not use the answer sheet provided, mark your answers on each test page by circling the correct answer for each question.

Directions: Choose the one best answer to each question.

Questions 1 and 2 are based on the information and the photograph below.

The first televised presidential debates were between Senator John F. Kennedy and Vice-President Richard M. Nixon. Nixon was recovering from a knee injury and came to the first debate looking pale and underweight. Kennedy, on the other hand, had taken time off the day before the debate. He had been campaigning out-of-doors in California and looked tanned and relaxed. People who listened to the first debate on the radio heard two politicians who were quite close in their views. People who watched the debate on television saw great contrasts in the way the two candidates presented themselves on camera.

1. Based on the information and the photograph, what difference between the two candidates did televising the debates highlight?

   (1) their debate experience

   (2) their political views

   (3) their understanding of key issues

   (4) their physical appearance and poise

   (5) their mental health

2. In an extremely close race, John F. Kennedy won the 1960 presidential election. What can you infer about the impact of the debates on the outcome of the election?

   (1) The debates had no effect on the outcome.

   (2) Richard Nixon's greater experience impressed voters.

   (3) Televising the debates prompted voters to be influenced by the candidates' appearance.

   (4) Voters felt that they could support a senator over the vice-president.

   (5) More people listened to the debates over the radio than watched them on television.

Questions 3 and 4 are based on the following paragraph from the U.S. government's *Occupational Outlook Handbook.*

"Applicants for reservation and transportation ticket agent jobs are likely to encounter considerable competition because the supply of qualified applicants exceeds the expected number of job openings. Entry requirements for these jobs are minimal, and many people seeking to get into the airline industry or travel business often start out in these types of positions. These jobs provide excellent travel benefits, and many people view airline and other travel-related jobs as glamorous."

3. Which statement best summarizes the paragraph?

    (1) It is easy to get a job as a ticket agent.

    (2) People who like to travel are likely to be good ticket agents.

    (3) Although getting a job as a ticket agent is easy, it is not desirable, because the job does not lead to career advancement.

    (4) Jobs in the travel industry are interesting and exciting.

    (5) Getting a job as a ticket agent may be difficult, but such a job can lead to advancement in the travel industry.

4. Which of the following statements is a fact, not an opinion, related to the passage?

    (1) There are qualifications for a ticket agent job.

    (2) It would be fun to become a ticket agent.

    (3) Taking a job as a ticket agent would be a foolish career move.

    (4) Travel-related jobs are exciting.

    (5) Only people who like to travel should become ticket agents.

Question 5 refers to the following information.

5. The Tenth Amendment to the U.S. Constitution reads: "The powers not delegated to the United States by the Constitution, nor prohibited by it to the States, are reserved to the States respectively, or to the people."

Which issue in U.S. political history is based on how the Tenth Amendment is interpreted?

    (1) state vs. local control of schools

    (2) federal government power vs. states' rights

    (3) the expansion of U.S. national boundaries

    (4) affirmative action for women and minorities

    (5) campaign finance reform

 Go on to the next page.

Questions 6 and 7 refer to the following map of the world.

Oceans and Continents of the World

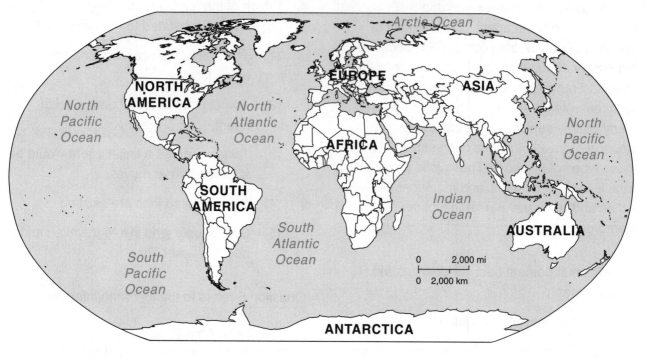

6. Which of the following statements is supported by information on the map?

    (1) Every continent is more than 4,000 miles wide.

    (2) The continents closest to the equator are the warmest.

    (3) Each of the world's oceans is divided into northern and southern regions.

    (4) Three of the world's oceans border the continent of Antarctica.

    (5) South America and Africa used to be part of a single, large land mass.

7. Who could make the best use of the information on this map?

    (1) a weather reporter

    (2) a family planning a trip

    (3) a geography teacher

    (4) an Asian tourist in North America

    (5) an international delivery service

Questions 8 and 9 are based on the following passage.

In 1830 Congress passed the Indian Removal Act, authorizing the federal government to take Native American lands in the East; in exchange tribes would receive land in Indian Territory (Oklahoma). By 1833 all of the southeastern tribes except the Cherokee had agreed to move.

In a letter to a principal Cherokee chief, members of the tribe wrote, "We the great mass of the people think only of the love we have to our land . . . . to let [the land] go will be like throwing away . . . [our] mother that gave . . . [us] birth." But in 1835 federal agents persuaded some chiefs to give up all Cherokee lands for $5.6 million and free passage west.

In 1838 the federal government forcibly removed the Cherokees from their lands. Many had no time to collect their possessions. The trip was harsh; about one-quarter of the people died. The Cherokee called this journey the "Trail of Tears."

8. What was a main reason the Cherokee did not want to move to Indian Territory?

(1) They had deep ties to their land.

(2) They did not like the land in Oklahoma.

(3) They did not have enough time to pack.

(4) There were not enough wagons for them.

(5) They did not accept the authority of the U.S. government.

9. What information supports the conclusion that Native Americans did not have the same rights as other Americans?

(1) Some tribes agreed to the removal.

(2) Some tribes were forced off their land.

(3) The Cherokee received only $5.6 million.

(4) The Cherokee had split leadership.

(5) The journey west was harsh.

Question 10 is based on the following information and the map.

Babylonia was one of the world's first civilizations. It developed in the area where the Tigris and Euphrates rivers flow into the Persian Gulf.

Ancient Kingdom of Babylonia

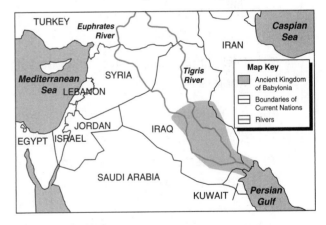

10. The area that was once the ancient kingdom of Babylonia is part of which modern nation?

(1) Kuwait

(2) Saudi Arabia

(3) Jordan

(4) Syria

(5) Iraq

   Go on to the next page.

Questions 11 and 12 are based on the following bar graph.

Percentage of Workers Using Computer Technology

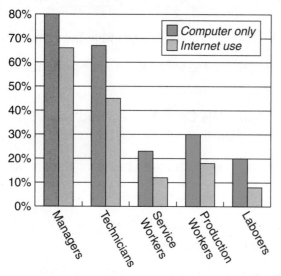

Legend:
- Computer only
- Internet use

Questions 13 and 14 are based on this political cartoon about the scandal surrounding the collapse of the Enron corporation in 2001.

11. What is the main purpose of this graph?

    To show a comparison of

    (1) managerial and technical computer use

    (2) service and labor computer use

    (3) Internet use among five categories of workers

    (4) computer use among five categories of workers

    (5) computer and Internet use among five categories of workers

12. In which category do a majority of workers use the Internet in their work?

    (1) managers

    (2) technicians

    (3) service workers

    (4) production workers

    (5) laborers

13. Which of the following statements is an opinion expressed through this cartoon?

    (1) A janitor should be Speaker of the House of Representatives.

    (2) It is not important to investigate corporate scandals.

    (3) Everyone knows that all politicians are crooks.

    (4) Washington politicians are too involved with big corporations.

    (5) Ordinary people are smarter than politicians.

14. What does this cartoon imply?

    (1) Corporate corruption is very rare.

    (2) Anyone can head an investigation.

    (3) Congress will conduct a thorough and fair investigation of Enron.

    (4) Congress needs to elect new leadership.

    (5) Congress will avoid vigorously investigating Enron.

Questions 15 and 16 are based on the information.

Think Before You Ink

The Voter Education Project has filed complaints against 10 ballot initiative petitioners so far this election season. As a result, two petitioners have been convicted of forgery. They admitted to state investigators that 70% of the signatures they turned over were invalid. Other investigations are pending.

Protect yourself from signature theft. Take a few simple steps before you sign:

Read the front and back of every petition.

Don't let a petitioner rush you into signing something you don't support.

Be wary when petitioners carry more than two or three initiatives. That means they are paid per signature and that's a high incentive for fraud.

Don't sign an initiative more than once.

Don't sign an initiative unless you are registered to vote at the moment you sign.

If you sign, make sure and fill out your **entire name and address** on every initiative. That makes your signature more difficult to forge.

If a petitioner tries to con you, report it immediately to the Oregon Secretary of State or the Voter Education Project.

15. Which of these statements is supported by the voter information in the document above?

   (1) In a ballot initiative, citizens elect candidates to public office.

   (2) By stealing signatures, corrupt people are perverting the political process in Oregon.

   (3) Oregon has been successful in stopping signature fraud.

   (4) You should sign petitions even if you are not registered to vote.

   (5) There is no reason for people to vote on initiatives.

16. Which of the following statements is an example of faulty logic?

   (1) If you are a registered voter, you can sign as many petitions as you like.

   (2) Don't sign any petitions because your signature might be stolen.

   (3) If you sign a petition, you should include your entire name and address.

   (4) Oregon should investigate petitioners who forge signatures.

   (5) Ending fraud on ballot initiatives is a good idea.

Questions 17 and 18 are based on the following passage.

In 1985 a photograph of a beautiful Afghan refugee appeared on the cover of *National Geographic magazine.* This became one of the magazine's most famous covers. However, the girl never revealed her name to the photographer, Steve McCurry. Therefore, McCurry was unable to contact the girl to let her know how famous she had become.

Seventeen years later, a team from *National Geographic* traveled to Afghanistan to try to find the now-grown-up woman. Through a list of contacts that finally led to her brother and husband, the woman was identified as Sharbat Gula. Sharbat's husband and brother agreed to let Sharbat be interviewed. To make sure that this was the right person, the magazine staff obtained proof through iris scanning and face recognition technology.

When they met again, McCurry told Sharbat that her image had become a symbol of the people of Afghanistan. "I don't think she was particularly interested in her personal fame," McCurry said. "But she was pleased when we said she had come to be a symbol of the dignity and resilience of her people."

17. Which of the following is an unstated assumption of this passage?

(1) McCurry photographed an Afghan girl of haunting beauty in 1983.

(2) The girl's name was Sharbat Gula.

(3) Sharbat's culture presented barriers to her being identified.

(4) Sharbat was recontacted through the men in her family.

(5) Sharbat had become a symbol of the Afghan people.

18. Based on the passage, which did Sharbat's culture value?

(1) modesty and privacy

(2) fame and fortune

(3) commercial uses of beauty

(4) art for art's sake

(5) independent action

Questions 19 and 20 are based on the timeline.

1939	1940	1941	1942	1943	1944	1945
Germany invades Poland. U.S. declares neutrality.	France surrenders to Germany.	Japan bombs U.S. Navy at Pearl Harbor. U.S. joins the war on the side of the Allies.		Italy surrenders to the Allies.		Germany surrenders to the Allies. Japan surrenders to the Allies.

19. The United States did not enter World War II until 1941. What spurred this action?

(1) Germany invaded Poland.

(2) France surrendered to Germany.

(3) Japan attacked Pearl Harbor.

(4) Italy surrendered to the Allies.

(5) Japan surrendered to the Allies.

20. The Axis powers—Germany, Japan, and Italy —were finally defeated by the Allies. Which year would you conclude was the turning point in World War II?

(1) 1939

(2) 1940

(3) 1941

(4) 1943

(5) 1945

Questions 21 through 23 are based on the following information.

ANARCHISM A philosophy that advocates the abolition of organized authority, and common ownership of land and the means of production

AUTOCRACY/DESPOTISM A supreme, uncontrolled, unlimited authority, where the right of governing is possessed by a single person

DEMOCRACY A form of government in which the supreme power is retained and exercised directly by the people or indirectly by popular representation

LIBERTARIANISM A philosophy of individual freedom, particularly from any unnecessary restraints imposed by governmental authority

SOCIALISM A system in which the means of production, distribution, and exchange are generally owned by the state and used on behalf of the people

21. If the government owns everything, and there is little or no private property, which political philosophy or system is in effect in the country?

    (1) anarchism

    (2) autocracy

    (3) democracy

    (4) libertarianism

    (5) socialism

22. A country that has one ruler or a single ruling party bases its government on which of the following?

    (1) anarchism

    (2) autocracy

    (3) democracy

    (4) libertarianism

    (5) socialism

23. "We stress that this opposition to hierarchy is not limited to just the state or government. It includes all authoritarian economic and social relationships as well as political ones, particularly those associated with property and wage labor."

    This quote best represents which political philosophy or system?

    (1) anarchism

    (2) autocracy

    (3) democracy

    (4) libertarianism

    (5) socialism

Question 24 is based on the following line graph.

Major Regions of Birth of Foreign-Born Americans, 1960–2000

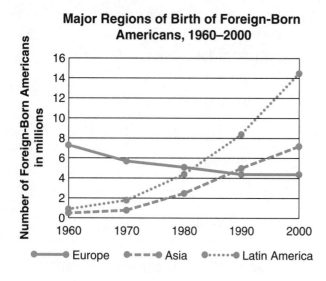

Europe ● Asia ● Latin America

Question 25 is based on the following circle graphs.

Annual Budget for St. Petersburg, Florida

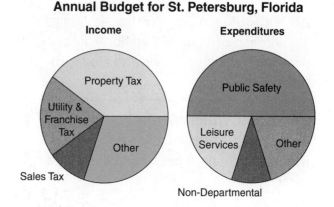

24. Based on the graph, which conclusion can you draw?

(1) Political instability in Asia caused more citizens of Asian nations to immigrate to the United States between 1960 and 2000.

(2) Political and economic conditions were better in Latin America and Asia than in Europe during the 1960s, so there were fewer Latin American and Asian immigrants than European immigrants.

(3) More immigrants were from Europe in the 1960s and 1970s, but by 1990 more Latin American and Asian immigrants lived in the United States.

(4) Today, more Asians than Latin Americans want to live in the United States.

(5) Most Europeans no longer want to live in the United States.

25. Which information from the graphs supports the conclusion that St. Petersburg plans to spend about half of its revenue on police, firefighting, and paramedic operations?

(1) Sales tax and property tax account for about half of the city's income.

(2) Expenditures for public safety account for about half of the city's budget.

(3) The city collects about the same amount for utility and franchise taxes as it spends on parks and other recreational services.

(4) The city has other sources of income in addition to the property tax, utility and franchise taxes, and sales tax it levies.

(5) The city has other expenditures besides those for public safety, leisure services, and non-departmental expenses.

Posttest Evaluation Chart

The chart will help you determine your strengths and weaknesses in social studies content areas and thinking skills.

Directions

Check your answers on page 253–254. Circle the number of each item that you answered correctly on the Posttest. Count the number of items you answered correctly in each row. (For example, in the *U.S. History* row, write the number correct in the blank before */6*, which means *out of 6.)*

Complete this process for the remaining rows. Then add the 5 totals to get your *Total Correct* for the whole Posttest.

If you answered fewer than 20 items correctly, determine the areas in which you need further practice. Go back and review the content in those areas. Page numbers for specific instruction appear in the left-hand column.

If you answered 20 or more items correctly, your teacher may decide that you are ready to go on to Steck-Vaughn's *GED Social Studies* book.

Thinking Skill/ Content Area	Comprehension	Application	Analysis	Evaluation	Total Correct
U.S. History (Pages 14–65)	2	5	1, 8, 24	9	____/6
World History (Pages 66–105)	10		19, 20		____/3
Civics and Government (Pages 106–145)	14	21, 22, 23	13, 16	15	____/7
Economics (Pages 146–185)	3, 11		4, 12	25	____/5
Geography (Pages 186–219)		7	17	6, 18	____/4

Total Correct for Posttest _____ out of 25

Boldfaced numbers indicate questions based on charts, diagrams, graphs, and maps.

PRETEST

PAGES 3–12

1. below 1,000 feet
2. the Great Plains
3. Deserts are dry and few plants grow there.
4. Some deserts are hot. Others are cold.
5. **(2) Living things have developed ways to survive in difficult environments.** Animals can live in all deserts so option 1 is incorrect. Options 3 and 4 are details stated in the article. The article does not discuss option 5.
6. to honor Zeus
7. **(4) way of life** The sentence immediately following *culture* lists things associated with the ancient Greek way of life.
8. North Korea invaded South Korea.
9. China joined North Korea. The U.S. and the United Nations joined South Korea.
10. **(1) North Korea gained control of South Korea's capital.** Option 2 and option 3 took place after China entered the war. Options 4 and 5 took place before China entered the war.
11. **(5) Neither side gained territory from the war.** Nothing on the timeline supports option 1. Option 2 is false. Options 3 and 4 refer to parts of the timeline, but do not reflect the outcome of the entire war.
12. Patriots wanted freedom from Britain. Loyalists wanted to remain under British rule.
13. Slave owners feared African Americans would use their guns to try to end slavery.
14. Many enslaved African Americans joined the British army. Patriot leaders allowed African Americans to join their army.
15. **(3) the loss of so many soldiers at Valley Forge** Options 1, 4, and 5 had no bearing on the policies of Patriot leaders toward African Americans. Option 2 resulted in Patriot leaders allowing free African Americans to join, but not slaves.
16. Idaho, Wyoming, Colorado, and Utah
17. **(1) In 1900 men influenced American government more than women did.** No information is given in the map about options 2, 3, and 5. Option 4 is false.
18. Sample answer: *Segregated* means "African Americans and white Americans did things separately."
19. to demand that Congress pass a civil rights bill
20. **(2) live up to the nation's values and beliefs** In his speech King was not asking Americans

to change their values or to follow Kennedy, so options 1 and 5 are incorrect. Americans were already marching in Washington, D.C., so option 3 is incorrect. Option 4 was the goal of the march but not the main point of King's words.
21. from state primaries and state caucuses and conventions
22. **(3) electors of the Electoral College** Voters elect the electors. The electors, in turn, choose the president and vice president from the national candidates.
23. A benefit tax is in proportion to goods and services used. An ability-to-pay tax is an income tax, with larger incomes taxed at higher rates.
24. The person who makes $25,000 would pay higher taxes under a flat tax.
25. **(4) fairness** Option 1 is not related to taxes. Option 2 is part of the flat-rate tax debate but has not been approved. Options 3 and 5 are not supported in the article.
26. the United States economy
27. The U.S. has saved itself by holding on to the branch with one hand and holding up the Asian economy with the other.
28. **(3) Global economies succeed or fail together.** The United States is holding up Asia, so option 1 is false. Option 2 is a literal interpretation of the cartoon. Option 4 is unlikely in light of what is happening to the U.S. and Asian economies. Option 5 contradicts the cartoon.

UNIT 1: U.S. HISTORY

LESSON 1

PAGE 16

Relate to the Topic

Answers should indicate your ethnic background and your feelings about how it has affected you.

Reading Strategy

1. Native Americans and new Americans
2. Native Americans arrived in North America before the "new" Americans.

PAGE 18

a

4, 2, 1, 3

PAGES 20–21

1. conquistadors
2. indentured servants
3. migrated
4. missions
5. pueblos
6. Immigrants
7. The first people from Asia were following wild game.
8. The Spanish sought wealth. The French sought profit in the fur trade. The British settlers wanted land, a better life, and freedom of religion.
9. disease, starvation, lack of supplies, and attacks by Native Americans
10. The founders of Rhode Island wanted more religious freedom than they had in Massachusetts.
11. **(2) Early English settlements lay north of Spanish settlements.** Option 1 cannot be determined from the map. Options 3, 4, and 5 are false.
12. **(4) The English settled at Jamestown, Virginia.** In chronological order, the other options are (3), (1), (5), and (2).
13. **(3) Pennsylvania** The other options, in chronological order, are (2), (1), (4), and (5).
14. Answers should indicate that later settlers were eager to profit from the land and stole the Native Americans' land instead of seeking their help.
15. Answers should indicate that most came to make a better living or to escape persecution.

LESSON 2

PAGE 22

Relate to the Topic

American colonists might have resisted Great Britain because they wanted to make their own decisions, much like teens resisting their parents' authority.

Reading Strategy

1. Boston, Lexington, and Concord
2. The article will explain why and how two groups of people clashed.

PAGE 23

a

PAGE 25

1. 1765
2. 1770
3. after

PAGES 26–27

1. exports
2. repealed
3. legislature
4. Minutemen
5. imports
6. boycotted
7. Angry colonists forced tax collectors out of town, protested the tax, and refused to buy British goods.
8. Parliament would not repeal the tea tax.
9. The Declaration of Independence explains to the world why the colonists were fighting to be free of British rule.
10. They hid behind fences, barns, and farmhouses along the road.
11. **(4) the Boston Tea Party** The British decided to punish the colonists for the Boston Tea Party by passing harsh laws, which the colonists referred to as the Intolerable Acts.
12. **(5) The American Revolution began.** All the other options were causes leading up to the battles.
13. **(4) 12** The war with France ended in 1763 and the Revolution began in 1775.
14. Sample answer: Many colonists in Spanish colonies may have wondered if they would be better off without their colonial rulers.
15. Sample answer: People might protest or rebel when laws are unfairly enforced.

LESSON 3

PAGE 28

Relate to the Topic

You should briefly describe the situation and how it was resolved.

Reading Strategy

1. a fierce battle
2. African-American soldiers

PAGE 30

My paramount object in this struggle is to save the Union, and is not either to save or destroy slavery.

a

PAGE 31

a

PAGES 32–33

1. Confederacy
2. Emancipation Proclamation
3. Abolitionists
4. discrimination
5. regiment
6. Union
7. cash crop
8. Plantation owners feared financial ruin if slavery was abolished.
9. They feared that allowing African Americans to join the army would upset the border states, who might then side with the Confederacy.
10. Answers should include two of the following: as camp cooks, barbers, spies, gravediggers, messengers, nurses, scouts.
11. Answers should include one of the following: African Americans were paid only half as much as white soldiers. They were not allowed to fight beside white soldiers.
12. **(1) African-American soldiers fought bravely for the Union.** Option 2 is not correct because the painting does not show who won the battle. Option 3 is false because the African-American Union soldiers, not the Confederates, are attacking. Options 4 and 5 are details that support the main idea.
13. **(4) a plantation owner** Options 1, 2, 3, and 5 would have applauded Smalls' heroics.
14. **(5) Freeing slaves in the Confederacy was a Union goal.** The other options are false.
15. Sample answer: The North had factories, while Southerners farmed plantations. Many enslaved African Americans lived in the South, but most African Americans in the North were free.
16. Sample answer: Minorities who move into the community feel uncomfortable. A possible plan is; (1) Welcome minorities who move into the community. (2) Introduce them to civic and religious organizations in the neighborhood. (3) Defend the minority neighbor's rights when other neighbors make racial or religious slurs.

LESSON 4

PAGE 34

Relate to the Topic

Answers will vary with the individual.

Reading Strategy

1. Answers will vary with the individual.
2. Possible answers include dates, statistics, and types of industries involved.

PAGE 35

b

PAGE 37

b

PAGES 38–39

1. Child labor
2. reformers
3. master
4. literate
5. apprentice
6. The master supplied clothing, food, and a place to live.
7. Some parents did not earn enough money to pay for their family's expenses so they needed their children's income to make ends meet.
8. The owners claimed that children could do some jobs better than adults, and they paid children less than they paid adults.
9. Factory owners did not want Hine to take photographs of the conditions in which children were working, nor did they want the state or Congress to pass child labor laws.
10. **(1) Work in garment factories as well as in coal mines posed health hazards for children.** This statement compares two of the places where children commonly worked in the late 1800s and early 1900s.
11. **(2) dirty workplace** The photo shows a floor covered with litter and stains. Options 1 and 5 are not detectable from the photograph. Options 3 and 4 are not supported by the photograph.
12. **(4) An apprentice learned more valuable skills than a factory worker.** Option 1 is true but is a comparison, not a contrast. Options 2, 3, and 5 are false.
13. Sample answer: The picture shows more clearly than any written description why factories are unsuitable for children.
14. Sample answer: Teenage workers should stop work by 9 P.M. on school nights. When a

teenager works more than five hours, he or
she should get a half-hour break.

LESSON 5

PAGE 40

Relate to the Topic
Answers should refer to the team's common goal
and team members' efforts to accomplish the
goal.

Reading Strategy
1. the number (in millions) of women at work
   during the time period in question
2. the years from 1940 through 1950

PAGE 41
a

PAGE 43
a

PAGES 44–45
1. defense contracts
2. defense industry
3. labor force
4. stock market
5. Allies
6. labor unions
7. It offered jobs that had not been available
   before and contributed to the Allies' victory.
8. Sample answer: The government was backing
   the campaign, and experts from New York and
   Hollywood worked on the ads.
9. Many women left their jobs or were let go.
10. They had enjoyed the benefits of a good job
    with good wages.
11. **(5) It ended discrimination in companies
    with national defense contracts.** Option 1 is
    incorrect because the order did not end all
    discrimination. Option 2 is incorrect because
    the order applied only to companies in the
    defense industry. The article does not discuss
    option 3. The article does state that women
    and African Americans earned more than they
    had before the war. However, it does not say
    this was an effect of the presidential order. So,
    option 4 is incorrect.
12. **(1) Many women were unwilling to return to
    the way life was before the war.** Options 2
    and 4 are true but unrelated to changes on the
    graph. Option 3 is related to only one change
    on the graph. Option 5 is false.

13. **(4) women working in the defense industry**
    Rosie the Riveter symbolized women in the
    entire defense industry, so options 1 and 3 are
    incorrect. Rosie the Riveter appeared in the
    movies and on the cover of a magazine but as
    a symbol of women in the defense industry,
    not as an actress or a model. So options 2 and
    5 are incorrect.
14. Sample answer: Yes, because World War II
    helped employ millions of Americans.
15. Sample answer: I would have joined the armed
    forces or worked in the defense industry.

LESSON 6

PAGE 46

Relate to the Topic
Sample answer: The war was fought in Southeast
Asia. The American people were sharply divided
over U.S. involvement in the conflict.

Reading Strategy
Sample questions: Why is there a North Vietnam
and a South Vietnam instead of just one Vietnam?
Were nearby countries involved in the fighting—
and, if so, how?

PAGE 49
Reading a Political Map: b
Drawing Conclusions: a

PAGES 50–51
1. Cold War
2. containment
3. draft
4. deferment
5. communism
6. guerrilla
7. One reason is that the Soviet Union wanted to
   gain back lands in eastern Europe that had
   once been theirs.
8. The United States wanted to stop the spread of
   communism to Southeast Asia.
9. Sample answers: The war cost the government
   too much money. Young Americans were
   dying halfway around the world.
10. through demonstrations and educational
    programs
11. **(4) Guerrilla tactics made the job of American
    soldiers difficult.** Options 1 and 2 are
    opinions that cannot be substantiated with
    facts from the article. No facts in the article
    address options 3 and 5.

12. **(3) the 17° N parallel** The other options are features on the map but none was the boundary between North Vietnam and South Vietnam.

13. **(5) South Vietnam's capital is a far distance from North Vietnam.** North Vietnam's success in capturing South Vietnam would depend on its gaining control of South Vietnam's political center, its capital. Options 1, 2, and 3 are unrelated facts about Vietnam's geography. Option 4 deals with China, not North Vietnam.

14. The Soviets suffered hardships because of the destruction in World War II and wanted to punish the Germans. Americans had not suffered the same kind of hardships but wanted to avoid another war. They felt the best way to do this was to return German life to normalcy.

15. Your answer should describe what conditions are present in the other nation, what are the motives of the attacking nation, and what goal the United States has in sending such assistance.

LESSON 7

PAGE 52

Relate to the Topic
Answers might include telephone, television, radio, computer, and photocopy machine.

Reading Strategy
1. personal computers
2. 1989–2001

PAGE 54

a

PAGE 55

b

PAGES 56–57

1. technology
2. Transistors
3. Internet
4. telecommunications
5. laser
6. communicate
7. It allows them to communicate quickly and easily over long distances.
8. They mean telecommunications devices whose signals travel as radio waves through the air instead of as electrical impulses through wires.

9. Sample answers: individualized computer lessons, computer labs, research capability on the Internet, teaching by computer

10. Many people work at home and send their work electronically to their office.

11. Sample answers: breaking down the communication roadblocks of distance and high costs; encouraging discussions among people from all cultures

12. **(2) the percentage of U.S. homes with personal computers** The graph title indicates that the graph shows U.S. households with personal computers; the label on the vertical axis indicates that the bars represent the percentages of such households.

13. **(3) The percentage of U.S. households having one or more personal computers more than tripled between 1989 and 2001.** The graph shows that between 1989 and 2001, the percentage of U.S. households with personal computers rose from 15 percent to almost 57 percent.

14. **(2) voice broadcasts** The other options are false.

15. Sample answer: New communications technology helped scientists share information more quickly so applications came more quickly.

16. Your answer should reflect your experience.

HISTORY AT WORK

PAGE 59

1. **(3) hot coals** The passage indicates that hot coals were used to heat colonial irons.

2. **(4) Colonial irons were smaller than modern irons** Option 2 is not supported in the text. Options 1, 3, and 5 are false.

3. **(4) all of the above** The reasons are not stated directly, but all three are reasonable explanations.

4. Sample answer: We take the electricity we use today for granted. We think nothing of turning on the light at any hour of the day or night. Back in the colonial era, people did not have electricity. They used candles for light. It took dozens of candles to get the same amount of light we now get from a single light bulb. People had to carry the candles with them when they moved from room to room in order to light the way.

UNIT 1 REVIEW

PAGES 60–63

1. **(1) to protect Spain's claim to La Florida** The king claimed all of La Florida, and wanted to get rid of the French colonists, so option 2 is incorrect. Option 4 is incorrect because Spain reached the Americas long before England or France even tried. The article does not support options 3 or 5.
2. **(2) Juan Ponce de León came to the Americas from Spain.** The other options, in chronological order, are (4), (1), (5), and (3).
3. South Carolina
4. Tennessee
5. 11
6. **(4) They separated the Union and the Confederacy.** None of the border states were along the northern Union or southern Confederacy borders, so options 1 and 2 are incorrect. They did not all separate the states from the western territories so option 3 is incorrect. Option 5 is incorrect because none of these states border the Gulf of Mexico.
7. **(3) The government feared that Japanese Americans might be spies for Japan.** Options 1 and 4 were not causes of the internment. The article does not support options 2 or 5.
8. **(2) The internment of Japanese Americans was an injustice.** The U.S. government apologized many years later and gave survivors money for damages, thus admitting the injustice. Options 1 and 3 are incorrect because the opposites were true. Option 4 is true, but it is not a conclusion supported by the article. There is nothing in the article to support option 5.
9. 1945
10. Union membership steadily decreased to the present.
11. World War II; War production increased when more workers, including women and African Americans, joined the labor force. So more workers joined unions. Production increased even more after the United States entered the war in 1941. The war ended in 1945.
12. **(3) 1935 and 2000** Union membership was about 13 percent in both of these years.

MINI-TEST UNIT 1

PAGES 64–65

1. **(4) was in a confrontation with British soldiers** *(Analysis)* The passage indicates that Crispus Attucks was killed because he was in a crowd that was fired upon by British soldiers.
2. **(5) as a memorial to the Revolution** *(Analysis)* Attucks was remembered as "the first to defy, the first to die." which indicates that he is remembered as the first to die in the American Revolution.
3. **(4) 1931–1940** *(Analysis)* Comparing the two bars on the graph shows that the number of immigrants coming to the United States and the number of emigrants leaving the United States were the closest in the decade 1931–1940.
4. **(2) marched for jobs and against discrimination** *(Comprehension)* The people in the picture are demonstrating, and the signs are about the right to work for all people.
5. **(1) We must unite to fight for our rights.** *(Analysis)* This picture shows individuals united in a cause. They are holding signs that are about the right to work, have shelter, and be free from discrimination.
6. **(4) Supreme Court decisions are based on specific sections of the Constitution.** *(Application)* The paragraph explains that Justice Marshall's decision in *Marbury v. Madison* established that the Supreme Court had the final authority on the constitutionality of laws. This would need to cite specific sections of the U.S. Constitution when making decisions.
7. **(2)** *Marbury v. Madison* **ensured that the judicial branch became an equal partner with the other two branches.** *(Evaluation)* This is the only option supported by the paragraph. The paragraph states that this decision made the Court the final authority on which laws are constitutional and clarified the power of the judicial branch over the legislative branch, which makes laws, and the executive branch, which enforces the laws.

UNIT 2: WORLD HISTORY

LESSON 8

PAGE 68

Relate to the Topic

Sample answer: Large kingdoms and companies offer more power, more profit, and less competition than smaller ones do.

Reading Strategy

1. the location of the Great Wall of China
2. about 1,000 miles (about two lengths of the scale)

PAGE 70

a. s

b. d

PAGE 71

b

PAGES 72–73

1. barbarian
2. peasants
3. dynasty
4. civilization
5. empire
6. Shi Huangdi had the wall built to mark and protect China's northern border.
7. They built up the army instead of the wall.
8. The Mongols put themselves and foreigners into high positions. The Chinese also resented the way their Mongol rulers tolerated people who did not follow traditional Chinese ways.
9. The builders during the Ming dynasty used more durable materials than the earlier builders had used.
10. **(5) The Chinese valued learning over physical strength.** Option 1 cannot be determined from the text. Options 2 and 3 list similarities, not differences, and option 4 is false.
11. **(2) Sui and Ming** Option 1 cannot be correct because the Yuan were Mongols and the Ming were Chinese. Options 3 and 4 are incorrect because although they were all Chinese, one built the wall and the other built the army. Option 5 is not correct because the Mongols and the Yuan are the same.
12. **(3) Tang** Options 1, 2, and 5 relied on the wall rather than an expanded army and weapons

for defense. Option 4 attacked rather than defended.

13. Answers should point out that aircraft can go over the wall to deliver invaders and bombs.
14. Sample answers: Lincoln Memorial and the Hoover Dam. Both are awe-inspiring because of their sizes, and the imagination and effort that went into their making.

LESSON 9

PAGE 74

Relate to the Topic

Sample answer: Life would be less pleasant and life might be shorter.

Reading Strategy

1. inventions from a certain age or time period
2. Sample answer: As I read I will be looking for information about new devices and new ways of doing things.

PAGE 76

a, d, e, c, b

PAGE 77

Sample answers:

a. Dr. Edward Jenner observed that **milkmaids who had had cowpox did not catch smallpox.**

b. He experimented by **injecting a boy with cowpox and later injecting him with smallpox.**

c. The results of the experiment were **that the boy was protected from smallpox, vaccination was invented, and eventually, smallpox was eliminated.**

PAGES 78–79

1. smallpox
2. orchestra
3. vaccination
4. chronometer
5. century
6. immune
7. The harpsichord makes sounds by plucking strings, and the piano makes sounds by hitting strings.
8. The pendulum could not swing regularly on a rolling ship.
9. Timepieces with pendulums would not be very portable and people's movements would make them inaccurate. Harrison's clock was small and worked by springs.

10. He got the idea from observing that milkmaids who had cowpox never got smallpox. He then injected a healthy boy with cowpox, which prevented him from getting smallpox.

11. (2) **steam engine and steam-powered boat** Without a powerful steam engine, the steam-powered boat could not be developed. The pairs of inventions in the other options are mechanically unrelated to each other.

12. (3) **a century** All other options are false.

13. (4) **To win a prize, John Harrison spent 34 years inventing a seagoing chronometer.** Options 1 and 2 refer to important details in the paragraph but are not the best summaries. Options 3 and 5 are false.

14. Sample answer: the piano, which produces sound when the hammers inside hit the strings

15. Sample answers: AIDS, leprosy, cancer, the common cold. Sample reasons; how deadly the diseases are, how painful they are, or how common they are.

LESSON 10

PAGE 80

Relate to the Topic

Sample answer: Some people might appreciate the advice but not the idea that someone else claims to know what is good for them.

Reading Strategy

1. Mexico's gross national product
2. any two of the following: mining, manufacturing, oil, transportation

PAGE 81

a

PAGE 83

b

PAGES 84–85

1. capital
2. liberals
3. Duties
4. conservatives
5. diplomat
6. democracy
7. Díaz sent troops throughout the country. He made strikes illegal and prevented many workers from joining unions.

8. He wanted to show the diplomats that Mexico had a strong leader and hoped that their countries would invest there.

9. Overcrowding and the lack of proper housing led to illness and death.

10. (4) **All foreign diplomats to Mexico approved of its government.** The word *all* signals a hasty generalization. It is unlikely that all foreign diplomats approved of the government under Díaz. The other options state facts.

11. (2) **Manufacturing doubled while Díaz was in office.** Options 1, 3, 4, and 5 are contradicted by the table.

12. (1) **Americans invested more money than the combined investment from Europeans.** The facts in the graph contradict options 2, 3, 4, and 5.

13. Sample answer: The people ate better because the economy improved, but they had little freedom.

14. Sample answer: No amount of money or job security could compensate for the loss of any of my rights and freedoms.

LESSON 11

PAGE 86

Relate to the Topic

Answers should defend your position with a statement of your values or beliefs.

Reading Strategy

1. white people and black people
2. They are in both in the same boat, which is sinking because it is filling up with water.

PAGE 87

1. a
2. b

PAGE 89

b

PAGES 90–91

1. parliament
2. apartheid
3. civil rights
4. Racist
5. republic
6. sanctions
7. suffrage

8. They considered the land of southern Africa their own and wanted to remain in control.
9. Sample answers: They no longer had freedom to move where they wished. They could not get a good education. Their privacy was violated because they had to carry passbooks with personal information.
10. The African National Congress tried to set up private schools, encouraged protest among black Africans, and prepared to fight.
11. **(5) They tried to open nongovernment schools for black children.** Option 1 indicates the ANC valued self-defense. Option 2 indicates that it valued human rights. Option 3 indicates it valued cooperation. Information in option 4 was not indicated in the article.
12. **(2) They are proud.** The cartoonist's exaggerated expression of snobbery with the men's heads tilted back and noses in the air suggests this emotion.
13. **(3) the water** Option 1 stands for solutions to the problems. Option 2 stands for racial harmony. Option 4 indicates the white population of South Africa. Option 5 indicates the black population of South Africa.
14. Answers should indicate that South Africa's economy would suffer.
15. Sample answer: I would end all apartheid laws still in force.

LESSON 12

PAGE 92

Relate to the Topic
Your answer should recap a recent world news story involving conflict in a foreign country.

Reading Strategy
1. Sample question: Who are peacekeepers?
2. Sample question: Where are the countries that make up the Middle East?

PAGE 94
a

PAGE 95
a

PAGES 96–97
1. mediator
2. neutral
3. charter
4. deadlocked

5. provinces, cease-fire
6. Observers are unarmed and few in number. Peacekeeping forces are lightly armed and can number in the thousands.
7. The British had money in the company that ran the canal.
8. Fighting drove the farmers from their fields, which were producing very little anyway because of a three-year drought.
9. **(2) More than half the refugees were women and children.** The photo contradicts options 1, 4, and 5, and does not support option 3.
10. **(3) fighting between people of the same country** All other options are false.
11. **(2) countries that help each other** Options 1 and 3 refer to alternate meanings for *allies*. Option 4 defines *alloys*, and option 5 defines *alleys*.
12. Sample answer: The UN troops were successful in that they protected civilians.
13. Sample answer: If I took the side of one friend, the other will be less willing to let me help find a solution to the dispute.

HISTORY AT WORK

PAGES 99
1. **(2) statue** The excerpt states that "Liberty Enlightening the World" is "better known as the Statue of Liberty."
2. **(3) France** The excerpt states that the statue "was a gift from the French."
3. Sample answer: The Statue of Liberty's face is 14 feet long. "Liberty Enlightening the World" is the original name for the Statue of Liberty. The Statue of Liberty was a gift from the people of France. The Statue of Liberty is covered in copper.

UNIT 2 REVIEW

PAGES 100–103
1. **(4) Russia's new government is struggling.** This answer is supported by the details the passage presents on difficulties the Russian government and the Russian people have faced since the early 1990s in establishing a strong democracy.
2. Russia; the Russian leaders' version of democracy

3. Sample answer: Russia is having difficulty following the recipe for democracy.
4. The way Russia is "cooking up" democracy is not successful.
5. **(5) freedom, impartial justice, and honest elections** The passage points out that many Russians believe in the importance of free elections, freedom of expression, and freedom of religion, but that Russia's democracy is in question because of corrupt law enforcement and questionable election practices.
6. **(4) fleet of ships** The other options are false.
7. **(2) He named an inexperienced nobleman as fleet commander.** Option 5 is false. The other options are true, but only option 2 showed faulty logic that high rank makes up for ability and experience.
8. Sample answer: Because England is an island, its navy would have been its strongest defense. King Philip II was too confident in his nation's strength. Spain required an experienced seaman to plan the attack.
9. Spain used ships to carry riches from the distant parts of its empire back to Spain. So Spanish rulers established settlements on coasts where the riches could be loaded onto the ships.

MINI-TEST UNIT 2

PAGES 104–105

1. **(3) Almost all of these countries became independent within a fifteen-year period.** *(Analysis)* From 1811 to 1825, nine of the ten countries shown gained their independence.
2. **(5) Voltaire and Rousseau were part of the same movement but often disagreed.** *(Comprehension)* The passage focuses on the differences between these two Enlightenment thinkers.
3. **(2) reforming the government** *(Evaluation)* The passage discusses both writers' views on governmental reform.
4. **(4) was a woman** *(Analysis)* According to the table, Hatshepsut's gender made her distinctive.
5. **(1) Amenhotep I** *(Application)* Like Napoleon, Amenhotep I focused on building an empire.
6. **(3) How did the EU develop into more than an economic association?** *(Comprehension)* The passage traces how the association now known as the EU developed from an economic

association to an organization that cooperates on political and other issues as well.
7. **(5) Members never disagree about policy.** *(Analysis)* The word *never* identifies a hasty generalization. Even though the member nations have agreed to cooperate, there is no reason to believe that they always agree on policy issues.

UNIT 3: CIVICS AND GOVERNMENT

LESSON 13

PAGE 108
Relate to the Topic
   Sample answer: I recycle aluminum cans at work but have no storage space at home for other items.
Reading Strategy
1. Sample answers: recycling; getting rid of trash
2. Sample answer: people who do not want to bother recycling their garbage

PAGE 110
   b

PAGE 111
   a

PAGES 112–113
1. landfill
2. ordinances
3. recycling
4. groundwater
5. Constitution
6. Hazardous wastes
7. In the U.S., different levels of government, including federal, state, and local governments, all share the power to tax.
8. They burn, bury, compost, or recycle trash.
9. Some are full, and old landfills have been leaking poisons into the groundwater.
10. Recycling is reprocessing some trash for new purposes. Composting is letting plant and food waste decay on its own.
11. **(1) Americans are too lazy to recycle.** Option 2 does not take into account the symbols within a political cartoon. Option 3 may be true but is not the cartoon's focus. The cartoonist is likely to agree with options 4 and 5, but the character's words center on the cartoonist's main idea.

12. **(5) Local governments have set up different ways to get people to recycle.** The paragraph does not support option 1. Option 2 is a conclusion one might reach from reading the entire article, not just the one paragraph. The subjects of options 3 and 4 are not mentioned.

13. **(3) People care about trash when it hits their pocketbooks.** This statement summarizes that people produce less trash when they have to pay according to how much trash they produce. Options 1, 2, 4, and 5 do not relate to the success of these programs.

14. Sample answer: In many states, more trash is placed in landfills than is burned or recycled.

15. Sample answer: I recycle newspapers and magazines; I could collect aluminum cans that litter parks and streets.

LESSON 14

PAGE 114

Relate to the Topic
Your answer should describe what the action was, which branch was responsible for it, and how you felt about the action.

Reading Strategy
1. checks and balances in government
2. Sample answer: The diagram gives information about how the different branches of government exert checks to balance each other.

PAGE 116
c

PAGE 117
a

PAGES 118–119
1. judicial branch
2. bill
3. executive branch
4. separation of powers
5. legislative branch
6. checks and balances
7. The President can veto bills.
8. The Supreme Court can rule executive branch actions or orders unconstitutional.
9. The President and some members of Congress thought that the line-item veto would help control wasteful spending and thus lower the federal deficit.

10. The Constitution states that a President can veto only an entire law, not just parts of it, so the Supreme Court considered the line-item veto, which allows the President to veto part of a spending bill, to be unconstitutional.

11. **(2) Each branch of government checks the power of the other branches.** Options 1 and 3 are opinions, not facts. Nothing in the diagram is related to options 4 and 5.

12. **(5) The line-item veto was a powerful tool to protect taxpayers.** Options 1 and 4 are facts, not opinions. Option 2 is an opinion, but it is unlikely to be true. Option 3 is also an opinion but not one that relates to the line-item veto.

13. **(4) It gave too much power over Congress to the executive branch.** State governors do have the line-item veto power and are not part of the federal government so option 1 is incorrect. Options 2 and 3 are false. Option 5 is an opinion.

14. Separation of powers divides the government's power into three equal branches with different functions. The checks and balances system gives each branch powers to check actions of the other two branches.

15. Sample answer: I would like the President to have a line-item veto, because it would allow the President to veto spending on items that seem to be a waste of the taxpayers' money.

LESSON 15

PAGE 120
Relate to the Topic
Answers will vary. You may think of being defended from foreign attack and being free to speak your mind and practice your religion. You may think of voting and volunteering your time as ways of giving back to the country.

Reading Strategy
1. Sample answer: I have heard the term used in a television news program about freedom of religion.
2. Answers should relate to personal experiences such as participating in political, religious, or social gatherings.

PAGE 122
a

PAGE 123
b

PAGES 124–125

1. Bill of Rights
2. warrant
3. Justice
4. amendment
5. Due process
6. indicted
7. Answers should include two of the following: the freedom to speak and write what one thinks, to assemble with other people, to worship freely; freedom of the press; the right to petition the government.
8. Answers should include one of the following: voting in an informed manner, running for office, volunteering time for public or political organizations, working to improve the community
9. They made plans for a community center that would serve all residents, organized neighborhood support, and succeeded in obtaining city council approval and funding.
10. (2) **Attacking guaranteed rights is as much a danger as terrorism.** The cartoon shows the Bill of Rights being targeted by a gun, and the caption compares this to terrorism. These ideas together suggest that weakening the Bill of Rights in order to combat terrorism is as much a danger to Americans as terrorism is.
11. (3) **the Fifth Amendment** The information states that one provision of the Fifth Amendment is that no one can be tried twice for the same crime.
12. (5) **by saying "This is it!" and giving the meeting date and time** These details give the message a sense of urgency that is meant to be persuasive.
13. Sample answer: Due process helps ensure that innocent people are not convicted of crimes, and that justice is equal for all Americans.
14. Answers should suggest ways of giving time and talent to help improve one's community.

LESSON 16

PAGE 126

Relate to the Topic

Answers should include the date of the last election held in your community and a description of a candidate, campaign, or issue that was important or noteworthy from that election.

Reading Strategy

1. political party, political action committees
2. Possible answer: Both relate to the process of electing people to office.

PAGE 127

b

PAGE 129

a

PAGES 130–131

1. campaign
2. media
3. political action committees
4. politics
5. primary election
6. political party
7. general election
8. A voter must be at least 18 years old, a citizen, and a resident of the state where he or she votes.
9. He or she may be running in a primary, which is in the spring, and also in the general election in November.
10. Sample answer: Candidates for president today have to spend a lot of money campaigning for office, and the media plays a much greater role in campaigns.
11. (4) **A magazine includes information about only one candidate for senator.** Options 1, 2, 3, and 5 are ways that the media try to present a balanced picture of a campaign.
12. (2) **to support candidates who share the group's views** The special interest groups want to elect people who have the same or similar views. So options 1 and 5 are incorrect. There is no evidence to support option 3 or 4.
13. (4) **The high cost of political campaigns has raised concern among many Americans.** All the other options express opinions.
14. Sample answer: Yes, television ads are a wise use of funds because people pay more attention to television than to any other media.
15. Sample answers: I would negotiate a deal with the major television stations to get a better rate for political campaign ads and would limit the number of weeks during which candidates can campaign.

PAGE 132

Relate to the Topic

Sample answer: I pay gasoline tax, sales tax, and income taxes now; perhaps I will pay property tax in the future.

Reading Strategy

1. Both relate to federal tax monies.
2. how the government collects and spends money for running the country

PAGE 134

1. a
2. b

PAGE 135

b

PAGES 136–137

1. excise tax
2. entitlements
3. revenue
4. Income taxes
5. flat tax
6. progressive tax
7. to collect the money needed to run the government and to provide services for citizens
8. Sample answers: (a) Social Security (b) education (c) public safety
9. **(2) personal income taxes, social security/social insurance taxes, corporate income taxes** The percentages are 50%, 33%, and 10%, respectively.
10. **(1) Social Security** The federal government spends 16 percent of its budget on national defense. Of the programs listed, only Social Security takes a higher percentage of the federal budget.
11. **(2) Individual states decide which kinds of taxes to levy.** According to the information, the majority of states levy income taxes and many also levy sales taxes. However, since some states do not levy these taxes, the information supplies adequate support for the idea that individual states decide which taxes to use to raise revenues.
12. Businesses contribute to the revenue for a state by paying corporate taxes and employing workers, who pay state income taxes.
13. Whichever type you choose, you should use your understanding about taxes to explain why.

CIVICS AT WORK

PAGE 139

1. **(3) to distribute election flyers at Stone Elementary School** Anita names the task in the first sentence of her memo.
2. **(2) giving flyers about the election to interested adults** Distributing flyers is an example of free speech, a right guaranteed by the First Amendment.
3. **(3) the local law specified she must be that distance from the entrance** Anita mentions the distance right after referring in her memo to "all the laws that you explained to me."

UNIT 3 REVIEW

PAGES 140–143

1. Answers should include two of the following: they both involve rape, the police questioned both men without advising them of their rights, neither man had a lawyer present during questioning
2. **(2) When suspects threaten public safety, their rights are not fully protected.** Option 1 is true but is not the point of the information. There is nothing in the article to support options 3, 4, and 5.
3. **(5) The council appoints department heads in the weak-mayor plan.** The voters go to the polls in both plans, so option 1 is incorrect. There is no information in the diagram about option 2. The council selects the mayor in the weak-mayor plan, so option 3 is incorrect. Voters elect the mayor in the strong-mayor plan, so option 4 is incorrect.
4. **(1) The power of voters is greatest in the strong-mayor plan.** Options 2, 3, and 4 are not covered in the diagram. Option 5 is not covered in the diagram and is also incorrect because the opposite is true.
5. public library and auto registration office
6. A person must be at least 18 years of age to vote.
7. **(5) Votes can make a difference in all kinds of elections.** According to the article, the outcome of past elections might have been different if more people voted.
8. The man with the beard is Uncle Sam and represents the United States.
9. Bill Gates represents big business and the computer industry.

10. **(2) Protecting the right to privacy is challenging because computers make information easily available.** The cartoon suggests that the federal government, businesses, and others use paper files and computers to collect key information about Americans.

SOCIAL STUDIES EXTENSION

A possible list at a city council meeting might include introducing new traffic signals at cross streets, repairing pot holes on main streets, and extending the 20-mile-per-hour speed limit near schools for an extra hour in the morning. The council may immediately approve the extension of the time the 20-mile-per-hour speed limit is in force. So you would circle that on your list.

MINI-TEST UNIT 3

PAGES 144–145

1. **(2) Rebels assaulted federal workers.** *(Evaluation)* The paragraph points out that protesters rioted and violently attacked federal agents, tarring and feathering them.
2. **(3) taxing the sale of cigarettes** *(Application)* The Whiskey Rebellion was based on the imposition of an excise tax, and todays cigarette prices include a high excise tax.
3. **(2) demonstrators protesting U.S. involvement in a war** *(Application)* Like the people in the photograph, antiwar demonstrators would be exercising their First Amendment rights of free speech and assembly.
4. **(5) The king has restricted the powers of colonial governors.** *(Analysis)* This fact appears in the third paragraph. All of the other options express likes, dislikes, and other points of view.
5. **(1) Some colonists were very disappointed with the King of Great Britain.** *(Evaluation)* This disappointment is expressed in the list of repeated injuries and usurpations in the quotation.
6. **(3) During election season, attack ads insult television viewers.** *(Comprehension)* Slinging mud on someone is an expression that means "speaking negatively of someone." The mud pouring out of the television set, which is labeled *campaign ads,* represents attack ads used in a negative campaign. Pigs enjoy

rolling in mud, so the depiction of viewers as pigs suggests that viewers are being demeaned.

7. **(4) be ashamed of the nastiness in negative political campaigns** *(Analysis)* The little heart above the pig's head implies love of the negative politics being shown on the television. By implying that viewers who love negative campaign ads are acting like pigs, the cartoon is trying to persuade viewers to feel shame.

UNIT 4: ECONOMICS

LESSON 18

PAGE 148

Relate to the Topic

Sample answer: Cheerios® brand breakfast cereal has lasted because the manufacturer has created other flavors besides the basic recipe. Legos® brand blocks are durable, promote creativity and fine motor skills, and have universal appeal to children.

Reading Strategy

1. farms in the United States
2. changes in numbers of farms in the nation and changes in the average size of those farms

PAGE 149

a

PAGE 151

b

PAGES 152–153

1. free enterprise system
2. consumer
3. market
4. demand
5. cooperative
6. efficiency
7. New methods of farming allow farmers to increase the amount of crops produced, so they can make more money on their crop without increasing the price.
8. Sample answer: Consumers gain low prices and many choices as results of competition.

9. A market is a place where producers sell their products to sellers, or where people who buy products from producers sell to consumers. It can also mean all the potential customers for a particular product or service.

10. **(1) Farmers earn more when they produce goods that are in demand.** Options 2, 3, 4, and 5 are details stated directly in the paragraph.

11. **(1) Farms will be close to the same size as in 2000, and there will be about the same number of them.** The graphs show that the decline in the number of farms and increase in their size have slowed considerably, making it likely that the numbers will be similar ten years later.

12. **(2) If there was less competition among farmers, food prices would be higher.** Options 1, 3, and 4 are directly stated in the paragraph. Option 5 is not addressed.

13. Sample answer: A high demand can result in a product not being readily available and create competition among buyers, which raises the price. If demand for a product is low, however, the price will probably be low, too, even if the product is not easy to find.

14. Sample answer: Competition makes long-distance services lower their prices. I choose the service with low prices. If less competition existed, prices for long-distance calls might be higher, and my phone bill would probably go up.

LESSON 19

PAGE 154

Relate to the Topic
Sample answer: From talking with my siblings, I've learned that using a credit card for weekly expenses can lead to overspending.

Reading Strategy
1. Answers should name someone who has a spending plan and tries to follow it.
2. Sample answer: Look for the lowest interest rate and make sure the monthly payments are affordable.

PAGE 156
b

PAGE 157
b

PAGES 158–159
1. opportunity cost
2. net income
3. interest
4. annual percentage rate
5. fixed expense
6. budget
7. flexible expense
8. Answers should include two of the following: Sticking to a budget helps people know how much money they have to spend. It helps them know what they are spending their money on each month. It helps them know what the opportunity cost of a purchase will be. It helps them identify where money can be saved.
9. The person should consider the opportunity cost and the cost of borrowing the money.
10. Sample answer: Create and follow a spending plan. Consider all the costs involved in a purchase before deciding. Do not borrow money often. Read and understand the terms of a loan.
11. **(3) They had less money to put into savings.** The chart shows that they saved $25 less than planned.
12. **(3) They could switch to less expensive insurance.** Option 1 would increase, not reduce, the Riveras' fixed expenses. Options 2, 3, and 5 would affect their flexible expenses, not their fixed expenses.
13. **(5) It spends less on health care than it does on electricity, gas, telephone, and other utilities.** The graph shows that the average family spends 4.8 percent of income on health care, compared with 5.9 percent on utilities.
14. Sample answer: Lenders make money when a person takes out a loan for many years because interest is charged every month. When the loan is paid off early, the lender will charge a penalty to gain back some of the interest money it will lose.
15. Sample answer: After buying a TV on the spur of the moment, I did not have enough money to pay for car repairs.

LESSON 20

PAGE 160

Relate to the Topic
Sample answer: I bought several boxes of cookies when they were on sale and cookies are

a want; I did not buy a gold chain because of the price and the chain was a want.

Reading Strategy

1. the information on the price of baseball cards
2. The article might focus on supply and demand, using baseball cards as an example.

PAGE 162

a

PAGE 163

a

PAGES 164–165

1. inelastic supply
2. profit
3. elastic supply
4. scarce
5. inelastic demand
6. elastic demand
7. supply
8. The price usually goes down.
9. Sample answer: Elastic stretches. When a supply or demand is elastic, it moves either up or down in reaction to a price change.
10. Food and soap are things people always need and buy, so the demand for them is inelastic.
11. **(4) The new owner of the Ryan card will make a profit.** Option 1 is a fact, not a prediction. The paragraphs do not support a prediction of either option 3 or 5. Option 2 is wrong because the opposite is likely to happen.
12. **(5) Clemens' Fleer card is in shorter supply than his Donruss card.** Nothing supports option 1 or 4. Option 2 is true but does not explain the difference in values. Option 3 cannot be determined because the table gives baseball card values for only the year 2002.
13. **(5) Ichiro Suzuki** In general, there is a more limited supply of cards for older players, so they have higher values. Suzuki is the newest player, so Suzuki's card may increase in value but is not likely to match the value of the others within one year.
14. If demand is high, this will make supplies more scarce. So companies will enter the market to sell products, hoping to make profit by meeting the demand. If demand is low, companies will leave the market if they cannot sell enough of the product to make a profit.
15. Sample answer: I would advise against investing in baseball cards. Many companies

make baseball cards, and the value of the cards may fail to rise in the future.

LESSON 21

PAGE 166

Relate to the Topic

Answers might include finishing the GED, learning to use a computer, or enrolling in a community or four-year college.

Reading Strategy

1. Sample answers: bank employees, customer service representatives, skilled auto mechanics.
2. Answers should reflect your personal experiences.

PAGE 168

b

PAGE 169

1. b
2. a

PAGES 170–171

1. bachelor's degree
2. internship
3. apprenticeship
4. Service industries
5. work ethic
6. Mentoring
7. Job shadowing
8. health-care jobs, desktop publishing jobs, and some teaching jobs
9. Most jobs today require technical skills as well as the abilities to follow directions, to work on a team, to be punctual, to act responsibly, and to use common sense.
10. by pursuing more education and training, especially in modern technologies
11. Workers learn to do different jobs so that they can help other workers when needed.
12. **(1) Get an education or training in a field that interests you.** Options 2 through 5 are not discussed in the article.
13. **(4) Between 2000 and 2010, the need for special education teachers will grow, but not as quickly as the need for desktop publishers.** The graph shows that for 2000 to 2010, desktop publishing has an estimated growth over 65% while special education has an estimated growth under 40%.

14. **(3) Many jobs in the United States today use technologies that process information.** Option 1 is true but has nothing to do with high-paying jobs today. Option 2 is true but is not directly related to technological literacy. Options 4 and 5 refer to job programs, not technological literacy.

15. Sample answers: A business runs better when employees come in on time and act responsibly.

16. Answers should describe the subjects you would study from books and the skills you would learn on the job.

LESSON 22

PAGE 172

Relate to the Topic

Sample answers: shoes, clothing, televisions, electronic equipment, automobiles

Reading Strategy

1. U.S. imports and exports from 1970 to 2000
2. The graph traces the value of both imports and exports.

PAGE 175

Reading a Double Line Graph: b
Supporting Conclusions: a

PAGES 176–177

1. Free trade
2. currency
3. protectionist
4. interdependent
5. tariff
6. trade deficit
7. quota
8. Many nations depend on one another for raw materials and finished goods.
9. International trade creates competition among the companies of many countries instead of just among the companies of one country. When the competition is great, a company must make products more efficiently to make money.
10. An increase in international trade offers a nation a larger market for its goods and a greater supply of raw materials to make its products.
11. Answers should include *tariffs* and *quotas*.
12. **(4) sharper increases in imports than exports** Options 1, 2, and 5 are incorrect interpretations.

Option 3 is true but it is not the best and most complete interpretation of the graph.

13. **(2) 1991** The figures were rather close until 1982, when imports began to exceed exports dramatically. Only in 1991 did they approach a balance.

14. **(3) American consumers can choose from a variety of goods.** Options 2 and 4 are negative results of the global economy. Option 1 deals with a political or protectionist policy. Option 5 does not describe the United States, full of natural resources.

15. Protectionist policies use different kinds of barriers to block trade, whereas free trade encourages many nations and companies to conduct business with one another.

16. Sample answer: Cost is more important to me than the country where it was made; I would buy the car made in Japan.

ECONOMICS AT WORK

PAGE 179

1. Calla lily — in season
   Carnation — out of season
   Delphinium — out of season
   Hyacinth — out of season
   Poppy — in season
   Tulip — in season

2. **(2) Calla Lily—$2.25 per stem** The fact that the price of the Calla lily is near the highest price paid suggests that it is in short supply and thus, out of season.

3. Sample answer: I have noticed how the price of grapefruit fluctuates in the grocery store. Around October, the price of grapefruits begins to fall, and gets really low in December and January. As spring approaches, the price begins to climb again. This makes me think that grapefruits are in season in fall and winter and out of season in spring and summer.

UNIT 4 REVIEW

PAGES 180–183

1. **(5) people concerned about the environment** Cornstarch helps plastic decompose, which helps the environment. Corn has always been considered a food so options 1 and 2 are incorrect. Options 3 and 4 are incorrect

because these groups could possibly be hurt by the new uses of corn.

2. **(1) Demand for corn is likely to increase.** According to the article, the new products will increase the demand for corn so options 2 and 5 are incorrect. The supply is likely to increase also, so options 3 and 4 are incorrect.

3. the reception

4. Yes; for the average wedding, 50% of the budget is spent on the reception; the Lees spent $6,975 of their $14,000-budget on their reception; this is 50% of their budget.

5. **(2) The Lees spent about an average amount on flowers but less than average on music.** According to the graph, flowers and music each represent 9 percent of the average wedding budget. The table shows that the Lees spent 9 percent on flowers but only 3 percent on music.

6. The seller is using bait-and-switch advertising.

7. The seller is using the special-pricing method.

8. **(2) Let the buyer beware.** According to the article, buyers should be wary of selling methods used by some sellers. The article does not state that all sellers are dishonest, so option 1 is incorrect. Option 3 is incorrect, because although it may sometimes be true, it is not supported by the article. Option 4 is incorrect because the article implies customers should check prices. Option 5 may be true but it is not supported by the article.

9. computer software engineers, applications

10. moderate-term on-the-job training

11. **(5) The fastest growing jobs generally require education beyond high school.** Most of the occupations listed require a bachelor's degree; several of the others require postsecondary education, such as an associate degree or a vocational award.

SOCIAL STUDIES EXTENSION

A possible budget may resemble the average American family's spending habits. However, it should reflect your family's needs and wants.

MINI-TEST UNIT 4

PAGES 184–185

1. **(1) to help shoppers compare the value of similar items (Comprehension)** Unit prices allow an equal basis for comparison of products.

2. **(2) deciding which brand of corn flakes is the better buy (Application)** Cereal is measured in ounces, and a shopper can compare the price per ounce of the different brands to determine which is the better value.

3. **(4) Between 1992 and 1996, homes in San Francisco and in Los Angeles gained little or no value. (Analysis)** Between 1992 and 1996, home prices in the San Francisco region rose only slightly, and home prices in the Los Angeles region dropped.

4. **(5) As in 1999, cash and checks will be used for most purchases in 2005. (Evaluation)** The table shows that cash and checks make up more than half of all transactions in both years: 72.1 percent of transactions in 1999 and 61 percent in 2005.

5. **(3) It is better to pay cash for purchases than to borrow money. (Evaluation)** The table shows that most Americans do not buy on credit, but instead pay with cash and checks—money they already have.

6. **(3) Bears have sluggish periods and bulls sometimes charge or stampede. (Application)** The paragraph describes a bear market as a time when prices go down and the economy is slow or sluggish, like a bear in winter; during a bull market, on the other hand, stock prices are going up and the economy is generally fast-paced, like a charging bull.

7. **(2) poor earnings predictions from major companies (Analysis)** Poor earnings would discourage investors and create pessimism, leading investors to sell or at least to not buy stock. This could lead to a bear market.

UNIT 5: GEOGRAPHY

LESSON 23

PAGE 188

Relate to the Topic

Answer should mention the location of your home, and features that make your neighborhood different from others nearby.

Reading Strategy

1. the Arctic

2. Sample answer: The map indicates that summer temperatures average under 50 degrees Fahrenheit in the Arctic and that there are no trees there. So it is a very cold region.

PAGE 190
a

PAGE 191
a

PAGES 192–193
1. tundra
2. climate
3. Vegetation
4. tree line
5. region
6. The climate includes long, cold winters and short summers. The vegetation includes algae on the rocks near the Arctic Ocean and tundra.
7. The Inuit fished, hunted, and gathered food. They wore clothes made of seal skins and caribou hides. They traveled on foot or by boat during the short summer and by dog team during the rest of the year.
8. They organized an annual Inuit conference, began demanding control of their hunting grounds, worked with Canada's government to establish the state of Nunavut, and insisted the schools teach native languages and customs to Inuit students.
9. **(5) Greenland lies entirely within the Arctic region.** The map and other information do not support options 1, 2, 3, and 4.
10. **(1) The Inuit met their needs by fishing and hunting.** The statements described in options 2, 3, 4, and 5 are details that support the main idea.
11. Sample answer: Some people may feel that the land and mineral rights are most valuable since these are tangible assets. Others think that the gain of political power and keeping their way of life are most valuable because they give people self-respect.
12. Sample answer: The children might use words, dress, and other practices common in the other country. They may lose a sense of connection to their family and old way of life.

LESSON 24

PAGE 194
Relate to the Topic
Answers should describe the climate of a place where you would like to live, and the climate where you live.
Reading Strategy
1. What does *climate* mean?
2. How do water, wind, and mountains affect climate?

PAGE 195
b

PAGE 197
1. a
2. c

PAGES 198–199
1. equator
2. current
3. Precipitation
4. latitude
5. elevation
6. longitude
7. Answers may include: latitude, nearby mountains or bodies of water, ocean currents, and winds
8. Places in the tropics are warm year-round. The middle-latitude areas are temperate. The polar regions are cold all year.
9. In summer, ocean water stays cold long after the land has grown warm. So the summer winds blowing off the oceans bring cooling breezes to the land. Large bodies of water also hold the summer's heat as the land cools in fall. So winter winds blowing off the oceans bring warm air over the land.
10. **(5) The tropics receive almost direct rays from the sun.** Options 1 and 3 are false. Option 2 explains why a place in the tropics that is near the ocean might get more rainfall. Option 4 helps to explain why southern Alaska has a mild climate.
11. **(4) 10° N latitude** The area between the equator and the Tropic of Cancer is part of the tropics. Option 1 is the South Pole. Options 2, 3, and 5 lie in the middle-latitude areas.
12. **(2) South America and Africa** North America, Europe, and continental Asia lie north of the equator, and Australia lies south of it.

13. Western Montana gets more precipitation because when winds reach the Rocky Mountains, they rise and cool. Cold air holds less moisture than warm air, so clouds form and rain falls on the western side of the mountains. When the winds reach the eastern side of the mountains, the air is dry.

14. Your description should include climate words such as *temperature, precipitation,* and *wind.*

LESSON 25

PAGE 200

Relate to the Topic
Answers should describe specific actions, such as organizing friends to pick up trash.

Reading Strategy
1. You may already know about the glaciers, sea animals, oil, or other features of the Alaskan environment.
2. You may know about the Alaskan pipeline or about transporting oil in ocean-going tankers.

PAGE 201
Sample answers: sound; environment; glaciers; crude oil; iceberg; conclusion. The definitions you have written will depend on the other words you have circled.

PAGE 203
Sample answer: The oil spill was the largest any group had ever cleaned up; oil is a difficult substance to remove from water or the gravel beaches.

PAGES 204–205
1. sound
2. environment
3. glacier
4. crude oil
5. iceberg
6. In 1989 an oil tanker hit a reef in the bottom of the sound and started leaking oil into the sound.
7. Answers should include at least one of the following: wind, movement of water, the storm, ocean currents
8. Fish, animals, and birds died. The fishing and tourist industries suffered. The water in the sound was polluted.
9. **(3) a long inlet of the ocean** Options 1, 4, and 5 are definitions for totally different uses of sound. Option 2 cannot be correct because the map does not show the sound connecting two large bodies of water.

10. **(5) The cleanup helped some living things in the environment.** The article contradicts options 1, 3, and 4. No information in the article supports option 2.

11. Sample answer: Tourists probably stayed away from refuges and beaches spoiled by oil. As a result, hotels in the area probably fell on hard times and laid off workers.

12. Your answer should address whether or not the cost of the tax for the oil-spill cleanup fund is likely to be passed along to gasoline customers through higher gas prices.

LESSON 26

PAGE 206

Relate to the Topic
Possible answer: I ate bread, which is made from wheat, and cheese, which comes from milk, given by grazing cows. Preserving productive land is important because it is a source of food and of the jobs of the people who work on it.

Reading Strategy
1. desertification, drylands
2. irrigated land, rainfed cropland, rangeland

PAGE 208
1. b
2. a

PAGE 209
a

PAGES 210–211
1. displaced
2. overgrazing
3. topsoil
4. desertification
5. Ecotourism
6. drought
7. a long period of overfarming of the land, followed by a drought
8. droughts in the Sahel region of Africa, which caused the deaths of more than 200,000 people and millions of animals
9. zero tillage farming
10. **(4) Rangeland has suffered more damage than cropland.** In all six regions, rangeland shows the highest percentage of damage.

11. **(1) Desertification refers to land; drought refers to the weather.** Drought is a long period of unusually dry weather; desertification is turning of productive land into desert.

12. **(3) Black blizzards were raging dust storms.** The term is used in the first paragraph, but it is never actually defined. You must assume this to fully understand both the quotation and the paragraph.

13. Answers should include the fact that it often is poor people who practice the farming and herding methods that damage the land the most and lead to desertification.

14. Answers might suggest some compensation for the farmers whose land would be replanted with trees.

GEOGRAPHY AT WORK

PAGE 213

3 trains; numbers 18, 126 and 150.
12:29 P.M.; 9:44 A.M.
Baltimore

UNIT 5 REVIEW

PAGE 214

1. **(3) Peary and his group were the first people to reach the North Pole.** Option 1 is not true. Options 2, 4, and 5 are true, but are details, not the main idea.

2. **(5) Peary followed a northerly route along the 70° W line of longitude.** Options 1 and 3 are not true. Information on the map contradicts option 2. No facts presented in the map would lead you to option 4.

PAGE 215

3. Peary's final trip began at Cape Columbia on Ellesmere Island in Canada.

4. 85° N

5. 87° N

6. **(2) The North Pole is on the polar ice cap and is bitterly cold.** The article does not state this, although it mentions hardships and ice storms as reasons earlier expeditions did not reach the North Pole.

PAGE 216

7. **(4) to get water for their crops and animals.** According to the article, irrigation is used to create a water supply, so options 1, 2, and 3 are incorrect. Nothing in the article supports option 5.

8. **(1) Grassland covers much of the North Central Plains.** Grassland is key to successful ranching.

PAGE 217

9. As the key shows, these states are marked with a symbol of a cow.

10. Alaska, Wyoming, North Dakota, Louisiana, and Mississippi

11. **(3) how many states are top producers of both oil and cattle** The map uses symbols to shows the top ten cattle-raising states and the top ten oil-producing states; if a state is included in both categories, both symbols appear within the state's borders.

MINI-TEST UNIT 5

PAGES 218–219

1. **(1) A glacier is a mass of ice that moves over land.** *(Analysis)* The term *glacier* is not defined in the paragraph. It is assumed that you understand that a glacier is a large mass of ice that moves over land.

2. **(2) melting at the bottom of the glacier and gravity** *(Comprehension)* The paragraph explains that high pressure and heat from friction at the bottom of the glacier cause the glacier's lower surface to melt. The glacier can slide over water, pulled downhill by the force of gravity.

3. **(5) has 54% of the total volume of the Great Lakes** *(Evaluation)* With over half the total volume of the Great Lakes, Lake Superior is larger, in terms of volume, than the four other Great Lakes combined.

4. **(4) moving is a matter of survival** *(Analysis)* Push factors force people out, suggesting that they face death if they remain in the existing conditions. Thus, moving is a matter of survival.

5. **(4) Americans moving west to settle their own farms during the 1800s** *(Application)* The opportunity to farm one's own land is a pull factor. Options 1, 2, 3, and 5 are examples of push factors.

6. **(3) Honolulu, because its high and low temperatures are close.** *(Application)* When there are not wide variations of temperature, the same kinds of clothes can be worn most of

the year. Portland and El Paso have much more variation between high and low temperatures.

7. **(5) places in the north tend to be colder than places in the south** *(Evaluation)* The graph indicates that Portland's average temperature is lower than the average temperatures of El Paso and Honolulu. The fact that Portland is farther north and the graph together support the generalization that places in the north tend to be colder than places in the south.

POSTTEST

PAGES 221–229

1. **(4) their physical appearance and poise** *(U.S. History: Analysis)* Based on the information and the photograph, John F. Kennedy appeared to be the more attractive and poised candidate.

2. **(3) Televising the debates prompted voters to be influenced by the candidates' appearance.** *(U.S. History: Comprehension)* Televising the debates allowed millions of Americans to compare each candidate's physical appearance, as well as his political views. The election outcome implies that enough voters were influenced by Senator Kennedy's poise and good looks that he was able to win the election against the more experienced Vice-President.

3. **(5) Getting a job as a ticket agent may be difficult, but such a job can lead to advancement in the travel industry.** *(Economics: Comprehension)* This statement summarizes the main ideas of the paragraph—while competition may initially make it difficult to get a job as a ticket agent, such a job is a good entry point into the travel industry.

4. **(1) There are qualifications for a ticket agent job.** *(Economics: Analysis)* This fact is given in the second sentence of the paragraph. The other options are opinions.

5. **(2) federal government power vs. states' rights** *(U.S. History: Application)* The Tenth Amendment distinguishes between the power of the federal government and the power of the states, granting all powers to the states that are not specifically given to the federal government or prohibited to the states. The tension between federal government power and states' rights has been an ongoing source of conflict in U.S. history.

6. **(4) Three of the world's oceans border the continent of Antarctica.** *(Geography: Evaluation)* The map shows that Antarctica is bordered by the Atlantic, Pacific, and Indian oceans.

7. **(3) a geography teacher** *(Geography: Application)* A geography teacher could make the best use of a map that shows the major continents and oceans of the world. The other people and institutions would find other types of maps more suitable for their purposes.

8. **(1) They had deep ties to their land.** *(U.S. History: Analysis)* In the letter quoted in paragraph 2, the tribe members indicated how deep their ties to their land were when they compared the land to the mother who gave them birth, stating that leaving the land would be like rejecting their birth mother.

9. **(2) Some tribes were forced off their land.** *(U.S. History: Evaluation)* Congress passed a law giving the federal government the right to take land away from the Native Americans who lived in the East. The law does not allow the government to take land from other groups of Americans.

10. **(5) Iraq** *(World History: Comprehension)* According to the map, Iraq encompasses almost all of the land that made up the ancient kingdom of Babylonia.

11. **(5) computer and Internet use among five categories of workers** *(Economics: Comprehension)* According to the key, the bars show "Computer only" and "Internet use." There are bars for five different categories of workers. Therefore, option (5) is a complete summary of what the graph shows, giving the main purpose of the graph.

12. **(1) managers** *(Economics: Analysis)* The only bar for "Internet use" that is over 50% is for the category of manager.

13. **(4) Washington politicians are too involved with big corporations.** *(Civics and Government: Analysis)* A conflict of interest is defined as a conflict between a person's private interest and his or her public obligations. A politician who has a conflict of interest with a corporation may not fulfill his or her obligation to pass fair laws, but may instead vote for laws that favor corporations. The janitor in the cartoon implies that all politicians in Washington have conflicts of interest with corporations; thus, the cartoonist thinks that Washington politicians are too involved with corporate interests.

14. **(5) Congress will avoid vigorously investigating Enron.** *(Civics and Government: Comprehension)* Since members of Congress (not janitors) will investigate Enron, and since the cartoonist thinks that members of Congress are tied too closely to corporate interests, the implication is that Congress will not vigorously investigate Enron.

15. **(2) By stealing signatures, corrupt people are perverting the political process in Oregon.** *(Civics and Government: Evaluation)* All of the warnings in "Think Before You Ink" lead to the conclusion that people's signatures are being stolen by ballot initiative petitioners; this signature fraud is a perversion of a legitimate political process in Oregon.

16. **(2) Don't sign any petitions because your signature will be stolen.** *(Civics and Government: Analysis)* It is faulty reasoning to think that you should not sign any petitions simply because you have to take precautions to prevent your signature from being stolen.

17. **(3) Sharbat's culture presented barriers to her being identified.** *(Geography: Analysis)* The passage implies that the photographer needed permission from the woman's husband and brother to talk with her. The unstated assumption is that her culture was a barrier that made it difficult for the *National Geographic* staff to identify the girl.

18. **(1) modesty and privacy** *(Geography: Evaluation)* From the references to the protection of Sharbat's privacy and the references to her modesty about her fame, you can conclude that Sharbat's culture places strong value on modesty and privacy.

19. **(3) Japan attacked Pearl Harbor** *(World History: Analysis)* According to the timeline, the attack on Pearl Harbor caused the United States to reverse its policy of neutrality and enter the war.

20. **(4) 1943** *(World History: Analysis)* According to the timeline, the first surrender of an Axis power took place in 1943. From this, you can conclude that 1943 marked a turning point in the war against the Axis powers.

21. **(5) socialism** *(Civics and Government: Application)* A country in which there is little or no private property has employed the socialist system; as the description states, in socialism, "the means of production, distribution, and exchange are mostly owned by the state".

22. **(2) autocracy** *(Civics and Government: Application)* A country that has one ruler or a single ruling party is ruled by "a supreme, unlimited authority." Thus, this country's government is based on the political philosophy of despotism.

23. **(1) anarchism** *(Civics and Government: Application)* This clear statement of opposition to government and to all types of authority is an example of anarchism.

24. **(3) More immigrants were from Europe in the 1960s and 1970s, but by 1990 more Latin American and Asian immigrants lived in the United States.** *(U.S. History: Analysis)* The graph shows that European immigration was much higher than Asian and Latin American immigration between 1960 and 1980, but that European immigration was surpassed by Latin American immigration in the early 1980s and by Asian immigration in the early 1990s.

25. **(2) Expenditures for public safety account for about half of the city's budget.** *(Economics: Evaluation)* The graph on the right shows that public safety expenditures, which would include police, firefighting, and paramedic operations, account for about half of the city's expenditures. In other words, the city is spending about half of its revenue on these public safety services.

GLOSSARY

abolitionist a person who is against slavery

adequacy sufficiency; enough to be considered acceptable

alien a person living in the United States who is not an American citizen

allies countries that help each other

Allies all the nations who fought Germany and its supporters in World Wars I and II

amendment an addition or change

annual percentage rate (APR) the percent of interest a lender charges per year

apartheid a policy in South Africa that separated black Africans from white society

appeal to bring a court decision from a lower court to be reexamined in a higher court

apprentice someone who learns a trade from an expert called a master

apprenticeship a period of training that includes on-the-job training

aquifer an underground layer of rock or earth that holds water

assumption a statement accepted as true without proof; a belief

bachelor's degree a degree earned after a four-year college education

barbarian a person considered to be inferior and ignorant

bar graph a graph used to make comparisons

bill a proposed law

Bill of Rights the first ten amendments to the United States Constitution, listing the rights of individuals

bloc a group of nations that acts together for military, political, or economic purposes

boycott to protest by refusing to use a service or to buy a certain item

broadcast the sending of a radio or TV program by radio waves

budget a detailed plan showing earnings and expenses over a period of time

campaign a series of events designed to get people to vote a certain way

candidate a person who runs for public office

capital money, assets, or property used for investment

cash crop a crop grown for sale rather than for personal use

cause why something happens

cease-fire a pause in fighting

century a period of 100 years

charter a plan that sets up an organization and defines its purpose

checks and balances the idea that each branch of a government has powers that limit the other branches' powers

child labor the practice of using children as workers

chronometer a very accurate clock

circle graph graph used to show parts of a whole; also known as a pie chart

civics the branch of political science that deals with the rights and duties of citizens

civilian a person not in military or government service

civilization the society and culture of a particular group, place, or period

civil rights freedoms guaranteed to citizens, including the right to be treated equally

civil war a war between people who live in the same country

climate the general weather of a region over a long time

Cold War the struggle for world power between the United States and the Soviet Union

colony a settlement or group of settlements far from the home country

communicate to exchange information

communism a political and economic system that does away with private property and places production under government control

compare to tell how people, events, or things are alike

composer a person who writes music

composting producing rich organic matter by letting food waste and plants decay

GLOSSARY
255

computer an electronic machine for processing, storing, and recalling information

conclusion a logical judgment based on facts

Confederacy the southern states during the American Civil War

conquistador Spanish word meaning "conqueror"

conservative a person who wants to maintain traditional and established values and practices

Constitution the plan for the United States government, proposed in 1787

consumer a person who buys and uses goods and services

containment a policy to prevent the spread of communism to other nations

context 1) the rest of the words in a sentence 2) one particular situation

contrast to tell how people, events, and things are different

cooperative people who join together to ensure the best price for their products

corporation a business owned by stockholders

crude oil untreated oil

culture customs or way of life

currency a kind of money

current part of any body of water that flows in a definite direction

deadlocked unable to agree; a tie vote

defense contract agreement that government makes with a private company that produces weapons and supplies needed by the military

defense industry companies that produce military supplies

deferment a temporary postponement of military service

demand the amount of goods or services consumers are willing to buy at a certain price at a given time

democracy a system of government in which the power to make choices belongs to the people

desertification the turning of productive land into desert

detail small piece of information

diagram a drawing that shows steps in a process or how something is organized

diplomat a person who handles relations between nations

displaced forced to leave ones home, often by climate change, natural disaster, or war

discrimination the unequal and unfair treatment of a person or group

drought a long period of unusually dry weather

draft a system of required military service

due process steps in the legal process that protect the rights of an accused person

duty a tax collected on goods brought into a country and sometimes on goods sent out of a country

dynasty a family of rulers whose generations govern one after another over a long time

economics the study of how people use their resources to meet their needs

ecotourism travel that appeals to people with environmental interests

effect what happens as the result of a cause

efficiency the state of being productive without wasting time, money, or energy

elastic demand a willingness to buy that increases or decreases as the price of a good or service changes

elastic supply an amount of a good or service that increases or decreases as the price changes

elevation the height of the land above sea level

email a message a writer sends electronically using a computer

Emancipation Proclamation the statement made by President Abraham Lincoln declaring freedom for slaves in states fighting against the Union during the American Civil War

empire a group of widespread territories or nations under a single ruler or government

entitlement a governmental program, such as food stamps or veterans' pensions, available to people who meet its requirements

environment all of the living and nonliving things that make up a place

equator an imaginary circle exactly halfway between the North and South poles

estimate to guess an amount based on past experience

excise tax tax on a specific item, such as cigarettes, alcohol, or gasoline

executive branch the branch of government that carries out the laws

export 1) to send and sell a nation's goods to other nations 2) a good produced in one country and sent to another country for sale

fact a statement of something that can be proved

federal deficit the amount of money the national government spends in excess of its income

federal government the government with authority over the entire United States

fixed expenses costs that stay the same each month

flat tax an income tax under which everyone pays the same percentage of his or her wages

flexible expenses costs that vary from month to month

free enterprise system an economic system in which buyers affect which goods and services are produced

free trade importing and exporting without political barriers, such as tariffs or taxes

general election a regularly scheduled election for state, local, or federal officials

geography the study of Earth's places and peoples

glacier a huge mass of ice that moves slowly over land

glossary an alphabetical listing of important words and their definitions

government the system of laws and political bodies that make it possible for a nation, a state, or a community to function

graph a drawing that is used to compare numerical information

gross national product (GNP) the money value of all goods, services, and products of a nation's industries

groundwater an underground source of water, such as a spring, well, pond, or aquifer

guerrilla a fighter or style of fighting that uses irregular and independent tactics

hasty generalization a broad statement based on little or no evidence

hazardous waste something thrown away that is harmful to the environment

headings the names of sections within an article

iceberg a huge block of floating ice that has broken off from a glacier

immigrant a person who moves from his or her homeland to another country

immune protected against a disease

impeach to accuse a public official of misconduct; sometimes to additionally remove that public official from office

implied suggested, but not stated outright

import 1) to bring in or purchase goods from another country 2) a good brought into a country from another country

incentive a reason for action

income tax a tax on a person's earnings

indentured servant a person who works for a set period of time in exchange for something of value, such as fare to another country

indict to formally charge someone with a crime

inelastic demand a willingness to buy that is not affected when the price of a good or service changes

inelastic supply an amount of a good or service that cannot change

inference an idea a person figures out based on details in given material and on what the person already knows

interdependent several parts, such as nations, relying on one another to be successful

interest the fee paid for borrowing money

interned to be forced to live in a camp away from home

Internet a network of computers connected by telephone lines

internship a temporary job assignment

job rotation a system that trains workers in many tasks so they can step into other jobs when the need arises

job shadowing following a worker on a typical day to observe his or her job responsibilities

judicial branch the branch of government that interprets laws

judicial review the federal courts' power to determine whether a law or an executive action follows the Constitution

justice 1) fair and equal treatment under the law 2) a judge who serves on the Supreme Court

labor force all the people capable of working

labor union a group of workers organized to improve working conditions and to protect the interests of its members

landfill a place where trash is buried

laser a narrow beam of intense light

latitude distance north or south of the equator

legislative branch the branch of government that makes laws

legislature a group of persons that makes the laws of a nation or state

liberal a person who supports political change

line graph a graph using lines to show how something increases or decreases over time

literate able to read and write

logic a systematic method of thinking that is based on reasoning correctly

longitude distance east or west on Earth, measured from the Prime Meridian in Greenwich, England; also called meridians

main idea the topic of a paragraph, passage, or diagram

market 1) a place where buyers and sellers meet 2) potential customers for a product or service

master an experienced tradesperson

media agencies of communication, such as television, radio, newspapers, and magazines

mediator a person who settles differences between persons or groups

mentoring teaching a less experienced person about a job through example and discussion

meridians the lines on a map or globe that are used to measure distances east and west on Earth; lines of longitude

microchip a tiny electrical circuit

migrate to move from one place to another

minutemen American colonists who were ready to fight at a minute's notice

mission a settlement centered around a church, established for the purpose of winning people over to a religion

navigator a person who charts the position and course of a ship during a voyage

net income money left after taxes are paid

neutral refusing to be on one side or the other

nominate to choose a candidate to run for an elected office

opinion a statement that expresses what a person or group thinks or believes

opportunity cost the cost of choosing one thing over another

orchestra a large group of people who play a variety of musical instruments together

ordinance a law or regulation

overgrazing the practice of letting too many animals feed on an area's grasses or of letting animals feed in one place for too long

override to cancel the executive branch's veto or rejection of a proposed law

parallels the lines on a map or globe that are used to measure distances from the equator; lines of latitude

parliament a lawmaking body

peasant a poor person who owns or rents a small piece of land that he or she farms, especially in poorer countries

pendulum a suspended weight, usually in a clock, that swings back and forth at regular intervals

persuasive intended to encourage people to have a certain opinion or to take a certain action

point of view how someone feels or thinks

political action committee (PAC) a group that gives money to candidates who have interests similar to its own

political cartoon a drawing that expresses an opinion about an issue

political map a map that focuses on showing boundaries, such as those between countries or states

political party a group of people who have similar ideas about public issues

politics ideas and actions of government

precipitation moisture that falls to Earth as rain, snow, or some other form

predicting outcomes trying to figure out what the results of events will be

primary election an election in which voters choose the party's candidate for an office

prime minister the head of a parliament

profit to make money by selling something at a higher price than the original cost

progressive tax a plan under which the percentage of a person's wages paid as income tax increases as the wages increase

property tax tax on the value of something that a person owns

protectionist supporting tariffs on imports to protect a nation's own producers of goods and services

province a political region in some countries that is similar to a state in the United States

pueblo Native American settlements with apartment-like buildings

quality circle a group of workers who check the quality of products and services they produce

quota a set limit of something such as imports

racist favoring one race of people over another

recycling reusing solid and non-solid waste for the same or new purposes

reformer a person who works to change things for the better

regiment a large military group

region an area that differs in one or more ways from the places around it

register to complete a form with such things as name, address, and date of birth in order to vote

reparations money paid to make up for damages, such as suffering during wartime

repeal to take back or do away with something, such as a law

republic 1) a self-governing territory usually headed by a president 2) a government in which the power is given to elected officials who represent the people

revenue income collected or produced

sales tax tax on a purchase

sanction an economic or military measure used to force a nation to stop violating an international law or human right

scale a set of marks that compares the distance on a map to actual distance

scanning to look at quickly; to browse for specific information

scarce describes a limited supply of something that is in demand

separation of powers a system that divides the functions of government among independent branches so that no one branch becomes too powerful

sequence a series of events that follow one another in a particular order

service industry business that employs people who meet the needs of other people

skimming to quickly look over something to get the main idea

smallpox a deadly disease that has been virtually eliminated through vaccination

soft money money donated to a political party for supposedly nonpolitical uses, and which is not subject to the limitations on campaign contributions

sound a long, wide ocean inlet

stock market a place where shares in companies are bought and sold

strike to stop work in protest

suffrage the right to vote

summarize to reduce a large amount of information into a few sentences

supply the amount of goods and services sellers are willing to offer at certain prices at a given time

switchboard a device for controlling, connecting, and disconnecting many telephone lines within one building or location

table a type of list that organizes information in columns and rows

tariff a tax on imports

technology the tools and methods used to increase production

telecommunications ways to send messages over long distances

timeline an illustration that shows when a series of events took place and the order in which they occurred

topic sentence the specific sentence in a paragraph that contains its main idea

topsoil the soil on Earth's surface, in which the roots of most plants usually take hold

trade deficit the value of the nation's imports that exceeds the value of the nation's exports

transistor a small device that controls the flow of the electricity in electronic devices

tree line the beginning of an area where temperatures are too cold for trees to grow

tropics the area on Earth that receives almost direct rays from the sun year-round

tundra a treeless region with a thin layer of soil over permanently frozen earth

Union the northern states during the American Civil War

union *see* labor union

U.S. history history of the area now known as the United States of America

vaccination an injection that protects a person from a disease

values ideas or qualities that people feel are important, right, and good

vegetation the plants that grow naturally in an area

veto to refuse to sign a bill into law

warrant a document that permits a police search in connection with a crime

work ethic the belief in the value of work, demonstrated through commitment to job responsibilities

world history history of all of the people and nations of Earth